D1614398

SHAKESPEARE AMONG THE ANIMALS

EARLY MODERN CULTURAL STUDIES

Ivo Kamps, Series Editor

PUBLISHED BY PALGRAVE:

SHAKESPEARE
AMONG THE ANIMALS

NATURE AND SOCIETY
IN THE DRAMA OF
EARLY MODERN ENGLAND

Bruce Boehrer

palgrave

For Barbara DeMent

Te, dulcis coniunx, te sola in litore mecum,
te veniente die, te decedente canebam.

SHAKESPEARE AMONG THE ANIMALS
© BRUCE BOEHRER, 2002

First published 2002 by PALGRAVE™
175 Fifth Avenue, New York, N.Y.10010 and
Houndmills, Basingstoke, Hampshire RG21 6XS.
Companies and representatives throughout the world.

PALGRAVE is the new global publishing imprint of St. Martin's Press LLC Scholarly and Reference Division and Palgrave Publishers Ltd (formerly Macmillan Press Ltd).

ISBN 0–312–29343–7 hardback

Library of Congress Cataloging-in-Publication Data
Boehrer, Bruce.
Shakespeare among the animals : nature and society in the drama of early modern
England / by Bruce Boehrer.
    p. cm.
  Includes bibliographical references and index.
  ISBN 0–312–29343–7
  1. Shakespeare, William, 1564–1616—Knowledge—Natural history. 2. Literature and society—England—History—16th century. 3. Literature and society—England—History—17th century. 4. Social values in literature. 5. Animals in literature. 6. Nature in literature. I. Title.
PR3044.B64   2002
822.3'3—dc21

                                                        2001053136

A catalogue record for this book is available from the British Library.

Design by Letra Libre, Inc.

First edition: March 2002
10 9 8 7 6 5 4 3 2 1

Printed in the United States of America.

CONTENTS

ILLUSTRATIONS

ACKNOWLEDGMENTS

Of my three books, this one has been far and away the greatest joy to write, perhaps because in doing so I have incurred far greater and more numerous debts than ever before. The joy of the writing now redoubles my gratitude to all who have helped me in the process.

First mention must go to those scholars who have kindly read and commented upon part or all of the manuscript during its years of development: David Lee Miller, Sharon O'Dair, Harold Weber, Margreta de Grazia, Marshall Brown, Annabel Patterson, Gail Paster, Joseph Price, Goran Stanivukovic, Marcy North, and, most importantly, Douglas Bruster and Ivo Kamps, who have helped me see the work into print.

Next, I must thank those others who have contributed to this project by suggesting source material, sharing their own work with me, discussing possible avenues of research and writing, assisting me with out-of-field questions, and the like. These include Arthur Kinney, Stephen Orgel, Hunt Hawkins, Marjorie Garber, Bruce Smith, and Joseph Price. In addition, I am grateful for the impeccable professionalism of the staff at the various research institutions whose collections contributed to my research: the Folger Shakespeare Library, the British Library, the Library of Congress, the Tübingen Universitätsbibliothek, the Strozier and Dirac Libraries of Florida State University, the Biblioteca Estense, the Ringling Museum of Art, The Philadelphia Museum of Art, and the National Gallery of London. (My especial thanks go to the staff in Tübingen, whose efficiency was surpassed only by their patience with my German.)

Pieces of this book have been originally aired either as lectures or as published articles, or both; I am therefore deeply indebted to the various organizations and publications that have provided me with an outlet for early versions of my work. These include the South Atlantic Modern Language Association, at whose 1990 meeting I read a short version of Chapter 1; the Shakespeare Association of America and the English Department of The University of Texas at El Paso, for both of which I read early versions of Chapter 3 in 1997; the Group for

Early Modern Cultural Studies, for whose 1999 meeting I read a piece of Chapter 4; *The Production of English Renaissance Culture,* edited by David Lee Miller, Sharon O'Dair, and Harold Weber (Cornell University Press, 1994), in which an early version of Chapter 1 appeared ("Bestial Buggery in *A Midsummer Night's Dream*"); *Ovid and the Renaissance Body,* edited by Goran Stanivukovic (University of Toronto Press, 2001), in which a portion of Chapter 2 appeared; and *Modern Language Quarterly* (59.2 [June 1998]), which published an early version of Chapter 3.

Likewise, I am grateful for financial support from the National Endowment for the Humanities, during whose 1990 Folger Library Summer Seminar on "Shakespeare and the History of Taste" I pursued some of the earliest research for this study. I would also like to thank my home institution, Florida State University, for an internal summer grant and for sabbatical and leave time that has enabled me to complete this project. In addition, Trish Thomas has served diligently as my research assistant, while Kristi Long, Annjeanette Kern, and Adelle Krauser have overseen the production of this volume by Palgrave Press. I owe them a particular debt for their hard work, attention to detail, and patience.

Beyond all this, I have a broad range of personal debts to acknowledge. As ever, Gary White and Pam Ball have encouraged me, entertained me, and seen me through various more or less disgraceful personal mishaps. Jeff Tatum has offered various kinds of help in the area of classical studies while remaining in no way responsible for my offenses against the Greek and Latin tongues. My mother and sister, Katherine Boehrer and Susan Seeley, have supplied me with the unconditional support and acceptance one can only expect of family. Linda Hall has provided me with invaluable company and emotional relief during the final stages of manuscript preparation. Jenny Caneen's love deserves better recompense than this book could ever be. And finally, this work is dedicated to Barbara DeMent, my former wife and steadfast friend, who has contributed to it, both directly and indirectly, in ways that defy enumeration.

A Note on Texts and Translations

The principal dramatists discussed in this study are William Shakespeare, Ben Jonson, and Thomas Middleton. I have referred to the following editions of their respective works: *The Riverside Shakespeare*, ed. G. Blakemore Evans et al. (Boston: Houghton Mifflin, 1997); *Ben Jonson*, ed. C. H. Herford and Percy and Evelyn Simpson (Oxford: Clarendon Press, 1925–1952), 11 vols.; and Middleton's *A Chaste Maid in Cheapside*, ed. R. B. Parker (London: Methuen, 1969).

When citing foreign-language material, I have employed published translations whenever possible. As a general rule, if there is a major translation contemporary with the works I discuss (e.g., Hoby's *Courtier*, Marlowe's Ovid, the Authorized Bible), I have consulted it over more recent renderings. In the absence of available translations, I have rendered foreign-language material into English myself, and only in such cases have I also supplied the original foreign-language text for comparison. However, I have deviated from this practice in one instance: my discussion of Ovid's *Amores* in Chapter 2. I believe the treatment of this work is sufficiently lengthy, and the work itself sufficiently complex, to warrant that I print references to it not only in translation, but in the original as well.

SERIES EDITOR'S FOREWORD

Once there was a time when each field of knowledge in the liberal arts had its own mode of inquiry. A historian's labors were governed by an entirely different set of rules than those of the anthropologist or the literary critic. But this is less true now than it has ever been. This new series begins with the assumption that, as we enter the twenty-first century, literary criticism, literary theory, historiography, and cultural studies have become so interwoven that we can now think of them as an eclectic and only loosely unified (but still recognizable) approach to formerly distinct fields of inquiry such as literature, society, history, and culture. This series furthermore presumes that the early modern period was witness to an incipient process of transculturation through exploration, mercantilism, colonization, and migration that set into motion a process of globalization that is still with us today. The purpose of this series is to bring together this eclectic approach, which freely and unapologetically crosses disciplinary, theoretical, and political boundaries, with early modern texts and artifacts that bear the traces of transculturation and globalization.

This process can be studied locally and internationally, and this new series is dedicated to both. It is just as concerned with the analysis of colonial encounters and native representations of those encounters as it is with representations of the other in Shakespeare, the cultural impact of the presence of strangers/foreigners in London, or the consequences of farmers' migration to that same city. This series is as interested in documenting cultural exchanges between British, Portuguese, Spanish, or Dutch colonizers and native peoples as it is in telling the stories of returning English soldiers who served in foreign armies on the continent of Europe in the late sixteenth century.

Bruce Boehrer approaches the topic of cultural exchanges through an intense engagement with the animal world. Specifically, Boehrer's *Shakespeare among the Animals* explores the social instrumentality of animal metaphors in early modern English drama. In recent years, we have become used to studies that look at cultural or racial "others" to help us understand who "we" are or were. When we read *Shakespeare among the Animals* we begin to recognize that the animals Boehrer encounters in Renaissance plays and culture serve a purpose startlingly similar to that served by foreigners and natives in early modern travel narratives such as those anthologized by Richard Hakluyt and others. Just as racial, ethnic, exotic, or cultural otherness serves as a touchstone for "Englishness" or humanity, so the representations of animals are made to do a significant amount of cultural work in the definition of social identities and biological categories.

What separates us from the animals, according to renaissance writers? Is it our physical body, our rational mind, or our ability to speak? Proceeding from the premise that early modern dramatic literature "discovers" within the organization of the natural world its own ideas about cultural organization, Bruce Boehrer adapts three ecocritical concepts—absolute anthropocentrism, relative anthropocentrism, and anthropocentrism, which delineate, respectively, "man," "animals," and "monster"—to explore the ways representations of animals in the plays of William Shakespeare, Thomas Middleton, and Ben Jonson yield valuable insights into early modern conceptions of what it meant to be human. In a graceful and accessible style, Boehrer traces various formulations of social and biological identity to Biblical, classical, and medieval sources, and scrutinizes their deployment in the construction of early modern conceptions of gender, class, and race. In the process, Boehrer discovers that early modern writers define animals in a manner that is intimately connected with early modern society's understanding of both the *essence* and the *limits* of our humanity, and why and how it is possible that some humans are more (or less) human than others. To his credit, however, Boehrer resists any temptation to reify the categories that structure his analysis. Though "man," "beast," and "monster" may appear stable, and mutually illuminating concepts in particular instances or locales, it becomes clear that when they are examined in a broader cultural spectrum they turn out to be porous at their boundaries. With sensitivity, imagination, and humor, Boehrer negotiates his way through this complex field of cultural exchanges, fully aware that the supposedly firm distinction between nature and culture in the Renaissance is far more malleable and dependent upon context than some of us would like to believe.

The fictionalized character of the theatrical entrepreneur Philip Henslowe in the recent film *Shakespeare in Love,* shallowly professes that for a play to be truly successful it must have "a bit with a dog."

Reading *Shakespeare among the Animals,* we are reminded that we have to take the entertaining "bit with a dog" much more seriously than we have been, and that we should pay closer attention to the bits with the cuckoos, parrots, horses, and what have you, as well.

Ivo Kamps, series editor

INTRODUCTION

HOW TO DO THINGS WITH ANIMALS

1. THE DUKE OF SAXONY'S NEPHEW

Early in Shakespeare's *The Merchant of Venice* (ca. 1596), Nerissa questions Portia about her opinion of her various suitors. Portia dismisses each of the men with scorn, until her waiting-woman finally asks how she likes "the young German, the Duke of Saxony's nephew" (1.2.84–85). In this case Portia's acid response, capitalizing upon the German reputation for drunkenness, also frames itself in terms of the distinction between human and animal nature:

> [1 like him] very vildly in the morning, when he is sober, and most vildly in the afternoon, when he is drunk. When he is best, he is a little worse than a man, and when he is worst, he is little better than a beast. And the worst fall that ever fell, I hope I shall make shift to go without him. (1.2.86–91)

The insult here is of a sort that Shakespeare returns to again and again in his work, in ways that the present study seeks to document and explain. In effect, Portia's words register a slippage of identity. As she seeks to understand the Duke of Saxony's nephew in terms of the venerable and fundamental distinction between man and beast, the distinction sifts through her fingers, and she is left instead with an unresolvable ambiguity. On one hand, the young German suitor behaves in a way that Portia refuses to acknowledge as human; on the other hand, his form and breeding and articulacy unquestionably exclude him from the animal world. The result is that he ends up in a space of ontological indeterminacy—a linguistic in-between land

whose existence is both denied and enabled by differential constructions of human and animal nature.

This book seeks to understand the social dimension of such constructions as they operate within the drama of Elizabethan and Jacobean England. I seek, in other words, to explore a chain of
interrelated questions that include the following: How did citizens of
early modern England understand the difference between people and
animals? How did their understanding of this difference affect their
understanding of themselves and their relations with one another?
And how did the resulting formulations of biological and social identity operate within the popular dramatic entertainment of the day?
These are vast questions, and any response I may offer to them here
will necessarily be incomplete, reflecting the structure of my inquiry
as much as the structure of the subject matter itself. However, the
present study may nonetheless serve as a useful introduction to its
subject; and if it is to do so, it must adequately address certain bodies of primary historical material: the plays (by Shakespeare, Jonson,
Middleton, etc.) that are its principal focus; the nondramatic literature, visual arts, architecture, music, and other elements of social ornament contemporary with these plays; surviving philosophical,
theological, and legal arguments concerning the relation between
human and animal nature; and the remnants of material culture that
reflect the place of animals in the daily life of Renaissance Englishmen
and Englishwomen. These are the central resources upon which I will
draw in the course of my work here.

The following chapters are thus both self-consciously eclectic and
self-consciously limited in scope. They participate in a broad tradition
of Shakespearean scholarship on the role of the natural world in the
poet's work, scholarship that extends from traditional philological
and old-historicist studies to the postmodern perspective of contemporary feminism, materialism, and cultural studies.[1] In general, the
present work tends to complicate traditionalist views that "man's nature and his place in the world" were "universally agreed upon" in
Shakespeare's day (Spencer 1942, 1), while nonetheless acknowledging the existence of a broad official consensus on such subjects. In its
procedure and orientation, I thus hope this work will complement
current scholarship on the natural world not only in early modern literature, but in the other, related fields surveyed briefly in my final
chapter on recommended additional reading. Although the present
study cannot possibly do justice to the richness and variety of the textual record it seeks to investigate, it may nonetheless reasonably hope
to identify certain outstanding trends, motifs, and conflicts in its sub-

ject matter; and in the process it may also hope to suggest directions for further research into the records and issues it seeks to explain. If these goals are worth pursuing, in turn, that is because distinctions between human and animal nature are central to western cultural organization in a wide range of ways. Such distinctions help to license particular forms of material and economic relation to the natural world; they help to suggest and reinforce parallel social distinctions on the levels of gender, ethnicity, rank, and so on; in the process, they help human beings to define and conceive of themselves, both as groups and as individuals; and finally, thus, these distinctions also help to structure very specific patterns of cultural exchange—such as those of the Renaissance drama—that are arguably worth studying in their own right.

In *The Merchant of Venice*, Portia's reaction to her German suitor provides a case in point, both in terms of what it accomplishes and what it fails to accomplish. On one hand, Portia clearly uses the distinction between people and animals as a hierarchized opposition: a means of separating the *inferior* elements of creation (the animals) from the *superior* (men—and perhaps even women). Such binary discriminators are undeniably useful in organizing the world; hence, as Mary Douglas and other anthropologists have noted,[2] they furnish a central motif in numerous forms of social protocol and religious ritual (see Douglas 1966). However, Douglas has also shown (using the Mosaic dietary prohibitions as her classic example) that such distinctions tend to fall victim to the limits they inevitably presuppose. How does one account for elements of creation that do not conform to the particular modes of binary organization one has already chosen as significant? This is the problem that confronts Portia in the form of the Duke of Saxony's nephew, who redistributes the significant characteristics that divide men from animals in such a way as to frustrate binary discrimination altogether. On the one hand, he is presumably capable of conversation and social interaction, a fact that renders him no animal; yet on the other hand, his lack of temperance and discretion makes him no man, either. Thus, although the distinction between man and beast may help in numerous ways to make life possible for Portia, it signally fails to make sense of her German suitor.

However, this failure is by no means an entirely bad thing. At the very least, it opens up a new realm of conceptual possibilities by generating a second field of binary discrimination parallel to the first: the distinction between things that conform to the man/beast opposition and things that do not. This secondary distinction—described very often by Renaissance authors as the difference between things natural and things monstrous[3]—exists in a shadowy relation to the original antithesis between human and animal nature. On one hand, the validity of the man/beast opposition as a means of sorting out the world is challenged by anything—like the distinction between nature and monstrosity—that eludes the terms of the opposition itself. Yet on the other hand, the classification of aberrant phenomena as such—the act of defining them as contrary to the natural order of things—paradoxically reinforces the perceived authority of the original, challenged binary terms by positing them as a given, normative state of affairs in relation to which the monstrous exists as a kind of degeneration or perversion.[4] On this level, the man/beast opposition ceases to stand for the world as it absolutely is, but stands instead for the world as it absolutely *should be*.

Hence the complexity of Portia's insult: on one hand, she represents the Duke of Saxony's nephew as a degenerate man who nonetheless occupies a position on the great chain of being at least nominally superior to that occupied by the beasts ("when he is worst he is little better than a beast"). However, the fact that he eludes "natural" binary categories simultaneously renders him inferior to the properly conceived elements of creation from which he differs; as an instance of the perversion of natural order, he is, in a sense, worse than any dog or cat or rat. Thus Portia concludes her remarks by observing that if "the worst fall that ever fell, I hope I shall make shift to go without him." Her attributive adjectives move from superlative to comparative to inverted superlative forms ("Best . . . worse . . . worst . . . better . . . worst that ever fell") in a way that parallels her suitor's supposed ontological degeneration.

Moreover, the biological discriminations Portia thus invokes also lend themselves to further use on the social level, where they supply a paradigm for various sorts of distinctions between persons. In the case of the Duke of Saxony's nephew, such distinctions operate on the level of national identity; Portia's German suitor is identified with the beasts as a result of a particular vice—drunkenness—that was conventionally associated in early modern England with such northern European peoples as the Dutch, the Germans, and the Danes (compare, e.g., *Hamlet*, ca. 1599–1601). Such identification tends to represent otherness of custom and nationality as a degeneration from a naturally instituted, normative pattern of human behavior correlative to the biological patterns that mark the order of physical nature. I do not think it accidental that Portia's animal references should articulate national difference in this way. *The Merchant of Venice*, after all, is also as deeply concerned with the emerging concept of racial

difference as any work in the Shakespeare canon; the play's formulations of race not only identify ethnic others with animals (Shylock is
"a cut-throat dog" [1.3.111], a "stranger cur" [1.3.118], a "dog"
[1.3.121], a "cur" [1.3.122], and a "dog" again [1.3.128] within
the space of 18 lines), but they also interrogate the supposed biological basis for racial discrimination: "Hath not a Jew eyes? Hath not a
Jew hands, organs, dimensions, senses, affections, passions; fed with
the same food, hurt with the same weapons, subject to the same diseases, heal'd by the same means, warm'd and cool'd by the same winter and summer, as a Christian is?" (3.1.59–64).

Scholars have spent much time and effort debating the particular
view of race promoted by *The Merchant of Venice,* and my personal
reaction to this one of Shakespeare's plays will inevitably interest few
readers. Still, it seems clear to me that this comedy of Shakespeare's
contains what we might now, anachronistically, call both racist and
antiracist elements, and that it invites the audience to identify with
both. For instance, Portia's dig at her Saxon suitor becomes funny
only to the extent that one accepts the cultural stereotype it presupposes; however, it is still hard to deny that Shylock's claim to humanity also solicits an audience's sympathetic identification. To this
extent, the play remains hopelessly inconsistent; critical efforts to
conform it to a traditional Christian anti-Semitism or to an emergent
model of ethnic tolerance seem equally unsatisfactory. And if that is
so, in turn, it is perhaps because *The Merchant of Venice* presents
racism not as an issue to be resolved, but rather as a resource to be
explored and exploited. In this regard, at least, the play's inconsistency on matters of race parallels a broader inconsistency, discernible
within early modern English culture in general, concerning the relation between the regimes of nature and of culture, the regiments of
men and of animals.[5] To the extent that *The Merchant of Venice* employs the relation between culture and nature to underwrite that between Christian and Jew (or Italian and German), the latter must
unavoidably inherit the inconsistencies of the former.

In what remains of this introductory chapter, I would therefore
like to survey three of the most ubiquitous, important, and per-
durably incohesive ways in which early modern English authors
wrote and thought about the relations between culture and nature,
people and animals. All three of these patterns of thought are discernible within Portia's remarks about the Duke of Saxony's
nephew; indeed, they are largely responsible for the tension and
humor that inform those remarks. Moreover, these three general
modes of thinking about nature and culture all encompass a wide

range of interrelated axioms, commonplaces, and implications, most
of which were subject to debate among various individuals at various times within the late sixteenth and early seventeenth centuries.
To survey these attitudes at all is inevitably to oversimplify them, to
lend them an order and distinctness that they rarely if ever possessed
in their original context. To give these attitudes names as well, as if
they were from their inception a triad of separate, tidy, well-formu-
lated and self-consistent theories, is to compound the oversimplifi-
cation still further. But such reductionism is the besetting vice of
literary-historical discourse, and in this case it does at least contain a
kernel of insight, for it helps us to understand quite economically
the dynamic inconsistencies that lend these attitudes their social usefulness. Modifying terminology currently popular among ecocritics
and related scholars, I call these attitudes themselves "absolute anthropocentrism," "relative anthropocentrism," and "anthropomorphism." Between them, they furnish an almost unlimited range of
ways to understand the relation between the human and animal
realms, and to this extent I believe that they are vitally interdependent, that—despite and indeed precisely because of their inconsistencies—they work together to constitute the widest possible
repertoire of precedents and precepts for making use of the natural
world. Taken as a whole, these attitudes do to the natural world
what *The Merchant of Venice* does to racism: they present it not as a
set of problems to be answered in a single coherent fashion, but as
a set of discursive opportunities to be capitalized upon in accordance
with the needs of the moment. In Shakespeare's time these three attitude groups were—and I believe they remain today—our most
powerful tools for dealing with the nature of nature.

2. ABSOLUTE ANTHROPOCENTRISM

The views I identify with absolute anthropocentrism are distinguished by their common adherence to three central principles: 1)
that human beings are radically—at the root of their nature—different from all other life on earth; 2) that this difference renders humankind superior to the rest of earthly creation; and 3) that this
superiority, in turn, designates the natural world as an exploitable resource, with the spheres of nature and culture replicating the traditional relationship between servant and master. As Keith Thomas
notes in his indispensable study *Man and the Natural World* (1983,
17–18), these principles can be traced to scripture, where they surface as early as the first chapter of Genesis:

God created man in his own image, in the image of God created he
him; male and female created he them.

    And God blessed them, and God said unto them, Be fruitful, and
multiply, and replenish the earth, and subdue it: and have dominion
over the fish of the sea, and over the fowl of the air, and over every living thing that moveth upon the earth. (1.27–28)

Uniquely endowed with God's image, Adam and Eve are distinct in
kind from all other earthly creatures; created last of all, they occupy
the place of honor in the hexameral order of things; and this mark of
superiority is then equated with absolute mastery through God's
command that Adam and Eve "subdue" the earth and "have dominion" over all the beasts of sea and air and land. Nor is this merely a
prelapsarian arrangement; on the contrary, God reaffirms it to Noah
after the flood:

Be fruitful, and multiply, and replenish the earth.

    And the fear of you and the dread of you shall be upon every beast
of the earth, and upon every fowl of the air, upon all that moveth upon
the earth, and upon all the fishes of the sea; into your hand are they
delivered. . . .

    Every moving thing that liveth shall be meat for you; even as the
green herb have I given you all things. (9.2–4)

Thus, as recent environmentalist scholars have argued (e.g., White
1996, 8–12), the Judaeo-Christian tradition encourages believers to
conceive of themselves as distinct from, superior to, and in a sense *entitled* to the rest of earthly creation. But the nature of the distinction
thus adduced by scripture is troublesomely vague: "Man" alone among
the creatures may be invested with the image of God, but what does the
Bible mean by "image"? Saint Augustine (388–389 A.D.; see *Two Books
on Genesis,* 1991) supplies the standard answer when, responding to the
Manichaean tendency to read "image" as "physical appearance," he
counters, "The spiritual believers in the Catholic teaching do not believe that God is limited by a bodily shape. When man is said to have
been made in the image of God, these words refer to the interior man,
where reason and intellect reside" (1.17.28). And likewise, for Augustine, humankind's superiority over the animals is not primarily a physical condition (as the Manichees note, beasts are often capable of
eluding human pursuit and even doing harm to people), but instead a
mental one, "for though [man] can be killed by many wild animals on
account of the fragility of his body, he can be tamed by none, although
he tames very many and nearly all of them" (1.18.29).

In this way a particularly influential and durable line of scriptural commentary not only reinforces the model of absolute anthropocentrism propounded by the Bible, but in the process also equates human hegemony with humankind's exercise of reason. For Augustine, this elision of hegemony with reasoning ability must have seemed natural and even inevitable. After all, Augustine was not only the Bishop of Hippo; he was also the recipient of an outstanding classical education, and classical philosophers had long viewed the capacity to reason as a distinctively human property. Thus Aristotle, in the *De Anima* (ca. 350 B.C.; see *The Complete Works of Aristotle*, 1984), famously subdivides "the psychic powers" into five categories: "the nutritive, the appetitive, the sensory, the locomotive, and the power of thinking" (414a). Of these, in turn, plants have only the nutritive, while different species of animals partake of the first four in varying admixtures. The most sophisticated of the beasts are those that possess not only the power of self nutrition, but also the faculty of growth, the capacity for sensation, and the gift of voluntary motion. However, it is only "man and possibly another order like man or superior to him" that can possess in addition "the power of thinking and thought" (414b).

To this extent, at least, certain major classical and Christian texts clearly agree: they regard humanity as different in kind from the beasts, and different precisely because of the assumption that people can reason and beasts cannot. To gauge the importance of this view for early modern English writers, one need look no farther than John Donne's plangent "Nocturnal upon S. Lucy's Day" (first published 1633; see *The Complete English Poems*, 1971), which employs Aristotle's taxonomy of the soul in order to depict the poem's speaker as emptiness incarnate:

> Were I a man, that I were one,
> I needs must know; I should prefer,
>   If I were any beast,
> Some ends, some means; yea plants, yea stones detest,
> And love; all, all some properties invest;
> If I an ordinary nothing were,
> As shadow, a light and body must be there. (30–36)

For Donne's speaker, the loss of his beloved is a personal catastrophe of cosmic proportions, depriving him not only of his human reason, but also of all the other qualities—of nutrition, appetite, sensation, and locomotion—by which living beings may be identified as such. A neo-Aristotelian idea of human uniqueness and psychic order is built so centrally into Donne's poem that for a reader unfamiliar with this concept the poem itself may be little more than gibberish.

A similar—albeit somewhat looser and more casual—principle of discrimination abounds elsewhere in the literary records of early modern Europe; again and again it is assumed that the crucial characteristic distinguishing human from animal life is the capacity for reason. When Hamlet declares that "man" is "like an angel in apprehension" (2.2.306), he may conceivably be alluding, like Donne, to Aristotle's attribution of reason to "man and possibly another order like man or superior to him." Certainly when Hamlet complains that "a beast that wants discourse of reason" would have mourned longer for its mate than did his mother (1.2.150); when Mark Antony exclaims that "judgment" is "fled to brutish beasts, / And men have lost their reason" (*Julius Caesar* 3.2.104–105); and when Friar Laurence tells the suicidal Romeo that his "wild acts denote / The unreasonable fury of a beast" (*Romeo and Juliet* 3.3.110–111), their words take for granted the idea that people can best be distinguished from the lower orders of creation by virtue of their rational faculties. Again, Cervantes's *Dialogue of the Dogs* (1612) makes this point very precisely; the dialogue's canine interlocutors (actually men subject to a metamorphic enchantment) first realize that there is something wrong with the order of things when they register their own capacity for speech and reason, for "the difference between man and animal is that man is a rational being and the animal an irrational creature" (85). And the Attendant Spirit in Milton's *Mask Presented at Ludlow Castle* (1634) offers the following account of the bestial transformation to which the sorcerer Comus subjects his victims:

> His baneful cup . . .
> The visage quite transforms of him that drinks,
> And the inglorious likeness of a beast
> Fixes instead, unmolding reason's mintage
> Character'd in the face. (525–530)

For Milton's Attendant Spirit, the human face and human reason apparently stand in the relation of signifier to signified; thus it is appropriate that when Comus's intemperate followers abandon reason and succumb to their bestial passions by drinking from his cup, they should lose their human features in the process.

In short, it is commonplace for early modern writers to regard reason as a definitive feature of humanity, and given the numbing

frequency of this view in sixteenth- and seventeenth-century literature, one may be surprised to find that it is also vigorously contested
in some quarters. But it is, and I will have more to say on this point
later when I address the attitudes I identify with anthropomorphism.
In the meantime, Milton's lines in the *Mask* raise a second, perhaps
even equally important point of differentiation between people and
beasts, for the Attendant Spirit implicitly concedes that reason itself
is never on unmediated display. Being an abstract quality, it cannot
be seen or felt or tasted or heard or smelled in itself; instead, it must
communicate its presence by way of secondary, sensible forms that
lend it more or less concrete expression. Between them, the lines
from Milton and Cervantes quoted above identify the two most
privileged vehicles for such communication. For his part, Milton's
Attendant Spirit gives particular emphasis to visible signs, and
among those particularly the contours of the human face, whose
eyes, high forehead, and relatively flattened and mobile features apparently betoken intelligence. It is an idea to which Milton will return in *Paradise Lost* (1667), where the signifying potential of the
human face is reinforced also by Adam and Eve's upright posture,
unique among earthly creatures:

> Two of far nobler shape erect and tall,
> Godlike erect, with native Honor clad
> In naked Majesty seem'd Lords of all. . . .
> His fair large Front and Eye sublime declar'd
> Absolute rule. (4.288–301)

But where Milton, at such moments, lends special emphasis to finding
visible bodily indices for the inward qualities of human reason and "absolute rule," Cervantes on the other hand foregrounds the importance
of acoustic signifiers, the linguistic sounds with which we make meaning. Thus his dogs note that the miracle of their articulacy is doubled
because "we speak using proper discourse, as if we were endowed with
the power of reason, and yet we are so lacking in it that the difference
between man and animal is that man is a rational being and the animal
an irrational creature" (*Dialogue* 85). Cervantes's dogs, that is, do not
simply babble like madmen or idiots or children, but they make refined
and sophisticated sense, their language registering through its diction
and syntax, its use of rhetorical ornament and logical structure, the
workings of two cultivated and civilized minds. Indeed, when the dog
Cipion points out that his articulacy is evidence of his reason, and that
his reason is evidence that the order of nature has been miraculously

suspended, his language, framed in syllogistic form, demonstrates the presence of the very reasoning ability whose existence he is in the process of deducing. For the present study, concerned as it is with literary artifacts, the importance of language as a marker of human rationality and human difference cannot be overestimated.

This importance, of course, is asserted, in some way or other, almost everywhere in early modern letters. When Ben Jonson famously declares that "*Language* most shewes a man: speake that I may see thee" (*Timber, or Discoveries,* first published 1640; see Herford, Simpson, and Simpson 8:625), his next words clarify the relation between manhood and speech by explaining that speech reveals the quality of the mind producing it: "It springs out of the most retired, and inmost parts of us, and is the Image of the Parent of it, the mind" (8:625). Again, while Milton can clearly draw attention to visible and bodily markers of human difference, he too is deeply interested in the ontological implications of the capacity for language. Indeed, he could hardly ignore such matters, given that one of the major characters in his major poem assumes the form of a talking snake; as Eve understandably inquires of the serpent in Book 9 of *Paradise Lost,* "What may this mean? Language of Man pronounc't / By tongue of Brute, and human sense exprest?" (9.553–554). Here and elsewhere, Milton is less confident than some authors regarding the assumption that muteness betokens irrationality; as Eve goes on to say, "Much reason . . . oft appears" in the "looks" and "actions" of the beasts around her (9.558–559). Yet even for Eve, articulacy indicates the presence of a special sort of "human sense" that is apparently a mark of distinction.

Shakespeare, too, foregrounds the relation between human speech and human reason in *The Tempest* (ca. 1611), a play whose interest in "the apparently straightforward distinction between monster and man" at first appears to be one of its "central commitments" (Hawkes, *That Shakespeherian Rag* 54). Thus Shakespeare's Miranda differentiates her own humanity from Caliban's "vild race" through Caliban's original lack of both language and "meaning":

> When thou didst not, savage,
> Know thine own meaning, but wouldst gabble like
> A thing most brutish, I endow'd thy purposes
> With words that made them known. (1.2.355–358)

Morton Luce's gloss on this remark for the original Arden *Tempest* (preserved by Frank Kermode in his successor edition) draws attention to Miranda's assumption of a mutually constitutive relation between language and reason:

> When you were so savage that you could not express your thoughts, nor even think intelligently, and when your only language was a gabble of meaningless sounds like those of the brutes, then I taught you the use of language. . . . [The passage] may also include Whateley's "Words are the prerequisites of thoughts." (qtd. in Kermode 32, n. 357)

For Miranda, at this moment, the human may be distinguished from the "brutish" equally by the capacities for both reason and language. Furthermore, these capacities are equally important, self-referential, and mutually sustaining; the ability to speak, in a sense, creates the thinking processes to which it then attests, while the capacity for thought supplies language with its necessary motive and referent.

However, in these latter two literary cases—of Milton's Eve and Shakespeare's Miranda—readers will have noticed that the absolute character of humankind's superiority is already subject to qualification. For Eve, that superiority manifests itself through two parallel qualities, human speech and human reason, but while she conceives the former to be the exclusive property of humankind, she suspects that animals partake of the latter to some extent. Thus, whereas her attitudes toward language preserve a classic sense of humanity as sui generis, a class unto itself, her thoughts on the nature of reason suggest that, in this latter regard at least, the difference between people and beasts is one not of kind but simply of degree. Miranda, working with the same two markers of discrimination—human speech and human reason—asserts her absolute difference from Caliban in terms of both, and even goes so far as to suggest that one of these qualities cannot exist without the other. But her assertion is undermined, in classic Shakespearean fashion, by the very circumstances that enable her to make it, for she does so in conversation with Caliban himself, whose inconvenient articulacy disrupts the very distinction that Miranda is laboring to establish. Thus both of these passages, which may from one perspective be taken to exemplify the attitudes I associate with absolute anthropocentrism, also display conflicting characteristics that I will describe at length in the next two sections of this chapter. I make this point here for two reasons: first, to clarify the particular sense in which I take *Paradise Lost* and *The Tempest* as representative of absolute anthropocentrism; and second, to provide a cautionary instance of how deeply this set of attitudes is interconnected with others that are more or less at odds with it. What I present as a self-contained and self-consistent set of beliefs is nothing of the sort, and in fact loses most of its social and ideological usefulness if it is employed in a self-contained and self-consistent manner.

But still and all, early modern authors can and sometimes do make startlingly aggressive claims about the uniqueness of the human capacity for thought and for speech. A good example of the former comes from the indefatigable author of Elizabethan husbandry manuals, Gervase Markham. According to Markham (in *Markhams Maister-Peece*, 1610) the intellectual difference between men and horses is so absolute that:

> Many Farriers, and those of approued good skils, haue strongly held opinions, that horses haue uery little or no brains at all: and my selfe for mine owne part, being carried away with their censures, did at last upon good considerations cut up the heads of diuers horses, some dead, some in dying, and I could neuer find any liquid or thin braine, as in other beasts, . . . and so resolued with others that a horse had no braine. (57)

Markham eventually qualifies this position, concluding that horses do have brains, but he still insists that these brains have taken a form answerable to the physical severity of the typical horse's life: a form "tough and hard, euen vnpenetrable, and not to be pierst by any reasonable motion" (57). Or again, for a particularly uncompromising Renaissance statement of humanity's linguistic uniqueness, one might consider the case of Henry Swinburne. Swinburne, a lawyer and author of *A Brief Treatise of Testaments and Wills* (1637), offers the following rule of thumb for determining whether an individual is compos mentis and therefore legally entitled to make bequests:

> If a man be of mean understanding, . . . such an one is not prohibited to make a Testament: unless he be yet more foolish, and so very simple and sottish, that he may easily be made to believe things incredible or impossible; as that . . . Beasts and Birds could speak, as it is in *Aesop*'s fables. (48)

For linguists, cultural theorists, biologists, and developmental psychologists at the cusp of the twenty-first century, the nature of animal communication has become a remarkably thorny issue. If even so unsophisticated an organism as a bee can communicate information to other bees, and if one of the daughters of Thomas Mann can induce a dog to compose a coherent sentence upon a specially designed typewriter, to what extent can language be viewed as an exclusively human property?[6] And if a laboratory-trained parrot can correctly answer, in English, questions that are put to him, in English, concerning the relative size, shape, color, and material of different physical objects, to what extent can the bird be viewed as irrational?[7] Such questions bedevil contemporary scholars; for Henry Swinburne, however, the belief that animals might talk is so absurd as to constitute prima facie evidence of mental incapacity.

And it is upon beliefs such as those of Markham and Swinburne that the broader edifice of absolute anthropomorphism resides. If "man" differs in kind from the rest of creation, the argument generally goes, the qualities that render him different also make him superior. Thus the language/intellect dyad reemerges as a marker of preeminence in Jonson's *Timber, or Discoveries,* in which speech becomes "the only benefit man hath to expresse his excellencie of mind above other creatures" (8:620). As Terence Hawkes has helpfully shown (*Shakespeare's Talking Animals* 1973, 9–10), this view finds an influential classical precedent in Cicero's *De Oratore* (55 A.D.; see *De Oratore* 1959), which argues that, "the one point in which we have our very greatest advantage over the brute creation is that we hold converse one with another, and can reproduce our thought in words" (1.8.32). Nor (as Hawkes also notes) is this idea even new with Cicero, who in turn could have found it in the *Antidosis* of Isocrates (354 BC; see *Isocrates* 1929):

> For in the other powers which we possess . . . we are in no respect superior to other living creatures; nay, we are inferior to many in swiftness and in strength and in other resources; but, because there has been implanted in us the power to persuade each other and to make clear to each other whatever we desire, not only have we escaped the life of wild beasts, but we have come together and founded cities and made laws and invented arts. (253–254)

It is in deference to this same tradition that Hamlet identifies humankind's "large discourse"—the noun here simultaneously and appropriately signifying both reason and power of speech—as the race's definitive feature and marker of superiority:

> What is a man,
> If the chief good and market of his time
> Be but to sleep and feed? a beast, no more.
> Sure He that made us with such large discourse,
> Looking before and after, gave us not
> That capability and godlike reason
> To fust in us unused. (4.4.33–39)

Once again, it is "discourse" that makes humanity more—and better—than the animals.

Finally, this sense of human superiority, founded in the capacities for reason and speech, helps frame the natural world as a consumable asset: in effect as human property, to be employed at the human community's behest and for the human community's convenience and advantage. At present, this is perhaps the most notorious of the principles I identify with absolute anthropomorphism, and it has been subjected to severe recent critique by bioethicists, who have branded it as "speciesism" (Singer 1975, 7); by environmentalists, who view it as derogatory to the ecological balance that sustains life on earth; and by advocates of cultural diversity, who associate it with various sorts of Eurocentrism, capitalism, and imperialism. For many early English writers, however, this principle is more or less taken for granted, and like the other two we have considered, it also can be traced both to scriptural and to classical sources. Thus Pliny the Elder, of all people, might as well be echoing Genesis 1.27–28 ("Have dominion . . . over every living thing") when he remarks (77 A.D.) that "The first place [in creation] will rightly be assigned to man, for whose sake great Nature appears to have created all things" (7.1.1). For his part, Sir Francis Bacon, whose advocacy of inductive over deductive reasoning is so revolutionary in other respects, justifies his new logic in 1620 on the ground that it better fulfills this same age-old imperative to master nature:

> For the end which this science of mine proposes is the invention not of arguments but of arts; . . . not of probable reasons, but of designations and directions for works. And as the intention is different, so accordingly is the effect; the effect of the one being to overcome an opponent in argument, of the other to command nature in action. (*The Great Instauration* 4:24)

More traditional thinkers also view nature as a manipulable resource, and none better represents this attitude than Bishop Lancelot Andrewes. Expounding upon the sixth commandment, Andrewes (*A Patterne of Catachisticall Doctrine*, 1630) specifically attributes humankind's proprietorship of nature to human superiority over the rest of creation, a superiority that he ascribes in turn to human reason:

> That the killing of beasts cannot be contained in this law [the sixth commandment] to be here forbidden, it is plaine by these two reasons . . . 1, . . . Beasts can have no right of society with us, because they want reason. 2, It cannot bee sinne to use things, to the ende for

which they were ordained; now the less perfect are for the more perfect, as hearbs for beasts: and hearbs and beasts both for man. (350–351)

Writing with the authority of mainstream Anglicanism at his back, Andrewes bluntly asserts the three principles of absolute anthropocentrism and extracts each of the latter two principles from its immediate predecessor. In the process, his assertion also returns us to the text of scripture, where our survey of these principles began.

But my discussion of absolute anthropocentrism cannot end without citing one final literary source. For if Lancelot Andrewes asserts the exploitability of nature within the context of spiritual discourse, Ben Jonson offers a parallel statement, within the context of secular patronage verse, in his famous country-house poem "To Penshurst" (*The Forrest* 2; published 1616). For Jonson, the Kentish estate of the Sidney family figures as a kind of postlapsarian paradise, distinguished by an egalitarian abundance—"The blushing apricot, and woolly peach / Hang on thy walls, that euery child may reach" (43–44)— and a social ethic of generous mutuality, whereby the tenant-farmers of the estate freely offer their produce to the lord and lady, not because that produce is necessary to anyone's well-being, but because it emblematizes the unconstrained character of the personal relations that structure the surrounding community:

> All come in, the farmer and the clowne:
> And no one empty-handed, to salute
>   Thy lord, and lady, though they haue no sute.
> . . . .
> But what can this (more then expresse their loue)
>   Adde to thy free prouisions, farre aboue
> The neede of such? (48–59)

Ultimately, we discover that this social ethic of freedom and abundance originates on the very grounds of the estate itself, whose fauna eagerly offers itself up for human consumption:

> The painted partrich lyes in euery field,
>   And, for thy messe, is willing to be kill'd.
> . . . .
>   And pikes, now weary their owne kinde to eat,
> As loth, the second draught, or cast to stay,
>   Officiously, at first, themselues betray. (29–36)

At Jonson's Penshurst, nature reachieves something like its originary, paradisal relation to humankind, and it does so by acknowledging and embracing its ordained subservience to culture. Moreover, this voluntary subservience also provides a model for the ideal behavior of the lower social ranks in the Penshurst community; by observing the partridges and pikes that volunteer to furnish the estate's larder, the farmer and the clown may encounter a naturally decreed model for their own proper deference to authority. Thus the relations between nature and culture pattern themselves upon—and in turn provide the originary pattern for—parallel relations between the lower and upper social strata. This complementarity, whereby the opposition between nature and culture simultaneously replicates and prefigures that between the lower and upper social ranks, supplies the enabling condition for the set of attitudes I describe as relative anthropocentrism, and to which I now turn.

3. Relative Anthropocentrism

The most obvious function of the beliefs I have identified with absolute anthropocentrism is to underwrite an exploitative or extractive mode of relation to the natural world: a mode of relation characterized by such activities as the hunting of game (which we have seen Lancelot Andrewes justify at length), the dissection and vivisection of animals (as practiced unselfconsciously by Gervase Markham), the domestication of beasts for purposes of labor, and the exercise of property rights over livestock and other wild and domesticated animals (as embodied in Jonson's Penshurst). However, this same complex of ideas also performs a second, equally important and far-reaching function, for it enables the parallel formation of a second set of attitudes, which I identify with relative anthropocentrism. These attitudes derive much of their force from their extreme similarity to the views I have already described above. Indeed, the only real difference between absolute and relative anthropocentrism is that the former distinguishes between humanity and the animal world without qualification, whereas the latter associates large and variable subsets of the human community to a greater or lesser extent with the realm of nature, while reserving full human status only for specific, arbitrarily defined social groups. In other words, relative anthropocentrism readily assents to all three of the central principles of absolute anthropocentrism: that humankind is different from, better than, and entitled to the use of the animal world. The only difference is that relative anthropocentrism adopts a much narrower definition of humankind.

The ways in which the definition can be narrowed are, of course, numerous, and they conjure up some of the ugliest practices in human memory, as well as some whose validity is hard to dispute. Among the former we must number various sorts of discrimination by nationality, ethnicity, gender, religion, social rank, and so on; among the latter, the special treatment regularly accorded to children, the insane, and the mentally challenged must figure prominently. In early modern England, notable objects of the first sort of discrimination include such groups as the Irish, Spanish, Italians, French, Germans, Scots, and Welsh; Africans, Turks, Arabs, and Native Americans; women; Jews, Muslims, Catholics, Puritans, and Protestants; apprentices, servants, farm laborers, the young, the poor, and the unemployed. One consequence of this pattern of discrimination is that, if we take it rigorously and cumulatively, the number of fully human human beings in the world must inevitably be much smaller than the number of human beings whose status as such is somehow impaired. A second consequence is that, by excluding the "impaired" groups, we may emerge with a fairly specific idea of what it takes to participate fully in the human condition. For example, in late Elizabethan England, one had to be white, English, Anglican, male, mature, mentally sound, and prosperous, at the very least. Of course, the patterns of discrimination enabled by relative anthropocentrism are not developed in any cumulative or rigorous way—at least not in early modern England, where a fully articulated ideology of racism, for instance, has yet to take hold.[8] But even in their isolated particularity, the patterns of bigotry I have described privilege certain social groups at the expense of others, and they uniformly do so by repositioning the disparaged other within the animal world.

However, one immediate obstacle to this repositioning would seem to be supplied by the text of scripture. As we have seen, Genesis clearly and repeatedly designates the human race, without limitation or qualification, as custodian of the rest of creation; so by identifying large parts of humanity with the animal orders, is one not directly contradicting God's own word? To escape this possibility, early modern writers on ethnicity develop a myth of racial degeneration tied to the legacy of Noah's children after the flood. Johannes Boemus, whose *Omnium Gentium Mores* was translated into English in 1555 as *The Fardle of Facions,* thus explains all ethnic diversity as a consequence of "that spiedie and unripe puttyng forthe of the children [of Noah] from their progenitours, before they had thoroughly learned and enured them selues with their facions and manners" (sig. B3v). The accursed son Ham naturally becomes the particular focus of this theory. As Boemus goes on

to explain, Ham was hastily expelled from the larger family after gaz-
ing upon his father's drunken nakedness; he and his wife and children
settled in Arabia; and, once there, he

> lefte no trade of religion to his posteritie, because he none had learned
> of his father. Where of it came to passe, that . . . beyng sent out as it
> ware, swarme aftre swarme into other habitations, and skatered at length
> into sondry partes of the world . . . some fel into erroures wherout thei
> could neuer unsnarle themselues. . . . Insomuch that some liued so
> wildely . . . that it ware harde to discerne a difference betweene them
> and the beastes of the felde. (sigs. B3v-B4r)

This myth of racial degeneration proves so useful that it endures for
centuries and migrates to such places as the United States, where it
installs itself within the proslavery politics of the antebellum South
and arguably contributes to the development of scientific racism in
the late nineteenth and early twentieth centuries.[9]

In the short run, however, theories like Boemus's yield two general consequences for any social group identified as degenerate and
therefore bestial. First, the group finds its human rights curtailed in
direct proportion to the curtailment of its human identity; second,
the group discovers that other, theoretically more human groups can
exercise rights over it, ostensibly on its behalf. As to the former of
these consequences: Early modern jurists expend a good deal of energy justifying the unequal distribution of rights under the law, and
they do so in ways that often presuppose the impaired humanity of
legally disadvantaged communities. For a relatively benign case in
point (and one of considerable interest for Chapter 3 of this study),
we may return to Henry Swinburne's *Brief Treatise of Testaments and
Wills* (1637), which patiently explains why a will framed by a mentally unsound testator has no legal validity:

> A Testament is an act to be performed with discretion and judgement.
> But a naturall fool, by the generall presumption of Law, doth not un-
> derstand what he speaketh, though he seem to speak reasonably; no
> more than did *Balam*'s Asse, when he reasoned with his Master; or
> doth a Parrat, speaking to the passengers. (50)

As I will argue later in this book—using the literary history of pet parrots as my illustrative case—animal articulacy greatly contributes to
the discriminatory capacities of relative anthropocentrism, and in a
way that is in fact quite counterintuitive. For where one might expect
talking animals to challenge the very nature of humankind's presumed

superiority to the beasts, instead they are most commonly understood as Swinburne understands them: as an archetype of the bestial inferiority of certain men and women. Given the emphasis that early modern culture places upon speech as a marker of human identity and reason, the bestial acquisition of language unfixes the boundaries that distinguish people from animals, and in the process it enables those boundaries to be redrawn within the human community itself.

Elsewhere in the cultural records of early modern Europe, this same tendency to bestialize specific social groups can acquire a far more threatening cast. When considering the relation of marriage practice to the crime of sodomy, for instance, the sixteenth-century Flemish jurist Joost de Damhoudere denies certain racial and religious groups the right to participate in marital relations with Christians. His justification for this denial coincides precisely with Swinburne's justification for denying "naturall fools" the right to make wills. In effect, Damhoudere says, the people in question are no better than animals:

> In consideration of our faith it is held by law to be true sodomy . . . when one engages in sexual intercourse with Turks, Saracens, or Jews. For law and the Christian religion openly attack, disregard, loathe, and hate all of this sort as nothing more than beasts. (*Practica Rerum Criminalium*, 1557, sig. X8r)

> [Consideratione nostrae fidei, pro vera Sodomitica iure habetur . . . cu[m] quis naturali Venere vtitur cu[m] turcis, Saracenis, aut Iudeis. na[m] huiusmodi omnes, Iura & religio Christiana non secus, quam bestias . . . aperte oppugna[n]t, negligu[n]t, fastidiu[n]t, oderu[n]t.]

Such language holds immediate and serious implications for a play like *The Merchant of Venice*, in which the "sodomitical" union of Christian with Jew is averted only by Jessica's timely baptism.[10] However, Damhoudere's precept is perhaps even more emphatically realized in Shakespeare's *Othello* (ca. 1604). There, although the wedding of Othello to Desdemona does not transgress the boundaries of the Christian religion, Iago repeatedly images the couple's miscegenous embrace in terms of bestial intercourse, which is of course the very model of comparison employed by Damhoudere to characterize interfaith, interracial marriages as sodomy. As Iago taunts Desdemona's father, "You'll have your daughter cover'd with a Barbary horse; you'll have your nephews neigh to you" (1.1.112–113).

Likewise, early modern commentators on property law make it clear that all human beings are not endowed with equal access to the

world's natural resources. In effect, that is, all people do not participate equally in God's command to "have dominion" over "every living thing"; and if this dominion, in turn, is taken to be a definitive
attribute of the human condition, then those whose dominion is limited are likewise limited in their humanity. In any case, Hugo
Grotius's *De Jure Belli et Pacis* (1625; see *De Jure Belli et Pacis*,
1853) specifically insists that

> The right of occupying moveable things (as wild beasts, birds, &c.)
> may be barred by the Civil Law. . . . For the right to take such things
> is from a permission of Natural Law; not from a command, directing
> that there shall always be such liberty. Nor does human society require
> that it should be so. If any one should say that it appears to be a part
> of *ius gentium* [the ancient law of nations] that such a liberty should
> exist; I reply, that although in any part of the earth this be or should
> be so received, yet it has not the force of a general compact among na-
> tions: but is the Civil Law of several nations distributively, which may
> be taken away by nations singly. (2.3.5)

Grotius's ultimate point here is that, although "lordship and ownership" (i.e., power and property) are "distinct" things, they "are commonly acquired by one act" (2.3.4.2), so that for most practical
purposes the former implies the latter. In short, as a general rule, political hegemony entails legal advantage with respect to the ownership of property.

Likewise—to return to a literary work we have already considered
at some length—this common elision of lordship with ownership lies
at the heart of Jonson's "To Penshurst," where the cheerful self-
sacrifice of the local game is framed specifically in terms of property
rights:

> Thy copp's, too, nam'd of GAMAGE, thou hast there,
>   That neuer failes to serue thee season'd deere,
> When thou would'st feast, or exercise thy friends.
>   The lower land, that to the riuer bends,
> Thy sheepe, thy bullocks, kine, and calues do feed. (19–23)

In this descriptive sequence the deer belong to Barbara Gamage's
copse, which belongs—like the kine, bullocks, and calves—to the estate (antecedent of all the poem's second-person singular pronouns),
which in turn belongs to the Sidney family, whose mistress's name is
associated (at least partly via ownership) with the copse with which
the sequence began. Moreover, this passage simultaneously enforces

a particularly tight parallel between the estate and its tenants. The copse, we are told, serves the estate "season'd deere," but the adjective in this phrase conflates two separate activities: the seasonal provision of game that one would expect of a hunting preserve and the seasoned preparation of such game that one would expect of a cook. As in the woods, so in the kitchen: both beasts and servants render unto the estate that which belongs to it, and in the process they become mirror images of one another, neither owning the other, both, in a sense, belonging to the institution and family that sustain them. It is perhaps a final irony, therefore, that I have already described Jonson's Penshurst as a place of "egalitarian abundance," where the smallest child may pluck apricots and peaches at will from the orchard fruit trees. In fact, this egalitarianism manifests itself specifically on the level of material prosperity rather than legal entitlement.

Thus we have considered certain representative ways in which relative anthropocentrism may be employed to curtail the rights of particular social groups in early modern England. However, this same cluster of attitudes and ideas may also be put to the second, complementary purpose of empowering other groups entirely. In classic Foucauldian terms, the ostensibly bestial status of "savages," women, children, Jews, and so on may be taken to license efforts to discipline these communities, thereby enhancing the authority of the community represented by the disciplinary apparatus. Hence, as Keith Thomas has observed,

> Animal domestication furnished many of the techniques for dealing with delinquency [in early modern England]: bridles for scolding women; cages, chains and straw for madmen; halters for wives sold by auction in the market, in the widely accepted informal ritual of divorce. The training of youth was frequently compared to the breaking of horses; and it was no accident that the emergence in the seventeenth and eighteenth centuries of more humane methods of horse-breaking would coincide with a reaction against the use of corporal punishment in education. (45)

Practices of the sort enumerated by Thomas have cast a long shadow across Western culture, and they arguably persist in various forms to the present day.

But for authors of the English Renaissance, as opposed to parents in twenty-first–century America, the temptation to view and to treat children as animals seems to have elicited relatively little self-scrutiny. Even the gentle and enlightened Roger Ascham (1570; see *The*

Scholemaster, 1967) could encourage schoolteachers to consider "the most special notes of a good wit for learning in a child; after the manner and custom of a good horseman, who is skilful to know, and able to tell others, how by certain signs a man may choose a colt, that is like to prove another day excellent for the saddle" (30). For Ascham, the comparison between children and colts remains largely figurative, but for other educators of the day it could acquire something like literal force, as manifest in the regularity with which both children and horses were beaten by their early modern parents and trainers. Of course, the identification of children with colts was not new to the early modern period; four centuries before Christ, Plato, in *The Republic*, could already advocate "introduc[ing] our . . . young to fear and, by contrast, giv[ing] them opportunities for pleasure," just as one exposes "a colt . . . to alarming noises" in order "to find out if [he] is nervous" (413d). Still, this homology seems to have particularly embedded itself in English linguistic practice in the late Middle Ages and early Renaissance. At any rate, it is during this period that the noun "colt" itself begins to acquire its common sense denoting "an awkward young person who needs to be broken in" (*Oxford English Dictionary* [OED] "colt" *sb.* 2); the OED's earliest examples of this usage date from 1225 and 1586 respectively.

In the early English drama, this association of colts with headstrong children leaves many traces (some of them documented by the OED), but perhaps nowhere more memorably than in *1 Henry IV* (ca. 1597), where it lends a certain irony to Hotspur's peculiar relationship with his horse. As the most popular and outspoken of his play's rebels, Hotspur is emphatically associated with the world of warfare and chivalric exploit, and he furnishes the standard of martial heroism whereby Prince Hal's emergence into maturity is to be measured. Thus it is highly appropriate that Hotspur should long for single combat with Hal, but even so, the terms in which he expresses this longing bear scrutiny:

> Come let me taste my horse,
> Who is to bear me like a thunderbolt
> Against the bosom of the Prince of Wales.
> Harry to Harry shall, hot horse to horse,
> Meet and ne'er part till one drop down a corse. (4.1.119–123)

"Harry to Harry . . . horse to horse": this line's formal antithesis, with men and animals balanced against one another on the fulcrum of the caesura, is undercut not only by the similitudes expressed in either hemistich (Harry opposed to Harry, horse to horse), but also by the unifying alliteration that connects all four of the line's nouns. In fact, the line conveys not so much a sense of antagonism or opposition as of amalgamation: of rider with horse, of warrior with opponent. Yet in the midst of this confusion (which Harry is which Harry? which horse is which Harry's horse?), the alliterating adjective "hot" stands out as a singular marker of difference, recalling the speaker's name and all it suggests about both his strengths and defects of character. Indeed, it is Hotspur's very heat—his impetuosity and lack of self-restraint—that distinguishes him as unfit for the mature exercise of sovereign power; as his own father remarks, Hotspur is "a wasp-stung and impatient fool" whose immaturity is betrayed by his fondness for the "woman's mood" of scolding resentment (1.3.236–237). Associated thus with women and fools and horses, the youthful Hotspur (his youth itself a deliberate departure from Shakespeare's source) is marked as a proper object for Prince Hal's disciplinary ministrations. In a sense, by killing Hotspur, Hal not only suppresses the bestial and childish impulses of a rebellious subject; he also evinces a parallel suppression of the bestial and childish impulses within himself. This act of interior governance, in turn, ostensibly authorizes him to discipline and govern others less fully realized—less fully human—than he himself.

Elsewhere in *1 Henry IV*, Hotspur's interest in horses marks not only his commitment to martial values and his boyish impulsiveness, but also what can only be called a brand of erotic transference. The outstanding scene in point is 2.3, where Hotspur takes leave of his wife on the way to battle:

> *Hot.*God's me, my horse!
>   What say'st thou, Kate? What wouldst thou have with me?
> *Lady.* Do you not love me? do you not indeed? . . .
> *Hot.*Come, wilt thou see me ride?
>   And when I am a' horseback, I will swear
>   I love thee infinitely. (2.3.94–102)

Here Hotspur's predictable fondness for equitation is coupled with something else: a conventional emblematic equivalency of women and horses that enables his fondness for the latter to parallel and ultimately to compete with his attachment to the former. As one scholar has recently observed, "There can be no doubt that the equation of women with horses was operative in Elizabethan culture" (Roberts 1991, 64),[11] and this is so for a variety of reasons. First, the ostensibly unruly nature of both woman and horse apparently invites a comparable exercise of physical discipline. Second, the relation of horse to rider supplies a paradigm for the right government of "man's" bestial attributes by his rational faculties, a model of governance that also implies the proper subordination of the bestial female to the rational male. Third, this proper relation of wife to husband may be powerfully inverted through the popular Renaissance iconography of the uxorious husband ridden by his spouse. And fourth, the identification of femininity with bestiality attaches in particular to the exercise of feminine sexuality, so that the mare becomes a powerful emblem of feminine unchastity. In the next chapter of this study, I will focus especially upon the last of these points; for now let it suffice that the management of horses provides a convenient animal referent not only for the governance of children, but for the discipline of women as well.

But such patterns of animal association can be multiplied almost at will; repeatedly invoked to license the dominion of one social group over a variously defined other, they proliferate in the representational idiom of early modern Europe. Women, for instance, are associated with many animals other than horses; among other things, they are repeatedly likened to hunting falcons that must be reduced to obedience and yet are capable of breaking their training at any moment. When, in Thomas Kyd's *Spanish Tragedy* (ca. 1587; see *The First Part of Hieronimo and The Spanish Tragedy*, 1967), Balthazar complains that his love for Bel-imperia is unrequited, Lorenzo urges persistence with a pair of beast-taming metaphors, the second drawn from falconry: "In time the savage bull sustains the yoke, / In time all haggard hawks will stoop to lure" (2.1.3–4). As Shakespeare's Othello contemplates his wife's supposed adultery, he vows to disown her as one would do an unreliable hawk:

> If I do prove her haggard,
> Though that her jesses were my dear heart-strings,
> I'ld whistle her off, and let her down the wind
> To prey at fortune. (3.3.260–263)

And Petruchio makes prominent use of the same imagery to characterize his treatment of Katharina in *The Taming of the Shrew* (ca. 1593):

> My falcon now is sharp and passing empty,
> And till she stoop, she must not be full-gorg'd,
> For then she never looks upon her lure.

> Another way I have to man my haggard,
> To make her come, and know her keeper's call,
> That is, to watch her, as we watch these kites
> That bate and beat and will not be obedient. (4.1.190–196)

It is perhaps noteworthy that this popular line of metaphor habitually conflates inward states and outward behavior, a conflation deriving from the fact that hawks cannot be bullied into obedience but must instead be persuaded into a kind of complicity with their handlers.[12] For Balthazar and Othello a woman's comportment (including, in Othello's case, her wifely obedience) is thus assumed matter-of-factly to presuppose a settled and satisfactory emotional state; if Bel-imperia comes to love Balthazar, she'll do what he wants, whereas Desdemona threatens to deceive Othello when her affections are settled elsewhere. In both cases, the falcon's training comes to represent not simply a compelled conformity but rather a heartfelt acceptance. When Petruchio employs the same metaphor, he does so less obviously with respect to Katharina's inward affective condition, yet one might be tempted to suppose that here, too, the elision of behavior with affect persists. On this logic, Petruchio's declared intention is not simply to transform Katharina's behavior, but to transform her heart as well.

Finally (although, as I hope is very clear, by no means exhaustively), similar beast associations form a stock-in-trade of early modern English discourse on race, nationality, and ethnicity. As I have argued elsewhere ("Shylock" passim), Shylock's canine character in *The Merchant of Venice* owes much to the traditional anti-Semitic characterization of Jews as feral, interloping scavengers; this characterization, in turn, apparently contributed to the historic practice of hanging Jews between two dogs in an inverted parody of the crucifixion. Once Jews had been discursively reconfigured as feral dogs, they were liable to treatment as such. Conversely, once dogs were identified with reprobate people, they in turn could become susceptible to human legal liabilities; they could be—and were—indicted, prosecuted, condemned, and punished by judicial and quasi-judicial tribunals throughout early modern Europe (hence the adjective "hangdog").[13] This reversibility of metaphorical association is a phenomenon we will encounter again, in connection with the history of early English laws on animal sodomy (see Chapter 1). It is as if the association of people with animals entailed a transference of attributes that was mutual rather than unilateral in nature.

Few dramatic characters have elicited more discussion on account of such transference than has Caliban in *The Tempest* (ca. 1610). Although Prospero acknowledges his servant's "human shape" (1.2.284), Shakespeare repeatedly compromises Caliban's humanity through patterns of animal reference; he is "a freckled whelp, hagborn" (1.2.283), a "tortoise" (1.2.314), a "fish" (2.2.25), and so on. Such epithets inevitably participate in a long tradition of racist namecalling similar to that which invests Shylock with canine qualities. However, *The Tempest* refuses to confine itself narrowly to the language of relative anthropocentrism, any more than it confines itself to that of absolute anthropocentrism; among other things, the play also describes Caliban in terms of a spiritual and physical inferiority that is more individual than general in form. He is a "monster" (2.2.30), a "lying slave" (1.2.344), "malice" incarnate (1.2.367), and a would-be rapist, and these modes of disparagement, rather than participating in the discourse of *group* degeneracy that governs Caliban's identification with the categories of "tortoise" or "fish," insist upon a personal, even unique sense of willful depravity and reprobation. If Caliban is a "monster," that is at least arguably because he refuses to conform to kind: Because, by choosing to lie, to be malicious, to violate Miranda, and the like, he himself is to an important extent responsible for being what he is. This perverse singularity, in turn, is the governing principle of anthropomorphism.

4. ANTHROPOMORPHISM

At first blush, anthropomorphism would seem irreconcilably opposed to the various attitudes I have already described. Where both absolute and relative anthropocentrism insist upon the distinctness of humankind from the rest of creation and upon humanity's superiority to the animal orders, anthropomorphism emphasizes humankind's animal nature and the unique capacity of human beings to sink below type—to become worse than they were created. This latter capacity, in turn, entails an obvious negative consequence, for if human beings, of all earthly creation, are alone able to become degenerate by an act of will, then humanity's preeminent status in created nature is compromised by the ever-present possibility that people will devolve. If, moreover, the capacity to degenerate is in fact fairly pronounced—if it can actually be described more as a *tendency* than as a *potential*—humanity's natural preeminence is compromised still further. Of course, this very devolutionary tendency is central to Christian accounts of the postlapsarian condition; as Saint

Paul observes, "The good that I would do I do not: but the evil which I would not, that I do" (Romans 7.19). In this view, to be human is to live constantly in a state of devolution from one's best self: to recognize and aspire to a standard of natural, right behavior that original sin has rendered unattainable.

Anthropomorphism speaks to this view of human experience by maintaining 1) that human beings, like all of creation, are imbued with divine goodness; 2) that human beings, alone of all earthly creatures, are endowed with the capacity for moral choice; and 3) that this capacity, when exercised improperly (as it always has been, and inevitably will be again, sooner or later), leads individual human beings into a unique state of rebellion against their better natures, as determined by and discernible from the order of nature at large. This state of rebellion, in turn, is typically described either as a violation of law (the root meaning of "sin" is "offence, wrong-doing, misdeed" [OED "Sin," *sb.* 1]) or as the act of wandering from a set course of behavior (the root meaning of "error" and "perversion" is "to wander" or "to turn away"), or as a warning to others (thus "monster" derives from the Latin *monere,* "to warn" [OED]). In this view, sinful, erroneous, perverse, monstrous humanity has chosen to neglect the original code of behavior by which God had required it to comport itself, and one consequence is that humankind has in the process grown alienated from its own original nature. In an important sense, the animals are better than we are, for they remember the fundamental principles of living—fidelity, physical courage, self-sacrifice, perseverance, contempt of pleasure, and so on—that we have chosen to forget.

As I have already noted, the general assumptions of anthropomorphism thus conflict with much of the thinking inherent to absolute and relative anthropocentrism. In a moment I will examine two of the most prominent points of conflict between these sets of attitudes: the nature of reason as a marker of human difference, and the use of such difference to license exploitative modes of social relation. But first, one must observe that despite their massive differences of emphasis and presupposition, these three sets of attitudes—absolute anthropocentrism, relative anthropocentrism, and anthropomorphism—are capable of fruitful, mutually enabling interplay with respect to a wide range of particular applications. The much-discussed figure of Shakespeare's Caliban provides a classic case in point. As I have already observed, Shakespeare's Miranda characterizes Caliban in terms that recall the traditional emphasis accorded to human reason and speech within the discourse of absolute anthropocentrism, and this characterization abets her efforts—typical of relative anthropocentrism—to figure difference of race as analogous to difference of species. Insofar as she must teach Caliban to speak, it becomes all the easier for her to describe him as less than human. But anthropomorphism also contributes certain tendencies to Miranda's racism, for it is not entirely clear whether Caliban's degeneracy derives from inherited qualities or from the exercise of individual will. On one hand, it is as if Caliban were a victim of bad breeding: "Thy vild race," Miranda tells him, "had that in't which good natures / Could not abide to be with" (1.2.358–360). Yet on the other hand, he is castigated for sinking below a standard of human behavior to which he should have been able to conform; thus Prospero insists that "I have us'd thee / (Filth as thou art) with human care, and lodg'd thee / In mine own cell, till thou didst seek to violate / The honor of my child" (1.2.345–348). The language of relative anthropocentrism ascribes to Caliban an inferiority for which he cannot reasonably be held responsible; that of anthropomorphism then holds him responsible for it anyway.

The resulting tension marks a classic point of convergence between two different ways of viewing nature. And in fact the conflict between these two points of view can be resolved into a kind of complementarity. On one hand, the inherited degeneracy described by relative anthropocentrism may be understood as a collective racial expression of individual moral acts; on the other hand, the individual acts of corrupted will that are the province of anthropomorphism may be taken as foundational moments in the history of racial difference. That, at least, is exactly how Johannes Boemus views matters in *The Fardle of Facions*. In his account of the history of Ham's descendants, as we may recall, individual conduct and racial degeneration are intimately interrelated; Ham never learns proper behavior himself, and after his exile from the bosom of Noah's family, Ham's children have no better standard of manhood to follow. Therefore they reproduce their father's errors, gradually hardening those errors into a pattern of racial depravity. Of course, bad personal behavior usually does not produce such broad and disastrous consequences; there is no absolute correlation between individual moral acts and racial character. But there is always the chance that under certain circumstances phylogeny may recapitulate ontogeny as it does for the offspring of Ham. In such circumstances, racial difference is simply bad manners writ large.

I believe this interplay between two broadly dissimilar views of nature may account for some of the instability in Shakespeare's presentation of Caliban as a degenerate being. If nothing else, the exile of Caliban's mother recapitulates that of Ham, propelling her into the seclusion of a desert island, where her son inevitably inherits her defects of character; yet *The Tempest* also exhibits a recurring tendency to hold Caliban accountable for his acts, to regard him as educable and to punish him when he fails to conform to an acceptable standard of human behavior. Likewise, a similar ambivalence invests the play's sense of human identity, which is both ascribed and denied to Caliban at various moments and by various characters. Perhaps most pithily, Prospero describes Caliban as a "freckled whelp, hag-born," but nonetheless endowed with "human shape" (1.2.283–284), and if Prospero himself has trouble deciding whether or not Caliban is human, so does the play as a whole. At its simplest, the problem here is that Caliban can reason and speak and learn. To this extent, he obviously resists classification with the animals—at least if one thinks of animals, in the tradition of absolute anthropocentrism, as incapable of sense. But anthropomorphism presupposes a very different view of what it means to be human, a view in which humanity is defined not so much by the capacity to reason as by the capacity for moral choice, so that by this measure, perhaps, Caliban may be found less than perfectly human. To be sure, some Renaissance authors tend to elide the intellectual with the moral; Ben Jonson, for one, sometimes seems to see little or no difference between being wrong and being bad. But at least from Augustine's *credo ut intelligam* forward, Christianity has fostered a sense in which moral goodness and spiritual regeneracy operate independently of the intellect. The heart, we are told, has its reasons.

Moreover, if reason is thus removed from its position as the definitive feature of humanity, it may then be assigned, to one extent or another, to the lesser creation. This is exactly what happens in a number of classical and Christian texts dealing with the intellectual capacities of beasts. Plutarch, for one, argues at length in his *Moralia* that animals can reason, and in his dialogue on "Whether Land or Sea Animals Are Cleverer," he offers the following instance in point:

> Logicians assert that a dog, at a point where many paths split off, makes use of a multiple disjunctive argument and reasons with himself: "Either the wild beast has taken this path, or this, or this. But surely it has not taken this, or this. Then it must have gone by the remaining road." Perception here affords nothing but the minor premiss, while the force of reason gives the major premisses and adds the conclusion to the premisses. (969a-b)

In its insistence upon the continuity, rather than the disparity, between humankind and the lower orders of creation, this argument
typifies anthropomorphism; it reappears almost verbatim in 1615,
when King James I attends a public debate, held in Cambridge, on
"whether dogs could make syllogismes" (see Thomas Ball, 1885,
23). The victor of this dispute, John Preston, quotes Plutarch without mentioning him by name:

> An Ethymeme [*sic*] (said he), is a lawfull & reall syllogisme, but dogs
> can make them; he instanced in a Hound, who has ye major proposi-
> tion in his minde, namely, the hare is gone either this way, or that way,
> smells out the minor wth his nose, namely, she is not gone that way, &
> follows the conclusion, "Ergo," this way, wth open mouth. (*The Life of
> the Renowned Doctor Preston* 23)

Plutarch's *Moralia* was far more widely read in early modern Europe than at present, and Plutarch himself—thanks largely to his
work "On the Cessation of the Oracles"—is regarded as an important figure in the transition from classical polytheism to early Christianity. Thus it may be no surprise that his views on the reasoning
ability of animals are popular in seventeenth-century England; at any
rate, those views emerge in yet another public debate at Cambridge,
this one staged in 1632 and later published by Milton as his Seventh
Prolusion. Here Milton, arguing that even the animals recognize the
superiority of learning to ignorance, notes how "Plutarch tells us that
in the pursuit of game, dogs show some knowledge of dialectic, and
if they chance to come to cross-roads, they obviously make use of a
disjunctive syllogism" (872). And arguments of this sort find an unlikely companion in Michel de Montaigne's great *Apology for Ray-
mond Sebond* (1575), which explicitly debunks the arrogance of those
attitudes associated with absolute anthropocentrism:

> Presumption is our naturall and original infirmitie. *Of all creatures
> man is the most miserable and fraile, and therewithall the proudest and
> disdainfullest* . . . It is through the vanity of . . . imagination, that he
> dare equall himselfe to God, that he ascribeth divine conditions unto
> himselfe, that he selecteth and separateth himselfe from out the rank
> of other creatures; to which his fellow-brethren and compeers, he cuts
> out and shareth their parts, and allotteth them what portions of
> meanes or forces he thinkes good. How knoweth he by the vertue of
> his understanding the inward and secret motions of beasts? By what
> comparison from them to us doth he conclude the brutishnesse, he as-
> cribeth to them? (398–399)

Montaigne offers his reader a counsel of humility, and to this extent his skepticism is well in keeping with the emphases of Plutarch and Milton, as well as with certain dominant tendencies within the discourse of anthropomorphism as a whole. Indeed, if anthropomorphism likes to contest human arrogance by denying the uniqueness of human reason, it also encourages humility through a concomitant inclination to present the natural world as a source of moral instruction. This tendency, formalized in the classical and medieval traditions of beast fable, beast epic, and bestiary, culminates in the theoretical construction of the Book of Nature, a revelatory text equivalent in value to scripture and deriving its equivalent authority from scripture itself. Thus—apart from the inevitable biblical exhortations to consider the lilies, to ponder the ant's ways, and the like—Ecclesiastes insists that "The sons of men . . . themselves are beasts. / For that which befalleth the sons of men befalleth beasts; . . . so that a man hath no preeminence above a beast: for all is vanity" (3.18–19). And likewise, Job declares categorically,

> But ask now the beasts, and they shall teach thee; and the fowls of the air, and they shall tell thee; Or speak to the earth, and it shall teach thee: and the fishes of the sea shall declare unto thee. Who knoweth not in all these that the hand of the LORD hath wrought this? (11.7–9)

But what is it, exactly, that the beasts shall teach us? One of the principal functions of early natural history—as it extends in a great sweep from Aristotle and Pliny through the mythical Physiologus and the bestiarists to Aldrovandi and Gesner and so on—is to explain the lessons of the beasts, in meticulous and expansive detail. *The Old English Physiologus,* for instance, claims that the panther, the inveterate enemy of dragons, exhales a fragrance "more transporting, sweet, and strong than any odor whatever, . . . [whereupon] from cities, courts, and castle-halls many companies of heroes flock upon the highways of the earth" (*The Old English Physiologus* 6–8). Then comes the moral: "Even so the Lord God, the Giver of joy, is gracious to all creatures, to every order of them, save only the dragon, . . . shackling him with fiery fetters, and loading him with dire constraints. . . . That was a sweet perfume throughout the world" (8). The twelfth-century English bestiary now known as Cambridge MS II.4.26 (see *The Book of Beasts,* 1984) is typically full of similar tales. After noting, for instance, that Echinus, the sea urchin, infallibly forecasts the coming of storms by latching itself onto a stone for ballast against the waves, the manuscript then comments, "Men often see the disorder of the atmosphere and are deceived—for the clouds frequently disperse without a storm. Echinus is not deceived, [and] we must believe that it is through the tenderness of God to all things that the urchin also gets his function of prescience" (*Book of Beasts* 212–213). Such tales may in many cases be easily traced to classical sources like Pliny, who maintains—among many other things—that "Owing to their modesty, elephants never mate except in secret, the male at the age of five and the female at ten; and mating takes place for two years, on five days, so it is said, of each year and not more; and on the sixth day they give themselves a shower-bath in a river, not returning to the herd before. Adultery is unknown among them" (*Natural History* 8.5.13). And, repeated many times, these very tales can likewise reemerge in Shakespeare's day; thus, for Saint Francis de Sales (1609), Pliny's story of the elephant can still serve as a compelling paradigm of sexual morality:

> The elephant, not only the largest but the most intelligent of animals, . . . is faithful and tenderly loving to the female of its choice, mating only every third year and then for no more than five days, and so secretly as never to be seen, until, on the sixth day, it appears and goes at once to wash its whole body in the river, unwilling to return to the herd until thus purified. Such good and modest habits are an example to husband and wife. (*Introduction to the Devout Life* 3.39)

But observations of this kind simply return us to the problem of Caliban. On one hand, we have seen that Caliban cannot be entirely dehumanized via the standard of human rationality presupposed by absolute and relative anthropocentrism. Yet the alternative index offered by anthropomorphism seems to do the job no better. For if the natural world embodies a system of moral organization from which humankind alone, by definition, can deliberately secede, then Caliban's deliberate secession simply confirms his humanity. By making the wrong moral choices, he proves that he is capable of moral choice, and thereby proves that he is indeed a man. Here relative anthropocentrism, with its theories of inherited racial devolution, may come to the rescue of anthropomorphism; perhaps Caliban's "vild race," hardening moral error into moral inevitability, renders him truly and irredeemably subhuman. But if, by this measure, Caliban is less than human, he is also, by the same measure, less than natural: he is a walking, talking error, a failure equally of reason and of morals, of manners and of natural law. In short, he is a monster.

As such, Caliban becomes appropriately subject to the teratological discourse that anthropomorphism develops to explain the effect
of moral error upon created nature. Not only can such error generate an entire subhuman race, as in the case of Ham's descendants; it
can also produce innumerable specific instances of prodigious birth
and physical disfigurement. Thus, for example, Ambroise Paré's influential survey of obstetrical abnormality, *On Monsters and Marvels*
(1573), asserts categorically that:

> Most often these monstrous and marvelous creatures proceed from
> the judgment of God, who permits fathers and mothers to produce
> such abominations from the disorder that they make in copulation,
> like brutish beasts, in which their appetite guides them, without re-
> specting the time, or other laws ordained by God and Nature. (5)

Paradoxically, in behaving as if they were "brutish beasts," men and
women become worse than the beasts they imitate, and the deformity
of their offspring attests to the moral chaos of the parents. Yet this
same deformity also seems to proclaim the moral unworthiness of the
self, too; thus, mining a rich vein of neoplatonic thought that believes
"the frame / And composition of the mind doth follow / The frame
and composition of body" (Ford, *'Tis Pity She's a Whore,* ca.
1629–1633, 2.5.15–17), early modern literature repeatedly reads individual appearance as an index of individual character. From Shakespeare's Richard III (ca. 1592)—that "lump of foul deformity"
(1.2.57)—to Curio in Lyly's *Euphues* (1578)—"in bodye deformed, in
minde foolishe" (1:240)—one never need look far to find literary figures that exemplify this principle. Even Ophelia, when she innocently
asks Hamlet whether "beauty [could] have better commerce than with
honesty" (3.1.108–109), takes the same association for granted.

Finally, however, the language of anthropomorphism provides a
means of opposing and critiquing the parallel discourses of absolute
and relative anthropocentrism (discourses, as we have just seen, with
which it is also capable of cooperating in a wide range of specific contexts). We may derive an outstanding case of this oppositional function from early modern theories of bestiality, which furnish subject
matter for the opening chapter of this study. By traditional standards,
of course, few sexual acts could better illustrate Paré's phrase "disorder . . . in copulation" than can zoophilia; its confusion of human
and animal leads people to imitate beasts and thus to become worse
than the beasts they imitate. Moreover, zoophilia is a clear—and relatively rare—case in which moral confusion and intellectual confu-

sion coincide. To mistake an animal for an appropriate sexual partner is not only to ignore a wide range of commands and prohibitions to be found in the Pentateuch and elsewhere; it is also to overlook obvious differences of physical appearance and mental constitution. Thus, as Milton's Adam observes in *Paradise Lost,* the sexual economy of Eden embodies a rule of like to like that is reinforced by the incommensurate capacities of different beasts:

> They rejoice
> Each with thir kind, Lion with Lioness;
> So fitly them in pairs [God has] combin'd;
> Much less can Bird with Beast, or Fish with Fowl
> So well converse, nor with the Ox the Ape;
> Worse then can Man with Beast, and least of all. (8.392–397)

By this measure, to confuse a beast with a woman is to engage in both moral and intellectual error of the gravest variety; but then what of the opposite mistake? Is it not equally erroneous to confuse a woman with a beast? That is certainly the view of Bathsua Makin (*An Essay to Revive the Antient Education of Gentlewomen,* 1673), who invokes the intellectual and moral confusion of bestiality as an argument in favor of cross-gendered education. Those traditionalists who would deny women equal schooling, she insists, would thus equate them with beasts:

> Meerly to teach Gentlewomen to Frisk and Dance, to paint their Faces, to curl their Hair, to put on a whisk, to wear gay Clothes, is not truly to adorn, but to adulterate their Bodies; yea (what is worse) to defile their Souls. This (like *Circes* cup) turns them to Beasts; whilst their Belly is their God, they become Swine; whilst Lust, they become Goats; and whilst Pride is their God, they become very Devils. (22)

And once this equation is accomplished, women become effectively indistinguishable from other objects of bestial desire:

> Had God intended Women onely as a finer sort of Cattle, he would not have made them reasonable. Bruits, a few degrees higher than Drils or Monkies, (which the *Indians* use to do many offices) might have better fitted some mens Lust, Pride, and Pleasure; especially those that desire to keep them ignorant to be tyrannized over. (23)

The broad implications of this argument are clear enough: To treat other human beings as animals is not only to do violence to them, but to do violence to one's own humanity in the process. Such views—as may be clear by now—are typical of anthropomorphism, and this fact may help clarify a paradox noted by Keith Thomas (1983):

> Nearly all the protests which were made on behalf of the poor and oppressed in the early modern period were couched in terms of the very same ideology of human domination that was used to justify their oppression. Slavery was attacked because it confused the categories of beast and man, while political tyranny was denounced on the grounds that it was wrong that human beings should be treated as if they were animals. (48)

In fact, while Thomas has identified a fascinating point of discursive ambivalence, it is not quite right to describe this ambivalence in terms of a single "ideology of human domination," any more than it would be correct to describe this same ambivalence as a product of opposed and irreconcilable lines of thinking. More precisely, it marks a point at which the discursive properties of absolute anthropocentrism and of anthropomorphism may be fused into a critique of relative anthropocentrism: God has drawn an absolute distinction between all human beings and all beasts (absolute anthropocentrism), and those human beings who ignore this fact (advocates of relative anthropocentrism) compromise their own human natures in the process (anthropomorphism). In such cases, the real monster is the person who cannot distinguish properly between people and beasts.

Here we may once again see how complexly nuanced early modern thought on the nature of nature could become. While my taxonomy of this thought is inevitably reductive, even so it may help to convey the startling ease and unexpectedness with which the early modern discourse of nature could transform itself in response to individual situations; how its constituent signifiers could combine to take advantage of particular opportunities; and how those same signifiers could simultaneously jostle one another for dominance within a superficially unified system of meaning. One of my aims here is to write a short book on the ways in which this vast and unsettled discourse manifests itself in early English drama, and to do so without speaking in theoretical tongues. But if there is one particular theoretical model that seems to me to accommodate the complexities and transformabilities of my subject most easily, it is the "nomad" theory of Deleuze and Guattari (1987), a theory whose refusal to privilege product over production, whose unconcern with linear reason, whose tolerance of inconsistency, and whose emphasis upon transformation all speak to various salient features in the material I survey.[14] For like the triad of man, animal, and monster that they delineate, the notions of absolute anthropocentrism, relative anthropocentrism, and anthropomorphism participate in a kind of intricate dance, joining hands and then separating, fading to the background or seizing the limelight, all in accord with the exigencies and opportunities of the moment. If politics is indeed the art of the possible, then this discourse is inherently political. And likewise, in terms of its effect upon the lives and experience of individual human beings, it is inherently social. To this extent, the present study concerns itself as much with people as with animals, as much with culture as with nature.

5. Into the Woods

In moving from this introduction to the ensuing chapters, we will be moving from general overview to particular interventions, and this move entails certain consequences. First, it requires that we move away somewhat from the triadic nomenclature that I have introduced. This nomenclature performs several necessary services by delineating certain dominant trends in the organization of my subject matter; reducing the broad and complex discourse of nature in early modern England to a manageable sequence of interrelated terms; and demonstrating the interdependence of those terms, as well as their potential for both harmonious and contradictory interaction. At the same time, however, this nomenclature may encourage an overly schematized reading of individual cultural and literary events; it may discourage us from recognizing the emergence of beliefs and attitudes other than those already described; and most certainly, no matter how many warnings one might give to the contrary, it encourages us to view each of its elements as a self-contained unit of ideology first, and only second as a unit in a larger system of cultural production. For all of these reasons, I have found it necessary both to generate the system of organization that is outlined in this introductory chapter, and then, having generated it, to leave it behind.

But the move from general to particular also entails a second consequence, for it must obey some further principle of selection. Just as early modern attitudes toward nature may be described in terms of general trends, those trends tend to interact with especial vigor when they are brought to bear on individual issues. The remaining chapters of this study will seek to focus upon certain of those issues so as to explain why they should have become sites for the expenditure of so much discursive energy, and to that end I have chosen to concentrate upon the simplest and most obvious issues I could identify. Thus Chapter 1 deals with the question of feminine nature: what makes women different from men, what makes women different from beasts, and how these notions of difference may be parlayed into dramatic capital on the early English stage. Chapter 2, in turn, addresses the complementary subject of masculine identity, as figured in terms of beast emblems, while Chapter 3 examines the role played by animal references in early modern constructions of racial difference. The fourth and final chapter then engages what one might call the question of beasts as beasts: given the metaphorical ubiquity of animals in early discussions of *social* difference, how did Renaissance Englishmen and Englishwomen make sense of the bestial as a category unto itself, independent of social overcoding? Woman, man, the racial other, and the bestial other: these four figures lie at the heart of the ensuing chapters.

Still further, in focusing upon these extremely broad and suggestive topics, I have also found it necessary to limit my inquiry to very specific animal associations. Early modern identifications of women with animals, for instance, are so numerous and various as to require their own library of scholarly documentation, and the case is no simpler with respect to men or to non-English races and nationalities. So to lend a manageable form to my discussion, I have had perforce to select certain animals, and certain animal images, for particular emphasis, and in doing so, I have inevitably sought out subject matter that answers to my own scholarly inclinations and experience. Chapters 1 and 2, for instance, deal in different ways with the history of sexuality, a subject upon which I have written at some length in the past. In Chapter 1, I concentrate upon the crime of bestiality: upon its legal formulation in Henrician England, its treatment in the disciplinary rhetoric of the Tudor and Stuart eras, and its intersection with the language of early modern misogyny via a traditional emblem for feminine unchastity, the mare. In Chapter 2, I deal with masculine identity as it seeks to evade, avoid, acknowledge, and accommodate the single most ubiquitous sexual emblem of the English Renaissance: the cuckold's horns. Chapter 3, with its focus upon race and ethnicity, cannot boast any grounding as such in my prior scholarly experience. However—perhaps to counter my own insecurities in this regard—I have chosen to deal with racial difference as it is relayed in the English Renaissance through the figure of the articulate bird par excellence, the parrot. As a cheerfully besotted psittaculturist of 20 years and counting, I can at least claim some small expertise on this head. Finally, Chapter 4 concentrates on those moments when Renaissance culture presented animals *as animals:* those moments when animals were scripted into the stage business of the early English theater, and those parallel moments of bull-baiting and bear-baiting, cock-fighting and bear-dancing that coexisted with the early theater as its marginalized and disreputable double.

Finally, however, I have had to perform still one more act of selection so as to make my subject matter manageable and coherent. I have had not only to limit my work to a series of basic general issues and a limited range of animal references, but I have also had to investigate those issues and those references through a limited number of literary texts. In each of the upcoming chapters I draw broadly and desultorily upon English Renaissance drama and verse, prose fiction and nonfiction, supplemented where appropriate by comparable continental sources. Most of these works will be familiar to any informed reader of early modern English texts, and taken together they provide a fair representation of the canon of such texts as it has survived. But against this diverse background of brief literary references, I also seek to focus more or less tightly upon individual dramatic works that illustrate my concerns particularly well. To this end, I have chosen five plays for relatively sustained study: Shakespeare's *A Midsummer Night's Dream* and *Two Gentlemen of Verona,* Jonson's *Volpone* and *Every Man Out of His Humour,* and Middleton's *Chaste Maid in Cheapside.* Between them, these plays furnish us with the early drama's most outstanding treatments of the issues I have outlined above; they also, by fortunate happenstance, provide a selection of both the best-known and least-known work to have been produced by Jacobean England's three most successful playwrights.

Specifically, then, the next chapter will focus upon the crime of bestiality as it is refracted through a near-zooerastic encounter on the English stage: Bottom and Titania's interlude in *A Midsummer Night's Dream,* together with the various echoes of their relationship that occur elsewhere in the play. In Chapter 2, we will read *Volpone* and *A Chaste Maid in Cheapside* as complementary texts, presenting in an extreme form two opposed but equally popular modes of masculine accommodation to the threat of cuckoldry. Chapter 3 returns to *Volpone,* this time to concentrate upon the play's two most outstanding talking birds, Sir Politic and Lady Would-Be, and their relation to notions of racial difference. And in Chapter 4, we will turn our attention to *Two Gentlemen of Verona* and *Every Man Out of His Humour,* both of whose use of animals onstage is virtually unique in the early English drama. In studying these works, we will find ourselves continually reencountering the terms with which this introduction has been concerned; the figures of man and animal and monster interanimate one another constantly within the works we will examine, just as they coexist in the dramatic character with which our discussion began: the Duke of Saxony's unfortunate nephew. For us, as for Portia and Nerissa, the problem of disengaging man from animal from monster will no doubt prove insuperable. For it is by virtue of their deep—and deeply unstable—interconnection that these figures are able to perform the far-reaching social work that this book seeks in part to document and explain.

CHAPTER ONE

SHAKESPEARE'S BEASTLY BUGGERS

1. ENAMOUR'D OF AN ASS

Although no one has paid much sustained attention to the fact, Shakespeare's *A Midsummer Night's Dream* (ca. 1596) is patently about bestiality.[1] On the most immediate level, Titania's animal passion for the asinine Bottom climaxes the play's fairy subplot. In the process, this passion tests the bounds of Elizabethan theatrical decorum; Titania leads Bottom to a bed of flowers, embraces and kisses him, and woos him with some of the play's most extravagantly sensuous verse:

> Come sit thee down upon this flow'ry bed,
> While I thy amiable cheeks do coy,
> And stick musk-roses in thy sleek smooth head,
> And kiss thy fair large ears, my gentle joy. (4.1.1–4)

Oddly enough, this humid rhetoric emerges from an exercise in household discipline: Oberon's plot to drug his wife with an aphrodisiac and thereby reassert his own domestic sovereignty—what Paul Olson (1957) has called "an orderly subordination of the female . . . to the more reasonable male" (97). Apparently, that is, one enforces traditional marital order and decency by indulging certain kinds of *in*decency, both within the moral economy of Shakespeare's play and within the political economy of Oberon's marriage. This contradiction reappears elsewhere in the play as a symbolic coupling of human erotic desire to animal objects.

Oberon, for his part, expresses at least two different—and not fully compatible—attitudes toward his queen's humiliation. On the one hand, he warns Titania that it will be a kind of just recompense for her insubordinate refusal to surrender her changeling page: "Well; go thy way. Thou shalt not from this grove / Till I torment thee for this injury" (2.1.146–147). The torment, these lines imply, is entirely merited, and later Oberon almost suggests that it is technically necessary—as if there were no way to win his quarrel with Titania other than to force her to make love to a jackass (or at least a "lion, bear, or wolf, or bull" [2.1.180]): "Ere I take this charm from off her sight / (As I can take it with another herb), / I'll make her render up her page to me" (2.1.183–185). From this standpoint, Titania would seem in fact to be punishing herself, and thus Oberon can emerge as her benefactor at play's end, taking "pity" on her (4.1.47) and moving—out of his own native goodness and decency—to "undo / This hateful imperfection of her eyes" (4.1.62–63).

Yet alongside this view of matters, Oberon also expresses a distinct sense of pleasure—indeed, almost a salacious delight—in his wife's degradation. Thus when Puck first reports to him that "Titania wak'd, and straightway lov'd an ass" (3.2.34), Oberon's response is one of unqualified satisfaction: "This falls out better than I could devise" (3.2.35). He later refers to the spectacle of Titania sleeping in Bottom's arms as a "sweet sight" (4.1.46). And his treatment of his enfeebled queen involves a good measure of open ridicule:

> Meeting her of late behind the wood,
> Seeking sweet favors for this hateful fool,
> I did upbraid her, and fall out with her.
> . . . .
> When I had at my pleasure taunted her,
> And she in mild terms begg'd my patience,
> I then did ask of her her changeling child;
> Which straight she gave me. (4.1.48–60)

In short, Oberon may claim to regret Titania's disobedience and to desire nothing more than to be "new in amity" (4.1.87) with his queen, but he also revels in the chance to make sexual sport of her.

For Oberon, then, Titania's plight is both hateful and delightful, and his language enables him to disavow any moral responsibility for degrading her while it simultaneously promotes her as an article of good theatrical fun. In the most obvious sense, such rhetoric legitimates fantasies of male authority: Titania is reduced to her husband's power, exposed to an audience, and placed in sexual bondage to a jackass, and all these events are represented as the inevitable consequence of her own misconduct. She has, as it were, brought them on herself, to both Oberon's and the audience's broad amusement. The play thus exacts a sort of "encoded revenge" upon womankind in general and the principle of female sovereignty in particular (Patterson, "Bottom's Up," 1988, 34)[2]; yet in the process, it places both Oberon and the audience in a potentially uncomfortable position, for it identifies the return to traditional domestic order with—of all things—bestiality. In short, Shakespeare's staging inadvertently illustrates Jonathan Dollimore's argument that through the concept of perversion "nature is always enacting or partaking of just that which it is required to repress" (Dollimore, *Dissidence* 1991, 154).[3] The fairy king solves his marital problems by openly transforming his wife into the erotic bondslave of an ass; and what, then, does that make him?

The present analysis takes this question as central to *A Midsummer Night's Dream*'s exploration of marital arrangements and household order. From this standpoint, the unproblematic distinction between human and bestial nature—a distinction to which this comedy of Shakespeare's might at first seem fully committed—ultimately emerges from the play as neither unproblematic nor particularly distinct. The play's various discursive mechanisms force human nature to amalgamate with animal nature and vice versa; Titania's unnatural wifely disobedience produces winds, fogs, floods, and diseases of cattle, as well as her amorous encounter with Bottom (2.1.81–117); and Bottom is clearly both man and animal, although various metonymic references to him as an ass (3.2.34, 4.1.76, etc.) invite us to consider him wholly beast. Moreover, as author of Titania's and Bottom's relationship, as well as the various other relationships that comprise the play, Oberon himself participates in the dalliance of people with animals, and this dalliance subtends the humanity of the very institutions (marriage, patriarchy, monarchy) he seeks to underwrite.

To this extent, *A Midsummer Night's Dream* derives its formative energy not just from various kinds of conflict between men and women, but from a broader conflict between the governing assumptions of absolute and of relative anthropocentrism. Scholars are fond, for instance, of claiming that Oberon's punishment of Titania suits her own relatively inferior position within the natural and social order of the play, and this model of "orderly subordination" (Olson 1957, 97) is just the sort of arrangement that relative anthropocentrism exists to affirm. But to construct Titania as Oberon's inferior is inevitably to risk associating her instead with the brute orders of creation, as those orders are conceived from the

perspective of absolute anthropocentrism; if she has more in common with the irrational beasts than with her rational husband, then
to what extent may she be viewed as his fit consort? One of the fascinating and daring qualities of Shakespeare's play is its determina-
tion to stage this question, in displaced form, through the
encounter of Bottom and Titania. And while the play itself may ultimately make light of the possibilities it thus raises, Oberon's own
behavior as a disciplinarian emphatically does not. In short, *A Midsummer Night's Dream* is about bestiality because the social
arrangements it promotes take bestiality as their raison d'être; they
assume that human nature is in constant danger of corruption from
the bestial and/or female other, and that it must therefore be con-
tinuously and rigorously policed. These arrangements then promote themselves as the proper vehicles for such policing. And thus
they manufacture the bestial prodigy—the Bottom and Titania—as
a means of political self-justification.

2. A MAN NEEDS A MARE

This argument assumes that the urge to bestiality finds its ultimate
source in the institutions that ostensibly oppose it—that, to use Foucault's words, it consistently provokes "a kind of generalized discursive erethism" within Western culture (32). In effect, that is,
conditions in *A Midsummer Night's Dream* should be at their most
bestial and disnatured exactly when the play promises that all is (or is
rapidly being) restored to order. Puck makes this promise very plainly
to the sleeping Lysander, and the terms in which he does so deserve
to be studied:

> The country proverb known,
> That every man should take his own,
> In your waking shall be shown.
>   Jack shall have Jill;
>   Nought shall go ill:
> The man shall have his mare again, and all shall be well.
>   (3.2.458–463)

According to Puck, the play's action will obey the dictates of the
proverb "all shall be well" when a proprietary relation is reasserted
between men and women, allowing "every man [to] take his own,"
and this proprietarism gains concrete illustration in the parallel
promises that "Jack shall have Jill" and "The man shall have his mare

again." Jack is to Jill as man is to mare—that is, as owner is to owned; the desire of characters and audience alike finds "its own natural, stable form" as male dominion within marriage (Eagleton 1986, 20); and this is apparently what it means for all to be well within the context of *A Midsummer Night's Dream*.

But of course these lines raise other possibilities as well. In particular, they do not really specify what it means to say that Jack is to Jill as man is to mare; the terms of the correspondence remain disturbingly imprecise. For if woman qualifies as man's fit sexual companion by assuming the status of commodity (i.e., by being like a mare), then a mare, too, may be a man's fit mate; the text's parallelisms acknowledge no qualitative difference whatever between a man's relationship with his woman and that same man's relationship with his horse. In fact, quite the contrary: Puck's language plays off a long-standing emblematic identification of sexually active women with mares. Described in medieval bestiaries as "the most lustful of female animals" (Clark 1975, 81), the mare appears in such early texts as the *Ancrene Riwle* (ca. 1215–1222) as a metaphorical placeholder for the wanton woman; thus the *Riwle* counsels unchaste women to unburden themselves to their confessors by bluntly exclaiming, "'Sir, God's mercy! I am a foul stud mare, a stinking whore'" (qtd. in Clark 81). Similar language pervades late medieval play-texts like *Mankind* (ca. 1475), where New-Gyse, interrupting Mercy's windy advice on how a man should govern his horse ("Yf a man have an hors, and kepe hym not to hye, / He may then reull hym at hys own dysyere" [233–234]), exclaims, "Ande my wyf were yowur horse sche wolde yow all to-samne" (242); apparently, that is, New-Gyse's wife is like a horse in that she can both resist male governance and at the same time "to-samne" (i.e., disgrace or shame) her male governors. In the same idiom, Heinrich Bullinger could declare in 1541 that "all old wyse and prudent men wold have wemen & horses kept in good nurtoure and governau[n]ce" (*The Christian State of Matrimony*, sig. IIr). Moreover, this traditional identification of woman with mare has a disturbing tendency to appear at unexpected places within the Shakespeare canon—as when Antigonus in *The Winter's Tale* (1610–1611) protests of Hermione, "If it prove / She [is unchaste], I'll keep my stables where / I lodge my wife" (2.1.133–135). Indeed, to carry the point further, Renaissance court records reveal the mare to be far and away the most commonly abused animal in cases of bestial buggery (see Table 2); it is almost as if, once woman had been made a mare by the processes of metaphor, mares then began to assume the qualities and status of women as well.

Of course, Bottom's asinine metamorphosis reverses the gender-troping of such identifications. Where Antigonus, Puck, the *Ancrene Riwle,* and generations of rustic Englishmen all seem determined to turn women into animals, Shakespeare's Oberon makes the *man* a beast and leaves his wife in her original form. Yet in either case the troping preserves a symmetry more important than any question of who gets to be the jackass this time, for all such transformations take as their immediate object the disparagement of the woman's identity. Hence Bottom's own personality remains outstandingly unimpaired throughout his interlude with Titania; indeed, a large part of his comic incongruity derives from the fact that his desires as beast—for headscratching, belly-cheer, and deferential service—remain so perfectly faithful to his human character. It is Titania, on the other hand, whose humanity is more fundamentally impeached by the entire exchange, for she—not Bottom—clearly cannot distinguish a bestial love-object from a human one. In this sense, at least, Bottom's transformation happens more to Titania than to Bottom himself. The result is an ideological identity of interest between locally dissimilar animal transformations, all of which offer roughly the same moral: turning a woman into an animal degrades the woman, and turning a man into an animal also degrades the woman.

The insistency of this message betrays its overdetermination. Emerging again and again out of contradictory circumstances, it repeatedly figures sexual difference in ways that privilege the man. Yet by the same token, such figurations place male privilege itself in a position of dependence upon the humiliated, bestialized female other—without whom male sovereignty could not possibly think itself and to whom it must therefore constantly refer for the invidious comparisons that lend it identity. Various theoretical models—Marxist, feminist, psychoanalytic, post-Saussurean, and so on—may arguably be invoked to account for this dependence, but it is not my intention to dwell upon any such model. Instead, I would argue that Renaissance bestiality texts typically concern themselves with exploring the boundaries of human character, and that in the process these texts repeatedly encounter social distinctions—such as those between man and woman, peer and commoner, virgin and pervert—that interfere with the equally fundamental distinction between human and animal nature. The unilinear moralizing of Renaissance bestiality texts can never finally foreclose this interference; underlying the obsessive formulation of social difference is an unavoidable sense of human mixedness—an ontological catachresis—that simply will not go away. Yet from the standpoint of the moralizing texts themselves, that is all the more reason for the moralizing to continue.

Thus, to use Harold Brooks's phrase, *A Midsummer Night's Dream* seems determined to construct men and women as "alien species" (1979 cxii), and as a result, all of the play's romantic couplings are in an important sense zoophilic. Hermia refers to the ardent Demetrius as a "serpent" (3.2.72), and in a much-discussed nightmare she envisions Lysander as "smiling" at her while another serpent eats away her heart (2.2.144–150).[4] More suggestively still, Helena can thus represent herself, in relation to her beloved Demetrius, as a dog:

> I am your spaniel; and, Demetrius,
> The more you beat me, I will fawn on you.
> Use me but as your spaniel; spurn me, strike me,
> Neglect me, lose me; . . .
> What worser place can I beg in your love
> (And yet a place of high respect with me)
> Than to be used as you use your dog? (2.1.203–210)

Helena's orgy of self-abasement finds its definitive expression as a sinister kind of puppy love. Hence the erotic charge of her remarks, which formulate her passion precisely as the state of being owned. Demetrius's eventual marriage to Helena comments further upon what it means to use a person "as you use your dog," for it is this very marriage that consummates Helena's erotic wishes and rewards her puppydog fidelity.

If, then, the moral of *A Midsummer Night's Dream* is that men should sow their oats among the most alien of mares, this mixed metaphor gains its ideal embodiment in the union of Theseus and Hippolyta. Carrying within her name the linguistic shadow of the Greek *hippos,* and herself the mother-to-be of a mythic figure famous for preferring horses to women,[5] Hippolyta is also preeminently an object to be possessed; thus, as scholars regularly observe (e.g., Montrose 1986, 70–71), Theseus wooes her "with [his] sword" and wins her love by defeating her on the battlefield (1.1.16–17). As a bride, Hippolyta becomes part of the spoils of war, only problematically distinct from such booty as weapons, gold, and horses; moreover, she relates to Theseus conspicuously through the medium of hunting animals. Thus she can kindle what at least one reader regards as a spark of sexual jealousy in Theseus by talking about a pack of hounds (Brooks civ):

> I was with Hercules and Cadmus once,
> When in a wood of Crete they bay'd the bear

> With hounds of Sparta. Never did I hear
> Such gallant chiding. (4.1.112–115)

Theseus responds with a peevish and aggressively phallic description of his own animals:

> My hounds are bred out of the Spartan kind;
> So flew'd, so sanded; and their heads are hung
> With ears that sweep away the morning dew;
> Crook-knee'd, and dewlapp'd like Thessalian bulls;
> Slow in pursuit; but match'd in mouth like bells,
> Each under each. A cry more tuneable
> Was never hollow'd to, nor cheer'd with horn,
> In Crete, in Sparta, nor in Thessaly. (4.1.119–126)

Theseus vies with Hippolyta's former male companions, Hercules and Cadmus, through the medium of their hunting dogs, and the dogs themselves, their heads encompassed by great folds of skin and their bodies dewlapped and bullish, serve implicitly as surrogates for the male member. Mine are the same as Hercules's and Cadmus's, Theseus argues—only better.

Thus *A Midsummer Night's Dream* seems determined to construct its various marital unions as analogues to (or extensions of, or coincident with) the sexual conjunction of people and animals. Given the play's peculiar discursive framework, zooerastia emerges as "integral to just those things it threatens" (Dollimore, "Perversion" 1990, 189), figured and refigured repeatedly within the space of human domestic relations. Moreover, bestiality arguably encompasses a large part of the play's overt eroticism; the spectacle of Titania and Bottom embracing and sleeping together comes as close to enacted sexual intercourse as any scene in Shakespearean comedy. In short, *A Midsummer Night's Dream* takes pains to establish sexual limits that it then transgresses, through metaphor and innuendo and overt representation, as often as possible, and this act of transgression constitutes a good measure of the play's appeal to its audience. In overall effect, *A Midsummer Night's Dream* is a strange amalgam of the moralistic and the salacious.

3. SOME MONSTERS

Documented cases of bestiality are rare in early English records (Lawrence Stone's lengthy *Family, Sex and Marriage in England*

1500–1800 does not mention a single one), but nonetheless they do occur. Indeed, despite the scarcity of prosecutions for this crime in the Tudor period, the English legal system expended a good deal of effort to remove buggery from the church-court purview and into that of the secular magistrate. Thus, as part of its attack on the papacy, Henry VIII's Parliament of 1533 declared "the detestable and abhomynable vice of buggery committed with mankynde or beaste" to be a felony without benefit of clergy and carrying an automatic death penalty (*Statutes at Large* 1786–1886, 25 Henry VIII, c. 6).[6] As B. R. Burg has observed, this act was an integral part of Henry's expansion of royal authority (Burg 1980–1981, 70), and as such it affords a prime instance of what one could call the rhetorical character of buggery laws. Created more to affirm the royal supremacy than to prosecute sodomites, the Henrician buggery statute's main job was, in effect, to make a political point; hence it was predictably rescinded under Mary and reenacted under Elizabeth. In the process, bestiality came to be formally regarded as "confusion of the natural order" (Bingham 1970–1971, 447), and thus Edward Coke claims in the third part of his *Institutes* (1628) that "Buggery is a detestable and abominable sin, amongst Christians not to be named, . . . against the ordinance of the Creator and order of nature" (sig. I3v).

Yet this fearsome rhetoric is not accompanied by any demonstrable obsession with buggery in Renaissance legal practice itself; buggery cases under Elizabeth I and James I are numerically insignificant. Bruce Smith rightly observes that prosecutions for homosexuality were far less frequent than for bestiality, and he notes that the assize records for Kent during the reign of Elizabeth list only two indictments for homosexual behavior out of approximately three thousand—"about .07 percent" (Smith 1991, 48). Against this minute quantity, the ten cases of bestiality listed in the same volume may seem a lot, but they still comprise only .3 percent of the overall records. Clearly courts were not much exercised by either offense.

For the reigns of Elizabeth I and James I, I have been able to identify forty cases of bestiality handled by the secular authorities. The aggregate character of these cases is illustrated in Table 1.1, and although Alan Bray correctly observes that "any statistical analysis [of this material] is out of the question" (1992, 40), the following points are still perhaps worth noting. First, given the fact that Elizabeth's reign was roughly twice as long as James's, the available records include about 33 percent more indictments for bestiality in the Elizabethan years than in the Jacobean. And second, the proportion of convictions to acquittals is spectacularly higher in Elizabeth's reign than in James's, comprising a ratio of 2 to 1 as opposed to a ratio of 1 to 3.5. Further, Table 2 demonstrates that horses (and, to a lesser degree, cattle) were easily the favorite objects of abuse in these cases. (Buggery indictments scrupulously document the species, color, and owner of the maltreated beast.)

It is worth comparing these figures, and the generally blasé attitude they embody, to the lurid rhetoric that Renaissance authors invariably attached to bestiality and that regularly associates such misconduct with women. The late Stuart pamphlet *Ravillac Redivivus* (1671), for instance, describes as follows the behavior of Thomas Weir, Mayor of Edinburgh during the Interregnum: Having seduced his sister when he was ten and lived with her incestuously thereafter, the violently antiroyalist Weir also "had sexual intercourse with cows and mares, and especially one of his mares, upon which he once rode to New Mills" (qtd. in Bloch 1936, 461). Again, Alan Bray has noted the passage in Marston's *Scourge of Villainy* in which a young voluptuary, deprived of his mistress, replaces her with a "perfumed she-goat" (Marston 1598, 1.3.37–42; see *The Poems of John Marston*, 1961; qtd. in Bray 16). And likewise, Coke explains in his *Institutes* that the original Henrician act declaring buggery to be a felony was occasioned because "a great Lady had committed Buggery with a Baboon, and conceived by it, etc." (1660, sig. I4r). Clearly the main work performed by Renaissance English attacks on buggery was discursive, rather than material, in nature.

In keeping with this fact, recorded prosecutions for bestiality during the sixteenth and seventeenth centuries acquire a literary/discursive character over and above the administration of physical punishment. This is not to deny that real people were tried, punished, and even executed for bestial buggery; they most certainly were. Yet the minuscule number of such trials; the extreme inconsistencies of sentencing, which could range from a virtual handslap from the church courts to hanging under the common law; the massive contrast between the heated language of Renaissance moralists and legal theorists and the trickle of prosecutions for buggery of any kind; and the occasional way in which bestiality charges were tacked on to other, more serious accusations as a kind of judicially unnecessary lily-gilding—all these things suggest that the rhetoric of bestiality was in some basic ways more important than the crime itself. This investment in rhetoric becomes clearer when one thinks of bestiality as being, in effect, a victimless crime; after all, in the absence of a vengeful or abused human plaintiff, what can bestiality prosecutions possibly redress? The offended party would seem to be not an indi-

Table 1.1 Indictments for Bestial Buggery in the Reigns of Elizabeth I
and James I

	Elizabeth I	James I	Combined
Cases	31	9	40
Convictions	18	2	20
Acquittals	9	7	16[a]

Sources: Calendar of Assize Records (London: Her Majesty's Stationery Office, 1980)
Elizabeth I vols. 1–5, James I vols. 1–5; Middlesex County Records, ed. John Cordy
Jeaffreson (Clerkenwell: Middlesex County Records Society, n.d.), vol. 1; County of
Middlesex: Calendar to the Sessions Records, ed. William Hardy (London: C. W.
Radcliffe, 1937), n.s. vol. 3.
[a]In four cases—all Elizabethan—the accused is listed as still at large or as having died
before sentencing.

Table 1.2 Animals Abused in English Renaissance Bestiality Indictments

	Number	Percentage
Sows	3	7.5
Sheep	1	2.5
Dogs	1	2.5
Cattle	13	32.5
Mares	20	50
Unspecified	2	5

Sources: Same as Table 1.1.

vidual human being, but rather a kind of abstract linguistic principle
of what human beings ought to be. To this extent, bestial buggery is
a crime against ideas, not people.

As such, it elicits inevitable judicial displays, some of which culminate in the execution of the offending party. But the execution becomes largely subservient to the discourse that demands it, and
indeed, as long as the discourse itself is satisfied through some ritual
of exorcism or purgation, capital punishment may even be deemed
unnecessary. The really important thing is not that a particular poor
bugger be hanged, but that the judiciary apparatus be seen to work.
To this extent, Renaissance buggery laws may parallel Jean-
Christophe Agnew's sense of the function of the medieval marketplace; they comprise "a ritually defined threshold" of the human
community (1986, 32), a threshold that is progressively blurred by
"the new liquidity" of Renaissance social/theatrical relations (59).

Court buggery records themselves are therefore overwhelmingly concerned with maintaining or reestablishing the threatened boundaries. In 1519, for instance, the ecclesiastical court presiding over Tetchwick, Buckinghamshire, reports that one Richard Mayne, a watercarrier, "joined himself carnally with a mare, and a certain Elizabeth Parsons noticed this and reported it" (Hair 1972, 147). The court records, which take care to describe the process of human intervention whereby the suspect was brought to justice, do not mention a penalty; but later, in 1525, a certain William Franklin appeared "in the parish church of Brisley" in Norfolk, to answer the charge of "having had sexual intercourse with an animal" (152). In this case the defendant was found guilty, although he produced four testifiers in his defense; for punishment, he was ordered "to go in procession publicly, as a penance, and to offer a penny candle before the high image" (152).

Franklin's token penalty may or may not have been standard for such offenses; however, it is certainly out of keeping with the dire precept of Leviticus (20.15–16): "If a man lies with a beast, he shall be put to death; and you shall kill the beast. / If a woman approaches any beast and lies with it, you shall kill the woman and the beast; they shall be put to death, their blood is upon them." Thus the Catholic court's ruling also runs counter to the severe rhetoric of Puritans like Thomas Beard, whose *Theatre of Gods Judgements* (1596) is contemporary to *A Midsummer Night's Dream:*

> It is not for nothing that the law of God forbiddeth to lie with a beast, and denounceth death against them that commit this foule sinne: for there have been such monsters in the world at sometimes, as we read in *Caelius* and *Volterranus,* of one *Crathes* a sheepheard, that accompanied carnally with a shee goat, but the Buck finding him sleeping, offended and provoked with this strange action, ran at him so furiously with his hornes, that hee left him dead vpon the ground. (sig. 2A1v)

Beard's peasant, unlike William Franklin, suffers to the full extent of the Mosaic law, and ironically, the vehicle for his punishment is a kind of miraculous *caper ex machina.* Justice and piety emerge from the traditional animal symbol of lust, and Beard solemnly warns his readers against fornicating with beasts, noting that "there have been such monsters in the world at sometimes."

To this extent, of course, Beard is himself in the business of making (or at least repackaging) monsters, and of retailing them to the highest bidder; thus the *Theatre of Gods Judgements* regales its readers with a mind-numbing sequence of adulteries, murders, fornications, incests, and rapes—as well as tyranny, sodomy, dancing, and playacting (this last in a book that likens itself to a theater). Beard himself, despite the lurid and muckraking quality of his work, seems more or less oblivious to the irony of his own position; and yet it is not nearly as distant from that of William Franklin's judge as Beard himself might insist. For Beard's own authority, as writer and as moralist, demands a steady supply of William Franklins: of aberrations to be disciplined and exposed and yet not really exterminated, but instead preserved in discourse. Only thus—through the dynamics of what Kenneth Burke has called "pure persuasion"[7]—can Beard claim to be performing a necessary social service; his is a moral economy of monsters.

"My mistress with a monster is in love" (3.2.6): Puck fixes Bottom with Beard's own favorite epithet for sexual deviants. Indeed Beard's sense of the term recalls an early parallel to the animal voyeurism of Oberon in *A Midsummer Night's Dream*. The Borgia pope Alexander VI could enter popular myth as a libertine "who enjoyed nothing so much as watching with his daughter Lucrezia as horses copulated" (Frantz 1989, 45), and if this tale seems improbably removed from Shakespeare's England, consider its reappearance in Aubrey's *Brief Lives* (1680; see *Aubrey's Brief Lives*, 1949), where it attaches not to a pope but rather to Mary Herbert, Countess of Pembroke:

> She was very Salacious, and she had a Contrivance that in the Spring of the yeare, when the Stallions were to leape the Mares, they were to be brought before such a part of the house, where she had a *vidette* (a hole to peepe out at) to looke on them and please herselfe with their Sport; and then she would act the like sport herself with her stallions. (138)

Aubrey ends this passage by remarking that "one of [Mary Herbert's] great Gallants was Crooke-back't Cecill, Earl of Salisbury" (138), known affectionately to James I as his spaniel; the anecdote thus transforms its female subject into the figurative lover of literal beasts and the literal lover of figurative beasts, more or less simultaneously. Moreover, the same gesture—a lewd peeping from out of the established moral and/or social center—can occur with greater complexity in a work like Donne's "Satyre IV" (1593–1598; see *The Complete English Poems* 1971). There the narrator laments his recent conversation with an obnoxious courtier: "A thing more strange than on Nile's slime the sun / E'er bred; . . . / Stranger . . . / Than Afric's

monsters" (18–22). Indeed, the source of this fellow's monstrosity is
to a large extent the substance of Donne's own text: "Who wastes in
meat, in clothes, in horse, he notes; / Who loves whores, who boys,
and who goats" (127–128). The narrator himself stands "more
amazed" at this discourse "than Circe's prisoners" (129), and the
poem therefore fashions a moral diatribe out of its own latent
voyeurism. In effect, it ends up satirizing itself.

In the process, the bestial metamorphosis of Donne's narrator parallels the dynamics of Shakespeare's comedy. Donne's speaker in effect
becomes an animal—"more amazed . . . than Circe's prisoners"—by
attending to the represented bestial behavior of others, and he then
hands his amazement on to his audience through yet another level of
representation. Aubrey turns himself—and his readers—into a series of
duplicate Mary Herberts, peeking through the cracks of his text at the
original Mary Herbert peeking at her rutting horses. Likewise, Shakespeare's Oberon, himself the principal audience at a scene of bestial
transformation and misbehavior, constructs that bestiality as entertainment for another set of viewers entirely. In the process, both Oberon
and Donne's narrator (and, in a less aggressive way, Aubrey as well)
claim to represent the stabilizing influences of domestic order and
moral indignation; they are, as it were, doing the wrong thing for the
right reasons.

For William Franklin's judge, for Thomas Beard, for Aubrey, and
arguably even for Donne, the discourse of traditional morality runs on
despite—even because of—its own slippages, unperturbed by the fact
that it depends for its existence upon the very categories of behavior
and of being that it seeks to extirpate. In Book 8 of Milton's *Paradise
Lost* (1667), our grand forefather Adam is demonstrably smarter. He
recognizes that something is wrong when the Son implicitly offers
him sexual companionship among the newly created animals—"with
mee / I see not who partakes"—yet he also recognizes that the solution to his problem—Eve—is not really a solution at all. The difficulty
with animals, after all, is that they are animals; they are inferior to
Adam, having been constructed with internal deficiencies of mind and
spirit that render them unsatisfactory as company or as mates:

> Among unequals what society
> Can sort, what harmony or true delight?
> Which must be mutual, in proportion due
> Giv'n and receiv'd. . . . Of fellowship I speak
> Such as I seek, fit to participate
> All rational delight. (8.383–391)

Yet Eve's own composition as Adam's mate pushes her relentlessly into the category of the unequal, away from the rational delight that Adam needs her, by definition, to share:

> For well I understand in the prime end
> Of Nature her th'inferior, in the mind
> And inward Faculties, which most excel,
> In outward also her resembling less
> His image who made both. (8.540–544)

Adam does not make the claim in so many words, but remarks of this sort unfortunately tend to situate Eve in the animal kingdom, precisely where we discover her distant descendants Helena, Hermia, Hippolyta, and Titania. Small wonder that scriptural exegetes like Jakob Boehme sought to bestialize Eve still further by accusing her of sexual intercourse with the serpent (cited in Turner 1987, 145). Such efforts comprise the logical endpoint of any rigorous attempt to hierarchize conjugal relations in accordance with the dictates of relative anthropocentrism.

How, then, does one mediate between the opposing claims of conjugal companionship and patriarchal authority? This question informs the "irresolvable doubleness" that scholars like James Grantham Turner have seen "at the heart of Milton's apprehension of wedded love" (286). Adam, for whom Eve's status is constantly threatening to accelerate out of the order of the inferior and into that of the all-too-equal (while just as constantly threatening to decelerate from equal to animal), sees this issue as a pressing one, and therefore he gives it pride of place at the end of his conversation with Raphael. Acknowledging Eve's deficiencies, Adam still cannot help regarding her as "more than enough" of himself (*Paradise Lost* 8.537), endowed with "too much of Ornament" (8.538); it is as if there were something inherently excessive about her very character as a human being, some equal-but-unequalness that assailed Adam's own personal integrity. Raphael's advice on this point is remarkable, for it initiates the order of language that this chapter has been busily surveying. Use your reason, he effectively counsels Adam; don't forsake it; keep it constantly on guard, elaborating, defining, affirming, and reaffirming the differences that make you what you are; never stop doing this job, for it is literally of your essence:

> [Nature] hath done her part;
> Do thou but thine, and be not diffident

Of Wisdom, she deserts thee not, if thou
Dismiss not her, when most thou need'st her nigh,
By attributing overmuch to things
Less excellent. . . . Weigh with [Eve] thyself;
Then value. (8.561–571)

This exercise of "Wisdom" (as Raphael calls it) evolves within the
compass of a conversation, coextensively with the linguistic distinctions between man and woman and man and beast. Moreover, it involves a vigorous, ongoing projection of Adam's own deficiencies
onto Eve—pulling the man's own beastliness out of himself in order
that he may recognize it in the woman instead. If this process is at all
suspended, male privilege evaporates; the man himself becomes the
beast, sunk in passion and ripe for the carnal blandishments of the
local fauna:

If the sense of touch whereby mankind
Is propagated seem such dear delight
Beyond all other think the same voutsaf't
To Cattle and each Beast. . . . Love refines
The thoughts, and heart enlarges, hath his seat
In Reason, and is judicious, is the scale
By which to heav'nly Love thou may'st ascend,
Not sunk in carnal pleasure, for which cause
Among the Beasts no Mate for thee was found. (8.579–594)

It is Adam's ceaseless responsibility to weed out the bestial pleasures in his human composition, and failure to do so will automati-
cally promote his inferior and wife to the position of "Guide / And
Head" (4.442–443).[8] In short, being a man—as opposed to a
woman or a beast—requires constant discursive police work. Milton,
concerned as always with preceding his historical predecessors, has
here created the great original of Renaissance morals critics, out-
Bearding Beard and outdoing Donne. In the process, he has paid the
same price the others have paid before him; he has constructed the
immoral and bestial as intrinsic to the human male subject himself,
requiring continuous surveillance and ongoing exorcism.
    Outside of *A Midsummer Night's Dream*, Shakespeare offers a fur-
ther perspective on the coupling of people with animals. For Falstaff
in *The Merry Wives of Windsor* (1597), zooerastia supplies a model
not just of heroic but of godlike behavior; wearing a buck's head for
his final rendezvous with Mistresses Page and Ford, Falstaff justifies
his appearance by invoking classical myth:

Now the hot-blooded gods assist me! Remember, Jove, thou wast a
bull for thy Europa, love set on thy horns. O powerful love, that in
some respects makes a beast a man; in some other, a man a beast. You
were also, Jupiter, a swan for the love of Leda. O omnipotent love,
how near the god drew to the complexion of a goose! A fault done first
in the form of a beast (O Jove, a beastly fault!) and then another fault
in the semblance of a fowl—think on't, Jove, a foul fault! (5.5.2–11)

Such transformations, Falstaff reasons, betoken extraordinary passion, and thus—although they may constitute a "fault" to be chuck-
led over indulgently—they ultimately redound to the lover's credit.
Mistress Ford continues the scene in a like vein by coincidentally
mocking Falstaff's animal pillow-talk: "Sir John? art thou there, my
deer? my male deer?" (5.5.16–17).

A Midsummer Night's Dream thus furnishes us with a king and
semideity who acts like a peeping Tom with a taste for animal forni-
cation. *The Merry Wives of Windsor,* by contrast, offers us a sodden,
horn-bedecked roue who justifies his antics in part by claiming that
they are of royal and divine inspiration. In either case, as in the works
of Donne, Beard, and the rest, the audience is left with the fundamental problem of sorting out morality—of determining where a
given social police-action ends and where the gratification of forbidden desire begins. And thus, despite their differences, Oberon and
Falstaff comprise a rhetorical continuum: a society of those who
claim to preserve the order of things by being above that order, while
resorting to the most grossly dehumanizing behavior in the name of
human values such as love and domestic harmony. Theirs is, as Falstaff would put it, a beastly fault.

4. SOULS AND BODIES

It is a fault writ large in the theological and sociopolitical discourse of
Shakespeare's contemporaries, who have regular trouble characteriz-
ing the precise relation of womankind to humankind. The problem
here should be clear by now; for most writers of the day, women are
essential and integral to the human race, while at the same time comprising a distinct and inferior order unto themselves. George Orwell's
famous maxim, "All animals are equal, but some are more equal than
others," could well have been written with this arrangement in mind.
Moreover, it is an arrangement with consequences for masculine identity as well as for feminine. The male intellectual of the early modern
period frequently finds himself in the position of Milton's Adam,

pulled simultaneously and almost irresistibly toward two opposed and equally unacceptable views of feminine nature; if he opts for either one, he compromises his own manhood in the process. On one hand, to accept a woman as one's equal is to commit the error Milton liked to call "uxoriousness," Adam's error; it is to abdicate manly excellence in favor of a fond (in the sense of both "emotional" and "foolish") subservience to one's wife. On the other hand, to deny women any commonality with men at all is to undo the human character of the marriage bond, and, in the process, to undermine the moral and physical distinctions that make bestial buggery a crime.

In 1595, at roughly the same time that Shakespeare is composing *A Midsummer Night's Dream,* an anonymous German humanist (sometimes identified as Valtin Havekenthal [Valens Acidalius])[9] apparently commits this latter error. He does so by publishing a brief theological treatise entitled *A New Discourse Against Women, In Which It Is Proven That They Are Not Human* (*Disputatio Nova Contra Mulieres, qua Probatur Eas Homines non Esse*). The work consists of fifty-one theses, arguing from scripture that women were not created as human beings; that they do not have souls and therefore are incapable of salvation; and that they have more in common with beasts than with men. Much of the discourse is patently outrageous. The author begins, for instance, by noting that "one can find neither in the New nor the Old Testament that woman is said to be or is called a human being" (*"Women,"* 22)—a point whose validity hinges upon the convenient fact that the Vulgate uses the noun *homo* to mean both "human being" and "man." Indeed, the argument continues, woman is created not as a human being, but after the physical likeness of Adam, as an instrument for the production of human beings: "A tailor does not take up an axe to repair clothing, but a needle, an apt helper. Thus for the procreation of man God did not wish to make a four-footed animal for Adam, or something else unlike him, for then a man would not be able to be born properly" (24). The fact that women are baptized says nothing about their humanity, in this view, since Catholics "also baptize bells and temples" (38). Nor is it any more helpful to point out that women may be possessed by demons, since the same was true of the Gadarene swine (33). Nor does it make any difference that Christ raised a little girl from the dead; on the contrary, "we read of Blessed Germanus, the British bishop, that he raised an ass from the dead . . . , but no one can reason on this basis that asses will be resurrected" (38). Quite the opposite, in fact: Christ specifically declared that "'No one will contract marriage in the resurrection'" because "no woman will be in heaven, but they [the resurrected souls] will be like the angels of God," which are "all male, of course, and not female" (35). In short, as the anonymous author declares in a particularly egregious display of misquotation and faulty deduction, God gave Adam dominion "'over all the beasts,'" and "since man also rules woman, who, unless he is insane, is able to believe her to be human and not, rather, a beast?" (25–26).

If these arguments sound sophomoric and ridiculous, they should. In fact, the misogyny of *A New Discourse Against Women* is clearly a satirical ploy, a fact rendered deeply ironic by the work's history and reception. From beginning to end, the treatise makes clear through the broadest of humor that it is a deliberate parody of the scriptural literalism popular with radical reformed Christianity in general, and with groups such as the Socinians and Anabaptists in particular.[10] The pamphlet's opening sentence directly sets forth its overall tone and strategy in this regard; since radical reformers argue, via the literal interpretation of scripture, that Jesus Christ "is not God," the anonymous author will prove by the very same exegetical method that women are not human beings (21). Working in the satirical tradition of Erasmus and Sir Thomas More, but with somewhat less delicacy of touch, the author seeks to discredit a highly popular mode of biblical interpretation by associating it with an argument of manifest and outrageous absurdity.

Unfortunately, however, the pamphlet's humor cut too close to the bone for many readers. The work received an immediate and massively negative reaction on the basis of its perceived misogyny; in the year of its publication, the prominent Lutheran scholar Simon Gedik (Gediccus) composed a response entitled *Defence of the Female Sex* (*Defensio Sexus Muliebris*), which set the tone for future responses as well. Gedik belonged to that venerable tribe of scholars who consider it a professional virtue to declare war upon irony and mirth. He shared Martin Luther's distaste for the Erasmian mode of discourse, and although he clearly understood that *A New Discourse Against Women* was not intended to be taken literally, he chose to do so anyway. The result is a line-by-line refutation of the original pamphlet's arguments, a refutation in which Gedik predictably hurls the charges of inhumanity back in his opponent's face. "I believe you are not a beast," Gedik says to the anonymous author, "but something worse than a beast" (*Defence;* in *"Women"* 48); and again, "Your most obscene deeds are not the impurities of men but of pigs" (68–69); and again, "You, you radical disputant, are a monster in nature, absenting yourself from your mind. For I would not dare to call you a man, who have not been brought into the world by a human mother" (73). Gedik's refutation proves ironic in any number of ways: It subjects *A New Discourse Against Women* to the very sort of humorless literalism that the original work was expressly designed to ridicule; it does so despite the fact that Gedik himself was opposed to the more radical forms of literal exegesis that the original work assails; and it was eventually placed upon the Index of Prohibited Books, alongside the very treatise it reprehends.[11]

Yet despite these ironies, Gedik's work paved the way for other responses to *A New Discourse Against Women*, both formal and informal rejoinders that appeared desultorily over the coming century. In the early 1600s, a student at the University of Cologne presented the theses of *A New Discourse Against Women* to an audience of outraged mothers who responded by beating him to death with their stools (Lehms 1714–1715, sig. B3v); the jurisconsult Johann Harprecht pronounced this action just because "whoever defends and affirms that women are not human beings was himself . . . worthy to be born not of a mother nor of humankind, but of a swine" ("Welcher wertheydiget and bejahet / dass die Weiber keine Menschen seyn / derselbe . . . ware wurdig / dass er nicht aus einer Mutter and Menschen sondern von einem Schwein gebohren wurde" [sig. B3v]). In 1639 the Dutch physician John Beverovicius followed in Gedik's footsteps with his own *Defensio Sexus Muliebris* (Des Maizeaux 2.2.539[C]). The Italian nun Arcangela Tarabotti (Galerana Barcitotti) published a treatise against the *New Discourse* in 1651, after the original pamphlet had been reissued in Italian translation (see *"Women"* 89–159). In 1672, the dispute was recapitulated in German, in dialogue form, as *A Basic and Provable Description, Argument, and Conclusion, Together with Appended Responses to the Question Whether Women Are Human Beings or Not* (*Grund- und probierliche Beschreibung, Argument und Schluss-Articul, samt beigefugten Beantwortungen der Frage: ob die Weiber Menschen seyen oder nicht* [Fleischer 1981, 110]). And in 1680 Johann Thilo published a detailed defense of women in his *Medulla Theologiae Veteri Testamenti Exegeticae* (Fleischer 118).

The controversy also left its mark upon seventeenth-century English letters. Most notoriously, it emerges in Ben Jonson's *Masque of Beauty* (1608), where Jonson's female masquers, led by Queen Anne herself, dance to the accompaniment of the following verses:

> Had those, that dwell in error foule,
> And hold that women haue no soule,

But seene these moue; they would haue, then,
Said, *Women were the soules of men.* (368–371)

Donne likewise begins his verse epistle "To the Countess of Hunt-
ingdon" (ca. 1605; see *The Complete English Poems,* 1971) by assert-
ing that "Man to God's image, Eve to man's was made, / Nor find
we that God breathed a soul in her" (1–2); then he predictably describes the countess herself as an example to the contrary. Indeed,
Donne seems to have been particularly drawn to the question of
women's humanity. He had addressed this issue earlier, in his *Para-
doxes and Problems* (1590–1600):

> It is agreed that wee have not so much from them [women] as any
> *part* of either our *mortall soules* of *sense,* or *growth;* and we deny *soules*
> to others equal to them in all but in *speech* for which they are behold-
> ing to their *bodily instruments:* For perchance an *Oxes* heart, or a
> *Goates,* or a *Foxes,* or a *Serpents* would speake just so if it were in the
> *breast* and could move that *tongue* and *jawes.* (20)

And toward the end of his life, with a classic gesture of Donnish self-
repudiation, he pointedly corrected this earlier opinion in his sermon
for Easter Day, 1630:

> Howsoever some men out of a petulancy and wantonnesse of wit, and
> out of the extravagancy of Paradoxes, and such singularities, have
> called the faculties, and abilities of women in question, even in the
> roote thereof, in the reasonable and immortall soul, yet . . . No author
> of gravity, of piety, of conversation in the Scriptures could admit that
> doubt, whether woman were created . . . in possession of a reasonable
> and an immortall soul. (369–70)

Later in the seventeenth century, the French author Paul Lorrain
published a translation of *A New Discourse* and dedicated it to
Samuel Pepys, who, he claimed, had introduced him to the argument
that women were not human (*"Women"* 5; See Herford, Simpson,
and Simpson 11:464, n. 370).

Thus *A New Discourse* cut a remarkably wide swath through the
world of seventeenth-century European letters. But the really remarkable thing about the responses to which this treatise gave birth
is their almost absolute univocality. With the possible exception of a
very young Donne and a very peculiar Pepys, no one actually asserts
that women are not human. As for Donne and Pepys, they may well
be jesting, as the author of *A New Discourse* was clearly doing, and in

any case we have seen that Donne makes a point of correcting himself later. (Pepys's remark, reported secondhand and out of context, proves little.) So the literature we are surveying here is far more unified than any body of controversy has a right to be. Pierre Bayle, writing of *A New Discourse* in his dictionary, asserts that "This little book was reprinted several times, and it found some people who thoroughly supported the view expressed in its title" ("On a reimprimé ce petit Livre plusieurs fois; & il s'est trouvé des gens qui ont soutenu tout de bon la These qu'n voit au Titre" [Des Maizeaux 1730, 2.2:538–539]); however, in his revision of Bayle's work, Pierre Des Maizeaux feels compelled to comment at this point that "I have put this remark to the test; but none of the examples I have adduced could truly be said to have taken the affirmative seriously" ("On en verra la preuve dans cette Remarque: mais tous les exemples que j'alléguerai ne sont point propres a montrer qu'on ai pris l'affirmative sérieusement" [2.2:539(C)]). But that is not to say that the affirmative doesn't exist. On the contrary, there is an important sense in which the negative *is* the affirmative. Again and again Gedik and his followers warn us not to believe that women are animals, and these warnings function rather like the repeated exhortation not to think about a fluorescent green hippopotamus; they return us officiously to the very thing they seek to eradicate. In short, from at least 1595 onward, the belief that women are not human is advanced and reiterated entirely by people who oppose it.

As with the other textual economies surveyed in this chapter, the figure of the monster ("worse than a beast," as Gedik says) is so essential to this economy of moral discourse that the discourse crafts the monster's existence more or less out of thin air. In a triumphant moment of exegetical bad faith, Gedik takes *A New Discourse Against Women* to mean practically the opposite of what it was designed to mean, and in this process his reputation as an interpreter of scripture is born. But what of the world prior to *A New Discourse*? For that pamphlet assuredly did not invent the idea that women are not fully human. On the contrary, one already hears this claim in 1567, in Lewis Wager's interlude of *Mary Magdalene* (see *Reformation Biblical Drama in England*, 1992). Here the opinion in question belongs to the vice Infidelitie, who seeks to dissuade Magdalene from repenting for her sins by claiming that "Women haue no soules, this saying is not newe, / Men shall be damned, and not women which do fall" (1184–1185). Within a decade or two of this play, the French jurist Jacob Cujas (Cujacius) had apparently made the same argument "in legal form."[12] Gaspar, in Castiglione's *Courtier* (1516; see *The*

Courtier, 1967), goes so far as to insist "wise men have left in writinge, that nature, because she is alwaies set and bent to make things most perfect, if she could, would continually bring furth men, and when a woman is borne, it is a slacknes or default of nature" (223).

In fact, one of the "wise men" in question was clearly Aristotle— a point made gleefully by the author of *A New Discourse* (37). It is Aristotle who lends the *New Discourse* its outrageous argument that man is to woman as tailor is to needle, for the *De Generatione Animalium* claims that the masculine principle is the efficient cause, and the feminine the material cause, of generation, and then additionally asserts that since "the first efficient or moving cause . . . is better and more divine in its nature than the material on which it works," therefore the male "is better and more divine" than the female (732a; see *The Complete Works of Aristotle,* 1984). Another such "wise author" was apparently Ambrosiaster, the fourth-century Pauline exegete whose influential commentary upon Romans declared that "there is a great distance between the glory of God and the glory of man, for man was made in the image of God, and woman was not" ("Multum distat inter gloriam dei et gloriam viri; vir enim ad imaginem dei factus est, non mulier" [*Ambrosiastri . . . Commentarius* 1968, 81]). This comment, in turn, could find at least indirect support in Paul's declaration that Christian men "are become dead to the law by the body of Christ," just as a wife "is loosed from the law of her husband" by the husband's death (Romans 1–4). The parallelism established here—man is to God as woman is to man—may, if taken one step further, lead to formulations of sexual difference in which woman is no more like man than man is like God. By the nineteenth century, in turn, it was fairly common in intellectual circles to maintain that an early church council had pronounced this indeed to be the case: that woman was not made in the image of God, and that she therefore had no soul.[13] Thus a lengthy tradition of commentary already lay behind *A New Discourse*'s tongue-in-cheek assertion that women are not human.

But once again, this tradition is perhaps more remarkable for what it does not say than for what it does. In *Mary Magdalene,* after all, Wager ascribes the opinion that women have no souls to the character Infidelitie; in Castiglione's *Courtier,* Gaspar serves as a straw man to introduce a lengthy discussion of feminine courtly perfection; Cujas's legal arguments have been dismissed as a jest promulgated "for personal amusement" ("*pour se devertir*" [Des Maizeax 1730, 2.2:539(C)]). The authority of Ambrosiaster's commentary—originally attributed to Saint Ambrose himself—was discredited during the sixteenth and seventeenth centuries, in part because it seemed incredible that such an eminent church father would even come close to denying the humanity of women (Donne, "Sermon for Easter Day, 1630," 369–370). As for the elusive church council that denied women souls, it has never been successfully located; there is only a brief remark by Gregory of Tours (ca. 586–594; see *The History of the Franks*, 1974) that a bishop at the council of Macon in 585 maintained that the vulgate term "homo" could not be taken to refer to both man and woman (8.20). However, Gregory notes, the bishop's brethren quickly set him straight.

So when we survey in its entirety the theologicoliterary tradition that women are not human, it seems to be constructed wholly out of refutations, misquotations, a couple of ill-conceived jokes, and a far greater number of willful misinterpretations of those jokes. At the root of this improbable catenation of errors lies the supposed authority of both Aristotle and Saint Paul, yet neither of these authors specifically denies women a soul, or membership in the human race. What they *do* deny is that women are equal to men. This denial becomes an article of faith for the socioliterary order that Shakespeare inherits when composing *A Midsummer Night's Dream*, and through the tradition that excludes womankind from humanity, this denial creates and sustains its own debased, self-parodic double, simultaneously inimical and essential to the dominant order itself. After all, if—as Aristotle and Saint Paul say—woman is to man as man is to God; if man is the efficient and woman the material cause of generation; if man is better and more divine than woman; and if he is likewise her domestic lord; then she may well appear to have more in common with the beasts than with him. It is as if the dominant order could only conceive of feminine difference in terms of difference of species, and then, having done so, felt compelled to disown its own monstrous conception.

5. DEERLY DEFLOWER'D

"To bring in (God shield us!) a lion among ladies, is a most dreadful thing; for there is not a more fearful wild-fowl than your lion living; and we ought to look to't" (*A Midsummer Night's Dream* 3.1.30–33): Bottom expresses tender concern for his audience's comfort at the upcoming ducal performance of *Pyramus and Thisby*, and his concern takes immediate shape as an awareness of sexual difference. The lion threatens not men but "ladies"; and the obvious way to countervail this threat is, in effect, to make the lion act the part of a man:

> Your lion . . . must speak through, saying thus, or to the same defect: "Ladies," or "Fair ladies, . . . If you think I come hither as a lion, it were pity of my life. No! I am no such thing; I am a man as other men are"; and there indeed let him name his name, and tell them plainly he is Snug the joiner. (3.1.32–46)

Thus, while seeking to straighten out the relations between men and women, Bottom's advice hopelessly confuses the relations between people and animals. Starting with the assumption that his play *does*, in fact, threaten to "bring in . . . a lion among ladies," Bottom's language foregrounds its own patent inability to keep species separate; the lion is a "wild-fowl," and (in arsy-varsy syntax allied to the rhetorical figure of the "preposterous," as delineated by Patricia Parker [1987, 66–69]) the beast winds up declaring himself "a man *as other men are*" (my italics). Bottom addresses a fictional audience of "Ladies," and urges Snug to frame words to "the same defect" as his own; that "defect" is coterminous with his own inability to conceive of men and women as comprising a single race.

Snug follows Bottom's advice in a way that once again thoroughly muddles the distinction between sex and species:

> You, ladies, . . .
> May now, perchance, both quake and tremble here,
> When lion rough in wildest rage doth roar.
> Then know that I as Snug the joiner am
> A lion fell, nor else no lion's dam. (5.1.219–224)

For the ladies, apparently, Snug threatens to assume the aspect of a "lion fell"—at least as like as not. Yet Snug's attempt to distinguish himself from his (other) dramatic character simply confuses matters further by claiming that Snug, as Snug, *is* a lion; and Snug then ends his explanation by triumphantly noting that otherwise he is no lion's dam. Beginning with the earnest concern that an alien sex might mistake him for an alien species, he ends up getting his own sex wrong; and that is arguably because, by adopting the character of another creature, his language has confused itself as to its own gender orientation.

Given such repeated confusion, Bottom's words as Pyramus take on a decidedly peculiar cast. "O dainty duck!," he exclaims upon discovering Thisby's bloody mantle (5.1.281); and his language quickly assumes the quality of a mock-heroic lament: "O, wherefore, Nature, didst thou lions frame? / Since lion vild hath here deflower'd my deer" (5.1.291–292). If Nature has framed Snug as a lion, one might reasonably wonder, has it then framed Thisby as a duck or a deer— or both? Further, the malapropism of "deflowered" for "devoured" hardly seems coincidental, given that Bottom/Pyramus utters it while holding aloft a piece of blood-stained fabric. And given Bottom's persistent tendency to conflate differences of species with differences of gender, this ambivalent use of the verb "deflower'd" seems fully preconditioned. For defloration in *A Midsummer Night's Dream* is almost by rule a thing done between total aliens: Athenian dukes and Amazon warriors, fairy queens and asses, men and their mares, lions and deer. As Stephen Greenblatt has remarked of *Twelfth Night*, "Licit sexuality . . . depends upon a movement that deviates from the desired object straight in one's path toward a marginal object, a body one scarcely knows. Nature is an *unbalancing* act" (*Shakespearean Negotiations* 1998, 68).

Of all the mechanicals, Bottom is presented as the one with the greatest taste for acting. Flute, who apparently would like to play "a wand'ring knight" (1.2.45), shrinks from the part of Thisby: "Nay, faith; let me not play a woman; I have a beard coming" (1.2.47–48). But Bottom is agreeable to the task, and he promises to do it justice in his tone of voice: "And I may hide my face, let me play Thisby too. I'll speak in a monstrous little voice, 'Thisne, Thisne!'" (1.2.51–53). In short, he proposes to impersonate a woman by speaking monstrously; then he further confirms his passion for histrionics by offering to act the other monster in *Pyramus and Thisby* as well—the lion: "Let me play the lion too. I will roar, that I will do any man's heart good to hear me" (1.2.70–71). For Bottom, that is, femininity presupposes monstrosity, and thus the lion becomes the one character in the play with whom Thisby has most in common; both require the hiding of one's face and form, both demand virtuoso modulations of voice and expression, and both provide outstanding opportunities for the display of one's histrionic skill. From an actor's (or at least *this* actor's) standpoint, the beast is Thisby's perfect mate. It is an attitude Bottom shares with Oberon.

Hence Shakespeare's burlesque subplot supplies a running commentary upon the concerns of the play's central characters, as well as upon itself. At the heart of this commentary lies Bottom's animal transformation, which offers him a very real opportunity to speak "in a monstrous little voice" and also, coincidentally, to join with Titania as the star attraction in a fairy freak show. Unable to distinguish between monsters and women, Bottom himself becomes a monster; and his metatheatrical appearance as Pyramus—"A lover, that kills himself most gallant for love" (1.2.23–24)—further deepens the irony of his situation by expanding its frame of reference. For while Shakespeare's audience watches Theseus, Hippolyta, and the others watching Bottom, it in effect watches itself; and the audience of *Pyramus and Thisby* sees Bottom's folly without recognizing it as a part of *themselves*—that is, as a product of the very discursive practices whereby they maintain social order. Their ox is gored, their deer deflowered.

6. SEPARATING THE MEN FROM THE GOATS

Peter Stallybrass and Allon White (1986) have advanced an attractive explanation for the relationship between low and high characters in *A Midsummer Night's Dream*. For Stallybrass and White, "the 'top' [of any social hierarchy] attempts to reject and eliminate the 'bottom' for reasons of prestige and status, only to discover . . . that the top *includes* that low symbolically, as a primary eroticized constituent of its own fantasy life" (5). Thus Shakespeare's wedding couples repeatedly signify their rejection of the Bottom through the condescending in-jokes that punctuate the play-within-a-play. Yet Bottom himself emerges as a prerequisite to the very social discriminations that privilege the wedding couples in the first place; he occupies the necessary place of the other, without which Shakespeare's aristocrats could not begin to think themselves. No quantity of in-jokes can sever this connection; nor can any quantity of male discipline deny the bestial/female other a controlling share in conventional models of "marital harmony . . . predicated upon the wife's obedience to her husband" (Montrose 1986, 70).[14]

In the governing terms of the present study, this complex interdependence repeats the ambivalence with which absolute and relative anthropocentrism relate to one another. On the one hand, of course, these two sets of attitudes remain starkly contradictory; to treat some human beings as if they were less than human, as relative anthropocentrism typically does, is to render indistinct the very opposition between human beings and beasts upon which the order of absolute anthropocentrism resides. Yet on the other hand, absolute and relative anthropocentrism are also clearly complementary formulations; the latter recapitulates, on the social level, the discriminations enacted by the former on the biological level. One result of this interdependence is that *A Midsummer Night's Dream* lent itself exceptionally well to the containment-subversion criticism of the late

1980s and early 1990s, which notoriously tended to resolve such ambiguities in favor either of a conservative or a radical Shakespeare, depending on the preferences of the critic of the moment. Sensing the complementarity of the play's tropes of authority and misrule, for instance, Leonard Tennenhouse could argue that "the introduction of disorder into [*A Midsummer Night's Dream*] ultimately authorizes political authority" (1986, 74). Yet, as C. L. Barber long ago observed, Shakespeare's play (and the clown subplot in particular) is pervaded by an acute "consciousness of the creative act itself" (1959, 148), and thus one may view the plot as deploying biology against institutions (like marriage and monarchy) that typically advertise themselves as natural and given. By equating social and sexual difference with difference of species, *A Midsummer Night's Dream* could be taken to contest the ultimate morality of class and gender distinctions; and to this extent, the play could be seen as conforming to Catherine Belsey's pro-subversion claim that "Shakespearean comedy can be read as . . . calling in question that set of relations which proposes as inevitable an antithesis between masculine and feminine, men and women" (*Alternative Shakespeares* 1985, 167).

But *A Midsummer Night's Dream* does not draw simply on the vocabularies of absolute and relative anthropocentrism; it is indebted to traditions of anthropomorphic thought, too, and this indebtedness can scarcely be accounted for by the binary logic of subversion and containment. While it is true, as has been recently argued, that "anthropocentrism—placing the human and human vision at the centre—leads . . . to anthropomorphism—seeing the world in our image" (Fudge 2000, 7), in *A Midsummer Night's Dream* the human image in question is so shifting and various as to defy description. It is not simply a case of seeing reflected in the bestiary tradition a society's prejudices concerning feminine sexuality; Shakespeare's play presents a world whose human characters represent—are aware of—only a fraction of the ambient sexual appetite. That, arguably, is why the play's hints of bestiality elicit so little attention, either from audiences or from the play's own characters; they are simply one aspect of the polymorphous universe of desire that Shakespeare's work envisions, a universe for which the dynamics of subversion and containment are not just inadequate but frankly irrelevant. As Theodore Leinwand has maintained, "a heteroglot Bottom . . . better captures the Shakespeare function . . . than does any univocal voicing" (1990, 487).

Indeed, Shakespeare's bestiality in *A Midsummer Night's Dream* resolutely resists critical attempts at univocal characterization; the play's weird, hybrid sexiness—or more importantly, the scariness of

its sexiness—has never been effectively foreclosed by efforts at interpretation. To this extent, Shakespeare problematizes the standard
Renaissance judicial approach to bestial sexuality, which relies upon
clear distinctions between the natural and the perverse, the bidden
and the forbidden, and which thus tends to obfuscate the very discursive conditions that make it possible in the first place. As Alan
Bray has observed in his book on Renaissance homosexuality (an offense that Renaissance law elided with bestiality under the common
name of buggery), individuals did not tend to recognize their own
acts as perverse; perversity was always the province of the other, not
of the subject in society (1982, 67–70). Shakespeare's Oberon might
have been created especially to illustrate the point; and indeed, by
following the discourse of sexual difference to its logically dehumanizing end, *A Midsummer Night's Dream* creates a world in which it
is impossible to separate the men from the goats, or the goats from
the audience.

The consequent ambiguity is best embodied in the protean figure
of Puck, who encompasses all shapes but holds to no proper shape
himself, and who thus furthers yet another of Oberon's Borgia-like
voyeuristic entertainments: "I jest to Oberon and make him smile /
When I a fat and bean-fed horse beguile, / Neighing in likeness of a
filly foal" (2.1.44–46). In a passage such as this, distinctions of biological category are buried almost as deeply as the sexual element itself. Puck—who is after all not a man, although he appears to the
audience in a human shape—becomes the perfect similitude of a "filly
foal," luring its mare (or perhaps its stallion—as assumed by at least
one nineteenth-century theater director)[15] forward to a consumma-
tion that is specifically Oberon's and that parallels the misrecognition
of species. It is a jest that Puck repeats at large for the play's audience,
when he both "follow[s]" and "lead[s]" (3.1.106) the mechanicals
"through bog, through bush, through brake, through brier"
(3.1.107): "Sometime a horse I'll be, sometime a hound, / A hog, a
headless bear" (3.1.108–109). These, for him and his master, are apparently the shapes of pleasure.

"O happy horse"—as another of Shakespeare's characters might put
it—"to bear the weight of Oberon!" Puck's multiform services for
Oberon depend repeatedly upon his ability to transgress limits—of gender, species, class, and even shape itself. To this extent Oberon's own
capacity to maintain order, including husbandly authority in marriage
and royal authority in the state, relies upon the violation of those very
kinds of order he himself constructs. As Stallybrass and White observe,
"the result is a mobile, conflictual fusion of power, fear and desire in the

construction of subjectivity: a psychological dependence upon precisely those Others which are being rigorously opposed and excluded at the social level" (1986, 5). In a word, the result is Puck.

If, then, the containment-subversion model used to ask readers of *A Midsummer Night's Dream* to choose between Theseus and Bottom, traditional patriarchalism or carnivalesque misrule, I would decline both options in favor of Puck. Admittedly, a Puckish Shakespeare is an uncomfortable Shakespeare; it deprives readers of social and ideological certainty, just as Puck himself (itself?) deprives the young lovers and bumbling mechanicals of confident knowledge about what is going on around them. Such a Shakespeare—and such a Shakespearean character—gains force and complexity from the persistent refusal to identify with a single binary term (human, male, conservative, traditional, moral) at the expense of its opposite. For this playwright, the inside is always the outside, and vice versa; he toys with the slippages—between woman and beast, for instance, or man and monster—that ground the system of meaning of which he is a part. However, he does so not for specifically disruptive or subversive purposes, nor yet against them, but rather because it is only through such toying, and such slippages, that the system ever emerges (or recedes).

The resulting Shakespeare is neither unambiguously conservative nor unquestionably radical, but complexly and unremittingly compromised. His work, in this sense, becomes a textual analogue for the processes of bestial copulation that this chapter has been about: a composite figure that blends from conservative into radical and back again, from human being into goat, in an incessant pattern of statement and self-interference. If *A Midsummer Night's Dream* supplies a particularly acute instance of this process, it is because this play dwells so centrally upon the imbricated issues of class and gender difference; its running metaphorical equations of low class, low gender, and low species eventually leave its characters with no real avenue for unimpaired commerce with others. In short, the play gives itself and its audience no place in which to be finally and unambiguously human; it attests to what Stephen Orgel has called "the radical instability of our essence" ("Nobody's Perfect" 1989, 16).[16] Shakespeare's comedy thus denies us the certitude—about who we are, and about what it means to be us—that Renaissance disciplinary texts on perversion uniformly, naively, and necessarily presuppose.

CHAPTER TWO

THE CUCKOO AND THE CAPON

1. *Bellum Amoris*

No animal image is more commonplace to English Renaissance culture, and at the same time more distinctive of that culture and its European contemporaries, than the horns of the cuckold. They are everywhere in sixteenth- and seventeenth-century English prose and poetry, legal records and visual iconography; and, if anything, they are at least equally pervasive in the dramatic literature of the period.[1] Their ubiquity has occasioned a fair amount of scholarly comment, most of which tends to view the theme of cuckoldry as an expression of anxieties related to patriarchy and the genealogical ascription of identity. Thus, as Marc Shell has noted (1988, 4–8), there is never any absolute guarantee of a child's paternity; the assignment of rank, opportunity, and privilege in Renaissance English society was accomplished largely through the facts of one's parentage; and therefore the possibility that a given husband might be a cuckold, raising another man's child, constituted a threat to the integrity of the social order in general and a challenge to the justice and determinacy of the terms that lent that order its particular expression.[2] Coppélia Kahn has emphasized the nature of cuckoldry as an emblem of "man's vulnerability to woman in marriage" (1981, 119), and Mark Breitenberg, following Kahn, has described the cuckold's horns as "a phallic symbol of male potency" whose displacement to the head signifies "male fears of dismemberment" (1996, 147–148). Likewise, Jeanne Addison Roberts has argued that the horns traditionally associated with the cuckold may suggest the degree to which a cuckolded husband has relinquished his status as a sexual pursuer and has assumed, instead, the status of his wife's "prey" (1991, 90–91). Douglas Bruster has noted the association between cuckoldry and various economic relations such as "the predator/husband rivalry" (1992, 55); for Bruster, the Renaissance preoccupation with cuckoldry, emerging as it does at a crucial moment in the development of market capitalism, provides "a carnivalesque celebration of an older and more fertile way of existence" (55). And Grace Tiffany has observed that the theme of cuckoldry articulates masculine fears of "*female* sexual betrayal" (1995, 84), fears to which every man must submit—at least theoretically—in the process of becoming a husband. To this extent, Tiffany concludes, "the embrace of eros requires the displacement of masculine ego" (81), and the cuckold's horns become an apt literary and visual emblem of that displacement.

These are all groundbreaking insights, and the present analysis is deeply indebted to each of them. However, in what follows I wish to address two problems that such arguments do not entirely resolve: First, if the early European imagery of cuckoldry expresses anxieties typical of a social order grounded in patriarchy and the genealogical ascription of rank, why is that imagery so localized in time and place? Why is it not to be found, in some form or other and to a similar degree, in such equally patriarchal social formations as those of classical Greece or imperial Rome or feudal Japan? And second, why is the discourse of cuckoldry so complex and contradictory in its derivation, involving as it does both a diverse and unrelated symbology and a tendency—equally contrary to legal precedent and common sense—to concentrate blame and ridicule upon the figure of the wronged husband? I believe that these points are interconnected, and that the wronged husband becomes the focus of ridicule in the early modern European discourse of cuckoldry because he represents manhood as a peculiarly embattled, and ultimately as a fictive, quantity. This notion of manhood as *masquerade*—to borrow a Lacanian term normally associated with the performance of femininity[3]—is in turn distinctively characteristic of early modern European formulations of sexual difference.

This argument takes the sexual discourse of early modern England as roughly representative of early modern Europe in general, and while one risks eliding important differences through this procedure, the language of cuckoldry was without doubt spoken equally by sixteenth-century Englishmen, Frenchmen, Italians, Spaniards, and Germans. In the following pages, thus, I seek to do three things. First, I attempt to trace the development of the complex vocabulary and symbolism associated with the theme of cuckoldry in early modern Europe. I then note some of the points that differentiate this vocabulary from its most immediate forebear: the sexual discourse of imperial Rome, as represented by the amatory verse of Ovid. And finally, I consider two of the most outstanding treatments of the cuckoldry motif in early English drama: Middleton's *Chaste Maid in Cheapside* (1613) and Jonson's *Volpone* (1605–1606).

In the course of this analysis, I attempt to formulate a sense of the cuckoldry motif as generated out of contradiction and fragmentation, and to this extent the following pages may find their counterpart in feminist and Lacanian theories of femininity as discontinuity. Such discontinuity has already been well documented both in classical literature and in its Renaissance avatars, and examples of it abound in the Ovidian materials under consideration here. Thus, for one instance, at the climax of his fragmentary *Hero and Leander* (1593; see *Hero and Leander*, 1979), Christopher Marlowe stages the initial sexual encounter between his poem's eponymous lovers as a kind of rape:

> Every kiss to [Hero] was as a charm,
> And to Leander as a fresh alarm.
> . . . .
> She trembling strove; this strife of hers (like that
> Which made the world) another world begat
> Of unknown joy. Treason was in her thought,
> And cunningly to yield herself she sought.
> Seeming not won, yet won was she at length,
> In such wars women use but half their strength. (2.283–296)

This assault comes as the crowning Ovidianism in a poem replete with Ovid; the base text here, first rendered into English by Marlowe himself some years before the composition of *Hero and Leander*, is *Amores* 1.5 (1 B.C.; see *Heroides and Amores*, 1977). There Ovid describes an assignation with Corinna in much the same terms employed later by Marlowe, terms that construct the sexual encounter as a struggle in which the woman withholds her favors so as, paradoxically, to provoke a more ardent desire:

> I snatched her gown; being thin, the harm was small,
> Yet strived she to be covered therewithal,
> And striving thus as one that would be cast,
> Betrayed herself, and yielded at the last. (1.5.13–16)[4]

> [Deripui tunicam—nec multum rara nocebat;
> pugnabat tunica sed tamen illa tegi.

> quae cum ita pugnaret, tamquam quae vincere nollet.
> victa est non aegre proditione sua.]

The correspondence between these two passages—their mutual emphasis upon the idea of feminine self-betrayal and the common-place of the *bellum amoris*—is only the most obvious aspect of a wide range of Ovidian attitudes toward feminine sexuality and physical con-straint, attitudes that surface repeatedly in the literature of the English Renaissance. Thus, as recent scholarship has shown, Renaissance poets like Marlowe derive from Ovid a sense of feminine identity as funda-mentally split, as a discursive site onto which patriarchal desire pro-jects its own contradictory impulses and behaviors, and clauses like "victa est . . . proditione sua" illustrate the resulting fragmentation of feminine consciousness very clearly.[5] On this view, figures like Mar-lowe's Hero (and Ovid's Corinna), whose subsidiary social status ren-ders them subject to sexual and economic exploitation, also provide evidence for the construction of a myth of femininity that justifies fur-ther exploitation of a similar variety. Hero and Corinna say no to mas-culine desire (so the story goes), but their eventual acquiescence proves that they never really meant it, and that—by extension—women in general may be defined by their inability to know what they want or say what they mean. Hence Marlowe's aphoristic summation: "In such wars women use but half their strength."

The present chapter extends this notion of sexuality to encompass Renaissance notions of masculinity as well. Hence I will focus here upon what I call the dilemma of the cuckold in the early English drama, a dilemma that complements the situation of women just ex-emplified in Ovid but that has elicited somewhat less scholarly atten-tion. Put simply, the dilemma of the cuckold is that by marrying, he has in a sense absorbed his wife's defects of character. Unable to cor-rect or to uproot her feminine inconstancy, he becomes a site onto which—in a reversal of the discursive process whereby the category of femininity is itself initially constituted—*she* projects her own innate bad faith. In other words, if femininity itself is a discursive space cre-ated through the repression of social contradictions proper to various sorts of patriarchy, the cuckold in turn serves as an exemplary mascu-line figure for the return of what has been repressed. To this extent, the early modern discourse of cuckoldry differs from its forebears in classical Rome by recognizing the failure of the repressions that Ovid-ian verse employs to construct the space of the masculine ego.

In terms of this book's broader preoccupation with animals and animal symbology, the present chapter draws on beast associations so broad-based and well attested to that they need little immediate documentation; Douglas Bruster, for one, has already noted "the parade of animals associated with the image [of the cuckold]" (1992, 52). I am less interested in proving the uncontroversial fact that cuckolds were regarded as beasts in the Renaissance than I am in exploring why they were bestialized as they were: What, precisely, was meant by the ubiquitous emblems of their bovinity? This question is rendered all the more intriguing, I believe, because the derogatory beast associations in question were applied at the very apex of the sociobiological hierarchy traditionally upheld by the structures of absolute and relative anthropocentrism. The cuckoldry motif represents a pejorative application of animal imagery at a spot in the cultural order where we should expect few, if any, pejoratives to apply. To this extent, I believe, the tokens of cuckoldry serve not simply as a slur directed at particular, otherwise privileged individuals, but as a broad expression of anxieties about how their privilege was constructed in the first place. The beasts who lend their horns to generations of cornuted Englishmen also lend their presence to the category of English manhood itself; they survive as a point of slippage at the heart of the anthropocentric discursive order that has conjured them into existence, and whose ultimate fictitiousness they confirm.

2. HIS OXCELLENCY

At the very least, the Renaissance vocabulary and symbolism of cuckoldry embody some remarkable discontinuities. First there is the fact that the cuckoldry motif tends to punish victims rather than transgressors. It exists, that is, to cast shame and ridicule on the party—the wronged husband—who has already been injured by an adulterous affair. In addition, the theme of cuckoldry, as handled by early modern European society, involves visual and linguistic symbols drawn from vastly disparate fields of reference. These symbols accumulate under the rubric of cuckoldry so as to project various notions of deficiency onto the figure of the injured husband, but the deficiencies thus invoked are not entirely consistent with one another.

The noun "cuckold" itself provides an outstanding example of the reversals and inconsistencies out of which the Renaissance cuckoldry motif is constructed. Etymologically, the term derives from the Old French *cucuault*, where it means both "cuckoo and cuckold" (OED s.v. "cuckold"). As the OED explains, "The origin of the [latter] sense is supposed to be found in the cuckoo's habit of laying its egg in another bird's nest." Moreover, cognate terms in German and Provençal

"were applied to the adulterer as well as the husband of the adulter-
ess, and [French lexicographer Maximilien] Littré cites an assertion of
the same double use in French; in English, where cuckold has never
been the name of the bird, we do not find it applied to the adulterer"
(OED s.v. "cuckold"). In other words, the term "cuckold" originates
as an animal metaphor for the genealogical instability created by wifely
infidelity, and to this extent its history supports efforts to interpret the
cuckoldry motif as an expression of anxiety regarding the bases of genealogically ascribed identity. Thus, in early usage, terms like *cucuault*
refer naturally to the adulterous lover, pointing to him as the origin of
this anxiety, that is, as the interloper whose sexual predation not only
destroys family harmony but also threatens the larger social order in
the process. However, as the word *cucuault* transfers from Old French
to English—and as its metaphorical sense becomes buried in the
process—it performs a "linguistic turnabout" (Kahn 1981, 120)
whereby it ceases to apply to the adulterer and becomes instead a term
of contempt employed exclusively for betrayed husbands. This transference, in turn, signifies a shift in the nature and focus of the social
condemnation conveyed by the word itself.

Hence, in the limited case of the noun "cuckold," we may trace a
process of etymological development whereby a wronged husband
eventually comes to be treated as if he were somehow responsible for
his own betrayal. This tendency to ridicule the husband, in turn, is
the only factor relating the noun "cuckold" to its principal visual emblem, the cuckold's horns. Indeed, the horns exploit a pattern of animal metaphor that has nothing to do with cuckoos or with
genealogically ascribed rank. Recent scholars have tended to view
these horns either as an extension of hunting imagery or—from the
psychoanalytic standpoint—as an "upward displacement" of the
cuckold's virility (Kahn 122); however, the surviving philological evidence derives them from the practice of northern European poultry
farmers, who would engraft "the spurs of a castrated cock on the root
of the excised comb, where they grew and became horns, sometimes
several inches long" (OED s.v. "horn" 7). These false horns, planted
deliberately to make for easy visual discrimination between cocks and
capons, also came to symbolize the impotence and fatness of the latter birds; moreover, the German terms "*hahnreh* or *hahnrei* 'cuckold', originally meant 'capon'" (OED s.v. "horn" 7).

Thus early modern European prejudices about cuckoldry are
marked by the convergence of disparate cultural materials, materials
that metamorphose, in the process of their convergence, into a consistent discourse of ridicule and blame. It is perhaps only an addi-

tional irony that all this ridicule and blame is directed toward a figure who is in many ways wholly deserving of sympathy and support.
So what makes this figure the object of scorn? Most immediately, the
European discourse regarding cuckoldry seems to evolve as a form of
nervous projection, as an effort to forestall or mitigate one's own
possible humiliation by directing it onto others instead. But if this is
the case, one must still determine the source and nature of the humiliation that is being deferred, and in the present instance it seems
to come from two different directions at once. On one hand, the emblem of the cuckoo foregrounds a given husband's inability to manage his domestic circumstances: to establish beyond doubt the
paternity of his children and to control without question his wife's
sexual appetite and reproductivity. On the other hand, the emblem
of the horned capon emphasizes the husband's inability to manage
his own body with respect to the central events of sexual arousal and
performance. To this extent, the cuckoo and the capon emblematize
very different varieties of sexual discomfiture, the former deriving
from spousal infidelity and the latter from personal impotence. Moreover, in the strictest possible interpretation of matters, infidelity and
impotence are not even compatible states, for in early modern canon
law impotence is a diriment impediment to marriage, whereas spousal
infidelity presupposes valid matrimony. Technically speaking, one
cannot be both impotent and a cuckold at the same time, except in
those limited cases where impotence develops subsequent to the con-
summation of wedlock. Yet the popular culture of early modern Europe insists upon conflating the two conditions.

I believe that this is the case because feminine sexual betrayal and
personal impotence function as complementary fantasies of masculine uncontrol, fantasies that engage the bodily exterior and the bodily interior, respectively, and that are both predicated upon certain
non-negotiable social and biological salients. In the case of sexual betrayal, notions of individual masculine authority are forced to yield to
the combined facts that heredity cannot be ascertained beyond doubt
(even, as the recent story of Kimberly Mays demonstrates,[6] in the age
of DNA testing), and that wifely fidelity cannot be produced or thoroughly verified by any available form of household discipline. In the
case of personal impotence, masculine self-sufficiency is likewise compromised by the simple but unavoidable facts that one cannot will an
erection, and that masculine sexual desire often diminishes over the
longue durée of marital cohabitation. Taken together, the threats of
infidelity and impotence suggest that any notion of masculine self-
sufficiency is in an important sense fictitious—that the ability of men

to establish a stable, sustainable lineage is at bottom dependent upon both external and internal factors beyond masculine governance. The fear of spousal infidelity is at heart a sexual fear of the outside world—even that part of the outside world that is presumably most close at hand and therefore most manageable. Conversely, for a man, the fear of impotence is at heart a fear of his own inadequacy. Between them, these two fears deprive him of any space within which to lay confident claim to his own self, and that is why they merge within the early modern discourse of cuckoldry, a discourse haunted by visions of masculine fecklessness and subjection and failure and gullibility. As the servant Vasques observes to his betrayed master in Ford's *'Tis Pity She's a Whore* (1629–1633), "A cuckold is a goodly tame beast, my lord" (5.2.7).

In any case, there is no doubt that in early modern Europe cuckoldry "was a slur on both [the husband's] virility and his capacity to rule his own household" (Stone 1977, 503), and perhaps no event in the period's history better illustrates the intimate relation between spousal infidelity and personal impotence than does the infamous marriage of Robert Devereux, third Earl of Essex, to Lady Frances Howard. The two were betrothed in 1606, while still in their mid-teens, in a match arranged to cement relations between the pro-Spanish, crypto-Catholic Howard family and various Protestant interests. The couple began cohabiting in 1609, but apparently there was trouble from the very first. Frances Howard conceived an immediate and profound aversion to her husband, perhaps because of his political affiliations and personality, perhaps because she had already settled her heart elsewhere. For whatever reason, she was later reported to have determinedly withheld her body from the Earl, despite all the blandishments and pressures exerted upon her to the contrary by her husband and relatives. At their annulment proceedings in 1613, both husband and wife testified that the relationship had never been consummated.

During the three unhappy years of their official union, the Countess of Essex humiliated her husband by consorting openly with various courtiers, most significantly with Henry, Prince of Wales, and with King James I's favorite, Robert Carr, then Viscount Rochester.[7] The latter of these flirtations developed into a public and unrestrained affair. By early 1613 the Countess of Essex resided separately from her husband; the relations between her and Rochester were common knowledge to anyone interested in news of King James's court; and the Countess and Rochester had begun the scheming that would eventually lead to their ruin via the murder of Thomas Overbury. Amidst this lurid atmosphere, the Earl and his Countess finally resolved to repudiate their marriage.

For his part, Essex had made every effort to control his adulterous wife, even going to the extreme of sequestering her for a time at Chartley, his manor house in Staffordshire. However, by 1613 she had become an unavoidable embarrassment to him. It was rumored that she had "prostituted herself" to Henry, Prince of Wales, who had thereby "reaped the first fruits of her virginity" (D'Ewes 1845, 2:90); her affair with Rochester was the object of open sneers at court (Arthur Wilson 1653, sigs. H4v, K3r; Weldon 1651, sig. F3v); and Essex himself was said, with more malice than logic, to be both impotent and a cuckold (Snow 1970, 41). In any event, this last rumor proved to be something of a self-fulfilling prophecy, for as the scandal and humiliation of his wife's adultery increased, Essex became less and less willing to endure it; however, the only way for him to escape it was to have his marriage annulled, and the most obvious ground for an annulment was impotence. So in May 1613 a court of delegates convened at Whitehall to determine the future of Essex and his estranged wife. Representatives of the Devereux and Howard interests had already met, and as it was clear that both husband and wife desired to part ways, both sides had already agreed to request an annulment on the ground of impotence. Still, the hearing continued, with much vacillation and acrimony, throughout the summer and to the end of September, and this fact belies the superficial concord of plaintiff and defendant.

At heart, the problem with securing an annulment on the ground of impotence was that, by destroying Essex's reputation, it also destroyed his ability to remarry and raise an heir. On one hand, if he admitted in a court of law that he was impotent, he would be consigning himself to a life of bachelorhood and his family to genealogical oblivion; on the other hand, if he did not admit impotence, he was doomed to spend his life separated from an estranged and adulterous wife whose children, if there were to be any, might have a legal claim on his family name and holdings. On one hand lay the Scylla of impotence, and on the other the Charybdis of infidelity; Essex would have to steer between the two to preserve a future in which he could raise his own children, hold his estate together, and achieve some measure of domestic contentment. As defendant in the annulment trial, he therefore settled upon a strategy that was legally insecure, but that seemed to offer his only hope of salvation. He admitted that his marriage with Frances Howard was unconsummated, and furthermore he admitted that he was impotent; however, he insisted that the impotence was specific rather than general, and that he was fully capable of having normal sexual relations with any woman in the world *other* than his wife.

Unfortunately, the law tended to understand impotence as a general rather than as a particular condition. Thus it was something near nonsense to argue that Essex was impotent with one woman and one woman only; as charged by the head commissioner overseeing the case, George Abbott, Archbishop of Canterbury, Essex's claim of "*Non potuit* was for lack of love, and not for want of ability" (Cobbett 1809–1828, 2:813). The supporters of Essex's claim could, at best, adduce only two cases in English law that they regarded as supplying precedent for their action; moreover, both of the cases they cited were clearly beside the point.[8] As Archbishop Abbott again observed of the Essex case, "It is the want of love which restraineth all motions of carnal concupiscency, and not any impotency: it is *defectus voluntatis,* and not *defectus potestatis*" (Cobbett 2:854). Indeed, Abbott sought to split hairs even more finely by distinguishing between legal impotence and the general diminution of sexual capacity that often accompanies lengthy marriages: "Married men best know these things . . . : many things they say fall out between man and wife, that for some good space of time there is no carnal conjunction, and yet no impotency concluded thereby may be" (Cobbett 2:854). However, the distinctions Abbott sought to draw here were easy to muddle or even to ignore, as subsequent events showed all too clearly. The commissioners themselves divided into two camps in rendering their verdicts upon the case. One group, loyal to King James and his favorite, officially supported the contention that Essex was impotent in the single case of his wife, while informally maintaining that he was in the broader sense "impotent for a woman" (Cobbett 2:814). A second group, taking its lead from Archbishop Abbott, denied that impotence had been proven and voted against annulment, regarding it as little more than a shift to cover the prior and more genuine fact of Frances Howard's adultery.

In any event, the former group prevailed. The marriage between Robert Devereux and Frances Howard was pronounced invalid; Devereux was officially declared impotent in the limited case of his betrothed; and Frances Howard, arrayed in the tokens of virginity (Arthur Wilson, sig. K4v), married Robert Carr shortly thereafter. On paper, at least, Essex had gotten what he wanted: annulment of his marriage on the basis of a uniquely limited sexual incapacity. In practice, however, he emerged with a peculiarly clouded reputation. On one hand, the supporters of King James, Robert Carr, and the

Howards naturally treated Essex's admission of impotence with contempt. He was placed under house arrest after quarreling with one of Frances Howard's brothers, who had apparently insulted his virility (Somerset 1997, 135–136, 139); Thomas Howard, Earl of Suffolk, derisively remarked that Essex "had no ink in his pen" (Le Comte 1969, 97; Somerset 114); and the Howards demanded that Essex return his wife's dowry. On the other hand, however, Essex's supporters tended to view him as the victim of a loose wife's dishonorable behavior. One sympathetic wit, for instance, exploiting the peculiarities of Jacobean spelling, extracted from Frances Howard's name the anagram "Carr finds a whore" (Le Comte 54).[9] And Essex's own efforts to assert his virility simply added to his reputation as a cuckold:

> Having five or six captains and gentlemen of worth in his chamber, and speech being made of his inability, [he] rose out of his bed and, taking up his shirt, did show to them all so able and extraordinarily sufficient matter that they all cried out Shame of his lady, and said, That if the ladies of the court knew as much as they knew they would tread her to death. (Cobbett 2:822)

Thus, even where he encountered friends, Essex could not escape sexual humiliation. Technically speaking, he had succeeded in his attempt to free himself from the combined blemishes of impotence and wifely infidelity; practically speaking, however, he was marked with both for life.

The consequences of Essex's embarrassment made themselves felt upon several levels. First, and perhaps most obviously, the Earl's discomfiture contributed to a singularly unhappy record of relations with the other sex. Essex did not attempt to remarry until 1631, 18 years after his admission of impotence, and when he did the results were not appreciably better than those of the first marriage. Essex's second wife did become pregnant, but the child died in infancy, and husband and wife separated under accusations of wifely infidelity (Somerset 38–39). As a result, when Essex died in 1646, his earldom perished with him. He may not have been impotent in fact, but from the dynastic standpoint he might just as well have been. Further, Essex's sexual humiliation may conceivably have fueled the Earl's growing efforts to style himself as "a man's man" (Snow 40). Even before his first marriage, he displayed a preference for male companionship, for rural life, and for such traditionally masculine pursuits as hunting, gaming, and dueling. After the annulment, these aspects of Essex's character acquired, if anything, greater and greater force, culminating in his leadership of the parliamentary army during the first English Civil War. It may seem overanalytical to suggest that Essex sought to recover on the fields of Edgehill and Turnham Green the manhood he lost in the chambers of Whitehall—although this view of matters strikes me, at least, as compelling and inevitable. But in any case, the events of Essex's first marriage can scarcely have bred in him a fondness for his Stuart sovereigns.

Still, try as he might to set the events of his first marriage behind him, Essex was doomed to reencounter them later in life. Thus his second marriage fell apart in 1642, and toward the end of that year the Countess, who had sought alternative companionship in the meantime, gave birth to a son of whose paternity Essex could by no means be certain. Here was personal history repeating and extending itself, much to the delight of Essex's political and military opponents. For virtually the rest of his life satirists referred to him derisively as "His Oxcellency" (Snow 343), an epithet that struck at his presumed impotence while also adorning his brows with the horns of a cuckold. This disparaging nickname, in turn, partook of well-established cultural and literary associations, reaching back at least to "King John's legendary request that the Miller perform his cuckold walk on St. Luke's day—the enduring ox being Luke's iconographic symbol" (52). In Richard Niccols's mythological-erotic poem *The Cuckow* (1607), for instance, Venus chooses in a moment of wrath to punish the inhabitants of Cyprus:

> And musing with her selfe, what plague should fall
> Vpon their heads, she chaunc'd to cast her eie
> Vpon an horne, which she did soone applie
> Vnto their browes, whereby they straight forsooke
> Their former shape, and Oxe-like was their looke. (sig. D1r-v)

But the victims of Venus's ire are oblivious to this punishment, and so it falls to the cuckoo to

> . . . wau[e] my wing,
> And cuckow in their eares aloud [to] sing;
> Which when they heard, like raging Buls they bore
> Their loftie heads, and with loud bellowing rore
> Did show their iealous thoughts: for which men say
> They called are *Cerastes* [horned creatures] to this day. (sig. D1v)

Likewise, when, in *The Merry Wives of Windsor* (ca. 1597–1601), Falstaff discovers that he has been betrayed into wearing horns for a false rendezvous with Mistresses Page and Ford, he remarks uneasily: "I do begin to perceive that I am made an ass"; the horn-mad Francis Ford responds with malice, "Ay, and an ox too; both the proofs are extant" (5.5.118–119). This latter remark nicely fleshes out Ford's character; obsessed throughout the play with the possibility of his own cuckoldry, he gleefully hands its attributes on to Falstaff at the earliest opportunity. As for Essex himself, we might recall how intimately his early history had conjoined the notions of cuckoldry and impotence. In Sir Thomas Overbury's character of "A Very Very Woman" (ca. 1613), which was commonly regarded as an attack upon Frances Howard, the doomed secretary had sneered that "The utmost reach of her *Providence* is the fatnesse of a capon" (see *The Overburian Characters* 1936, 6). He could hardly have known just how right he would prove to be in this estimate.

In sum, the Earl of Essex survives as a man whose reputation and family were undone by the conflation of two fundamentally disparate sexual aspersions. I do not think it accidental that the history of the cuckoldry motif in early modern England repeats this process of conflation on the level of language and iconography. To this extent, as I shall argue, notions of cuckoldry in sixteenth- and seventeenth-century England refigure the precursor discourse of ancient Roman sexuality, and they do so in a way that attests, as Roman models do not, to the illusory nature of masculine sexual integrity. When the Earl of Essex stakes his manhood on military endeavors rather than on marriage and family, that is arguably because martial exploits remain something over which he can at least pretend to exercise some control, whereas early modern English sexual discourse, with its pervasive and nervous awareness of masculine dependency, deprives him of any similar capacity for self-determination. The rest of this chapter draws upon selected texts—first of classical Rome, then of Jacobean England—in order to document the development of the particular nervousness that characterizes attitudes toward cuckoldry in the English Renaissance.

2. WHAT FLIES I FOLLOW

Ovid's *Amores* (1 B.C.) are as preoccupied with adultery as is any text of Roman antiquity, but they do not elide adultery with impotence in the manner discussed above. When impotence does become the focus of Ovid's elegies, it is in a limited and tangential way, in *Amores* 3.7. This poem generates a small but distinctive subgenre of pornographic verse—the imperfect-enjoyment poem—whose outstanding

English exponents include works by Nashe, Behn, and Rochester;[10] and Ovid's poem deserves brief discussion here precisely because of the ways in which it *fails* to contribute to the early modern discourse of cuckoldry. In the end, plays like *Volpone* and *A Chaste Maid in Cheapside* do not derive their notions of masculine sexual feebleness from *Amores* 3.7, but rather from cultural discontinuities discernible in certain other of Ovid's elegies—particularly, as I shall argue, *Amores* 2.19 and 3.4. But before we proceed to these latter and more central Ovidian texts, it is worthwhile to consider *Amores* 3.7 by way of contrast.

Amores 3.7 confronts the fact of its narrator's impotence head-on, but in such a way as to distance the physical shortcoming from the narrator's sense of masculine identity. Lamenting a failed sexual encounter with a beautiful young woman, the poem repeatedly questions its speaker's manhood, to be sure, but the questioning occurs in such a way as to displace all notions of blame and deficiency onto other objects. On one hand, the speaker complains, "I prove neither youth nor man" ("Nec iuvenum nec me sensit amica virum!" [3.7.20]); and again, "She had me in vain" ("vir non contigit illi"— literally, "No man touched her" [3.7.43]); and again, "Worthy she was to move both gods and men, / But neither was I man nor lived then" ("Digna movere fuit certe vivosque virosque; / sed neque tum vixi nec vir, ut ante, fui" [3.7.59–60]). Given this recent enfeeblement, the poem's speaker likewise presents himself as deficient both in manhood and in youth: "What will my age do . . . , / When in my prime my force is spent and done?" ("Quae mihi ventura est . . . senectus, / cum desit numeris ipsa iuventa suis?" [3.7.17–18]).

Yet on the other hand, these laments for lost masculinity contrast with various of the poem's other gestures. For instance, there is an exaggerated insistence upon the speaker's previous virility:

> Yet boarded I the golden Chie twice,
> And Libas, and the white-cheek'd Pitho thrice.
> Corinna crav'd it in a summer's night,
> And nine sweet bouts we had before daylight. (3.7.23–26)

> [At nuper bis flava Chlide, ter candida Pitho,
> ter Libas officio continuata meo est;
> exigere a nobis angusta nocte Corinnam
> me memini numeros sustinuisse novem.]

Again, Ovid's verses repeatedly seek to ascribe their narrator's impotence to the external intervention of "Thessalian charms" ("Thes-

salic[um] . . . venen[um]" [3.7.27]) and "magic[ae] . . . artes"
(3.7.35). And still further, the poem points ultimately to a resurgence of its narrator's physical capacities, a resurgence that in turn in-
spires a comic passage of mock denunciation directed at the
narrator's penis:

> Now, when he should not jet, he bolts upright,
> And craves his task, and seeks to be at fight.
> Lie down with shame, and see thou stir no more,
> Seeing thou wouldst deceive me as before.
> Thou cozenest me. (3.7.65–70)

> [Nostra . . . membra . . .
>   . . . nunc, ecce, vigent intempestiva valentque,
> nunc opus exposcunt militiamque suam.
> quin istic pudibunda iaces, pars pessima nostri?
> sic sum pollicitis captus et ante tuis.]

In sum, Ovid's elegy does everything possible to ascribe its
speaker's impotence to factors external to his identity as a man, with
the final result that the speaker's own penis becomes, as it were, a
separate and guilty party. When viewed against the background of an
Herculean sexual history, the possible interference of debilitating
drugs and enchantments, and the fact that the penis has a mind of its
own, the impotence of *Amores* 3.7 becomes an amusing sexual aber-
ration rather than a real threat to anyone's gender. Conversely, the
speaker's status as a man is confirmed by the insatiability of his sexual desire, a desire that survives any feebleness of the flesh and renders such feebleness somehow beside the point. The poem's speaker
may not have been able to make love at a given moment, but the important fact is that he wanted to, and this fact in itself redeems his
masculinity—indeed, constitutes it. By contrast, consider Edgar's famous apostrophe to Nature in *King Lear* (ca. 1605). There he
prefers the "lusty stealth of nature" (1.2.11) that inspired his adulterous conception to the semicomatose fumbling "[That] doth,
within a dull, stale, tired bed, / Go to th' creating a whole tribe of
fops, / Got 'tween asleep and wake" (1.2.13–15). What Edgar
mocks here is specifically the collapse of the masculine ego constructed in Ovid's *Amores*. Whereas Ovid celebrates a sexual desire
that survives irrespective of bodily infirmity and that renders such infirmity irrelevant as a marker of sexual identity, Shakespeare describes
a state in which sexual intercourse occurs despite rather than because
of individual desire, which is conspicuous only by its absence. This is

a considerably bleaker picture, created through the summary rejection of a cherished Ovidian fantasy.

As to the sources of this altogether more disheartening view of masculine sexuality, I believe they, too, may be found in repressed form in Ovid's *Amores,* in connection with the work's preeminent sexual interest: adultery. Ovid's *Amores* celebrate the exploits of a cuckold-maker. Insofar as they have a unifying narrative (and they do not have much of one), Ovid's elegies tell the story of an adulterous seduction—the poet-narrator's conquest of Corinna—and the situational force of many specific poems in the series derives from their unashamed elaborations upon the theme of adultery. Thus, for instance, *Amores* 1.4 instructs Corinna on how to convey secret messages to her lover when at a supper party in the company of her husband:

> When I (my light) do or say aught that please thee,
> Turn round thy gold ring, as it were to ease thee.
> Strike on the board like them that pray for evil,
> When thou dost wish thy husband at the devil. (1.4.25–28)

> [Cum tibi, quae faciam, mea lux, dicamve, placebunt,
> versetur digitis anulus usque tuis.
> tange manu mensam, tangunt quo more precantes,
> optabis merito cum mala multo viro.]

Again, *Amores* 2.7 defends the narrator against Corinna's suspicions that he has slept with her handmaid. This poem, ironically exploiting the unfaithful wife's fears of her lover's infidelity, is then immediately followed by a secret note to the handmaid in question (*Amores* 2.8), a note in which the narrator wonders how Corinna could have gotten wind of their liaison. At moments like these, the *Amores* take an especial delight in the perfidies and subterfuges of adulterous love.

Given such a context, Corinna's cuckolded husband can hope for little sympathy and still less respect; he is, at best, a figure of contemptuous fun. *Amores* 1.4 thus opens with the cheerful asseveration, "Thy husband to a banquet goes with me, / Pray God it may his latest supper be" ("Vir tuus est epulas nobis aditurus easdem—/ ultima coena tuo sit, precor, illo viro!" [1.4.1–2]). In similarly derisive fashion, *Amores* 2.12 exults,

> About my temples go, triumphant bays!
> Conquered Corinna in my bosom lays,

She whom her husband, guard, and gate, as foes,
Lest art should win her, firmly did enclose. (2.12.1-4)

[Ite triumphales circum mea tempora laurus!
vicimus: in nostro est, ecce, Corinna sinu,
quam vir, quam custos, quam ianua firma, tot hostes,
servabant, nequa posset ab arte capi!]

Indeed, it is no surprise that within the self-glorifying narrative of an adulterous lover, the injured husband may appear both base and ridiculous, nor is it unexpected that the husband in question should be mocked for failing to preserve his wife's chastity. The really remarkable thing in Ovid is the utter inevitability of the cuckold's situation; no matter what he says or does in his efforts to manage his wife's sexuality, he is always in the wrong, and always will be.

Two elegies—*Amores* 2.19 and 3.4—together provide a clear sense of the cuckold's dilemma in Ovidian amatory verse. On one hand, *Amores* 3.4 mocks as futile a jealous husband's efforts to place his wife in protective custody; on the other hand, *Amores* 2.19 upbraids another husband for not guarding his wife with sufficient vigilance. (Recall that at different times during his first marriage, the Earl of Essex employed both of these strategies for handling Frances Howard.) Between them, these two poems confront the Ovidian world's principal options for coping with a wayward wife, and neither course of action emerges as effective or attractive. Indeed, the only good news that Ovid's verse offers to wronged husbands is implicit, for the logic rendering one option unsatisfactory is in potential conflict with the logic that opposes the second option. Thus, finally, we may see the Ovidian cuckold's eternal wrongness as a projection of contradictions within the central consciousness, masculine and adulterous, of the *Amores* themselves.

Amores 3.4 mounts an argument that will become axiomatic to early modern English writers: that no amount of masculine surveillance is sufficient to prevent a determined woman from committing adultery, and that any limited fidelity the surveillance may produce is in fact a sham. Ovid makes both of these points early in his poem, admonishing his reader that

'Tis vain thy damsel to commend
To keeper's trust: their wits should them defend.
Who, without fear, is chaste, is chaste in sooth:
Who, because means want, doeth not, she doth.

Though thou her body guard, her mind is stained:
Nor, lest she will, can any be restrained. (3.4.1–6)

[Dure vir, imposito tenerae custode puellae
nil agis; ingenio est quaeque tuenda suo.
siqua metu dempto casta est, ea denique casta est;
quae, quia non liceat, non facit, illa facit!
ut iam servaris bene corpus, adultera mens est;
nec custodiri, ne velit, ulla potest.]

Ultimately, this argument becomes so pervasive in early English writing that it can detach itself from the immediate question of wifely fidelity and function instead in a metaphorical capacity. Thus it can appear, for instance, as an element of Milton's plea for unlicensed printing in the *Areopagitica* (1644): "I cannot praise a fugitive and cloister'd vertue, unexercis'd & unbreath'd. . . . That vertue therefore which is but a youngling in the contemplation of evill . . . is but a blank vertue, not a pure; her whitenesse is but an excrementall whitenesse" (1006). For Milton, readers are like the wives in Ovid's *Amores:* only truly virtuous if exposed fully to temptation. To seek to preserve their virtue by physical constraint is futile and self-defeating.

Indeed, *Amores* 3.4 continues, not only is physical constraint useless as a guarantor of chastity; it can actually serve as a temptation to vice, for jealousy by nature renders its objects attractive to others:

What's kept, we covet more: the care makes theft;
Few love what others have unguarded left.
. . . .
She is not chaste that's kept, but a dear whore;
Thy fear is than her body valued more.
Although thou chafe, stol'n pleasure is sweet play;
She pleaseth best, "I fear" if any say. (3.4.25–32)

[Quidquid servatur cupimus magis, ipsaque furem
cura vocat; pauci, quod sinit alter, amant.
. . . .
non proba fit, quam vir servat, sed adultera cara;
ipse timor pretium corpore maius habet.
indignere licet, iuvat inconcessa voluptas;
sola placet, "timeo!" dicere siqua potest.]

This insight, in turn, provides the impetus for *Amores* 2.19, in which the poet-narrator tauntingly demands that a cuckolded husband increase the guard upon his wife so as thereby to enhance the speaker's own adulterous pleasure:

> What flies I follow, what follows me, I shun.
> But thou, of thy fair damsel too secure,
> Begin to shut thy house at evening sure.
> Search at the door who knocks oft in the dark,
> In night's deep silence why the ban-dogs bark.
> . . . .
> Let this care sometimes bite thee to the quick,
> That to deceits it may me forward prick. (2.19.36–44)

> [Quod sequitur, fugio; quod fugit, ipse sequor.
> at tu, formosae nimium secure puellae,
> incipe iam prima claudere nocte forem.
> incipe, quis totiens furtim tua limina pulset,
> quaerere, quid latrent nocte silente canes.
> . . . .
> mordeat iste tuas aliquando cura medullas,
> daque locum nostris materiamque dolis.]

In effect, the *Amores* suggest, a cuckold's behavior is inevitably wrong because it is inevitably inconsequential. Since nothing a husband can do will restrain a wife who is determined to stray, the cuckold functions as a peculiar case of reverse coverture—the legal condition "of a woman during her married life, when she is . . . under the authority and protection of her husband."[11] Set inescapably at the mercy of his wife, the cuckolded husband may acquiesce to her infidelity with bad grace or with good, but acquiesce he must, and the best advice Ovid can offer a man in this dilemma is to submit good-naturedly:

> Kindly thy mistress use, if thou be wise,
> Look gently, and rough husbands' laws despise.
> Honour what friends thy wife gives, she'll give many;
> Least labour so shall win great grace of any;
> So shalt thou go with youths to feast together,
> And see at home much that thou ne'er brought'st thither.
>   (3.4.43–48)

> [Si sapis, indulge dominae vultusque severos
> exue, nec rigidi iura tuere viri,
> et cole quos dederit—multos dabit—uxor amicos.
> gratia sic minimo magna labore venit;

> sic poteris iuvenum convvia semper inire
> et, quae non dederis, multa videre domi.]

In essence, the adulterous wife's inalienable control over her own reproductivity comprises the external limit of masculine authority
within marriage, and the cuckold, subject to his wife's desire, exists
somewhere on the far side of that limit. Hence his eternal inadequacy, and the withering scorn that accompanies it in the works of
Ovid and others: In a sense the cuckold is not simply a failed husband, but an emblem of failed husbandship in general, or, worse yet
(and this, I think, is what happens at the hands of Renaissance authors), the cuckold intimates that husbandship can never really suc-
ceed on its own terms, as an institution created and upheld by
masculine authority.

   Given this broad iconic status, it is understandable that the very
forms of the cuckold's inadequacy, as set forth in Ovid, should be
contradictory and mutually discrediting. If, for instance, the husband
of *Amores* 3.4 actually takes Ovid's advice and throws his household
open to his wife's suitors, he will realize the condition to which Ovid
himself has strenuously objected in *Amores* 2.19, the condition in
which an absence of impediments to desire leads to the absence of
desire itself. Indeed, Ovid's aphoristic "*Quod sequitur, fugio; quod
fugit, ipse sequor*" would seem to offer the perfect course of action to
a husband intent upon preserving his wife's fidelity; all he need do is
offer her freely to all comers. But this gesture, the inveterate "Take
my wife—please!" of Henny Youngman, is unthinkable in the Ovidian universe. Even when the speaker of *Amores* 2.19 threatens to
abandon his girlfriend if her husband does not guard her more
closely (2.19.47–48), the threat functions as a jocular expression of
the unimaginable, for one of the main jobs of the *Amores* is to manufacture a notion of masculinity as boundless desire. This desire—so
vast and unmitigated that it even exceeds the limits of the male body
(as, for instance, in *Amores* 3.7)—defines itself not against its own absence, but against the jealous, ever-desiring impotence that the figure
of the cuckold represents. Thus the Ovidian cuckold has no choice
but to be eternally, contradictorily wrong, for he exists as the projection of two separate anxieties that Ovid's protagonist-narrator cannot
acknowledge as native to his own constitution: first, the anxiety that
feminine reproductivity can never be placed under masculine control,
and second, the fear that masculine desire, too, is beyond masculine
governance. The cuckold neutralizes the former of these anxieties by
functioning as an emblem for masculine sexual impotence—as the ef-

feminized masculine figure against which a successful, sexually dominant man defines himself. Likewise, the cuckold responds to the latter anxiety by being eternally jealous, for the idea of a pervasive masculine sexual apathy, even in the case of a failed husband, is anathema to Ovid's verse.

4. MY BLOOD, AND MY AFFECTIONS

In the early English drama, no play better approximates Ovid's contemptuous portrait of the willing cuckold than does Thomas Middleton's *A Chaste Maid in Cheapside* (1613). Indeed, Middleton's character of Master Allwit could be a deliberate response to Ovid's advice that a husband "honour what friends [his] wife gives." Thus Allwit introduces himself with a lengthy soliloquy in which he descants upon the material benefits he has realized from his wife's lover:

> I walk out in a morning; come to breakfast,
> Find excellent cheer; a good fire in winter;
> Look in my coal-house about midsummer eve,
> That's full, five or six chaldron new laid up;
> Look in my backyard, I shall find a steeple
> Made up with Kentish faggots, which o'erlooks
> The water-house and the windmills: . . .
> I see these things, but like a happy man
> I pay for none at all; yet fools think's mine;
> I have the name, and in his gold I shine. (1.2.22–40)

Allwit's situation fulfills the final promise of *Amores* 3.4, the promise that by indulging his wife a husband will discover "at home much that [he] ne'er brought . . . thither" ("quae non dederi[t], multa . . . domi"). As for Allwit himself, he is apparently so taken with the personal comforts generated by his sexual acquiescence that he recognizes no disadvantage whatever to his situation. Quite the contrary, in fact: Allwit imagines himself enriched by his wife's adultery not only in terms of material well-being, but in terms of reputation as well. Thus he congratulates himself on "pay[ing] for none at all" of his household comforts, and in the next breath he can refer scornfully to the "fools" who believe him responsible for his own prosperity. For Allwit, in short, wittolry is a wonderful confidence game, a supremely clever ploy through which the cuckold absorbs both the economic well being and the honor—the "gold" and the "name"—of his wife's seducer.

In this latter respect, Allwit would again seem to be reacting to the wittol's situation as described by Ovid, for Ovid makes a point of observing that the acquiescent cuckold will enjoy a high level of social popularity; as the *Amores* put it, "*gratia sic minimo magna labore venit*," and hence the wittol will find himself a popular guest at dinner-parties and similar festivities. But *A Chaste Maid in Cheapside* puts the wickedest possible twist upon the cuckold's popularity. Allwit may imagine that he "shine[s]" in the "gold" of his wife's lover, Sir Walter Whorehound, but he is an object of general contempt among the play's other characters. Thus his first appearance onstage—only a few lines before his long, self-congratulatory soliloquy upon the joys of a cuckold's life—is greeted by a serving-man's scornful exclamation, "Honesty wash my eyes! I have spy'd a wittol" (1.2.1). Later, when the goldsmith Yellowhammer learns of the arrangement between Allwit and Whorehound, he exclaims in disgust, "What an incomparable wittol's this! . . . What a base slave!" (4.1.218–220). And the most memorable scene of Middleton's play is arguably a rewrite of the Ovidian promise that an acquiescent husband will find himself always dining among the young. In the case of Middleton's play, the dinner in question is a christening ceremony, hosted at the Allwits' home, in honor of Mistress Allwit's latest child; the child's natural father, Sir Walter Whorehound, stands as its godfather; and the gathering is not the graceful and witty "*conviviu[m] iuvenum*" imagined by Ovid, but rather an assembly of sharp-tongued, gluttonous gossips who do not scruple to abuse Allwit in his own presence:

> 4 Gossip. I promise you, a fine gentleman [i.e., Sir Walter] and a courteous.
> 2 Gossip. Methinks her husband shows like a clown to him.
> 3 Gossip. I would not care what clown my husband were too, So I had such fine children. (3.2.29–32)

If this is the cuckold's paradise promised by Ovid to the complaisant husband, one may be excused for declining the proffered delights. But the remarkable thing about Allwit is that he remains highly satisfied with his circumstances. C. S. Lewis once famously described the discourse of courtly love as "Ovid misunderstood" (1936, 7), but the phrase may in fact apply even more perfectly to Allwit's character, which is drawn so as to take the advice of *Amores* 3.4 literally, with no awareness of the irony and derision that inform it. And Allwit's general satisfaction, in turn, is made possible by one signal variance from the Ovidian model of cuckoldry: his absolute lack of sexual interest or appetite. This lack, signaled of course by the charactonym "Allwit" (meaning all mind, no libido, as well as witall/witoll), is most manifest in contrast to Sir Walter Whorehound's anxious jealousy. On one hand, Sir Walter is so consumed with sexual possessiveness that he cannot abide the thought of Allwit approaching his own wife ("Yet, by your leave, I heard you were once off'ring / To go to bed to her" [1.2.94–95]); on the other hand, Allwit exults in his own lack of jealousy—a quality that, like all of the other traditional burdens of a husband, he seems to have passed on wholesale to his wife's paramour:

> These torments stand I freed of; I am as clear
> From jealousy of a wife as from the charge:
> O, two miraculous blessings! 'Tis the knight
> Hath took that labour all out of my hands. (1.2.48–51)

In effect, Allwit has happily developed into a full-blown portrait of the Ovidian wittol because he, Allwit, has failed to grasp the extent to which wittolry effeminizes its subject. Coppelia Kahn has emphasized the manner in which early English drama "defin[es] masculinity as the retention of exclusive sexual property in woman" (132); Allwit, on the other hand, exists specifically to give that property away. In his own self-aggrandizing fantasy life, he imagines himself as co-opting the emblems of Sir Walter Whorehound's masculinity: "I am like a man / Finding a table furnish'd to his hand" (1.2.11–12); "I have the name, and in his gold I shine" (1.2.40); "I live at ease, / He has both the cost and torment" (1.2.53–54). But the price Allwit pays for this fantasy (a price he cannot stand to admit to himself) is the abdication of his own manhood as figured through the exercise of domestic authority in general and sexual authority in particular. He stands bareheaded in Sir Walter's presence, a servant within his own home ("Now a stands bare . . . ; make the most of him, / He's but one pip above a serving man" [1.2.64–65]), not really even a household dependent, but rather the dependent of a dependent—his wife. Where he imagines that he has miraculously encompassed Sir Walter's income and reputation, surrounding circumstances suggest a contrary arrangement: one in which his own masculine status has been encompassed and obliterated by his wife's infidelity. Thus, if Allwit's lack of jealousy differentiates him from the pattern of the Ovidian cuckold, it ultimately reveals a model of unmanliness that Ovid's verse cannot bring itself to imagine: a model in which the cuckold himself is oblivious to just how completely his own identity depends upon his ability to control his wife's sexual behavior.

If *A Chaste Maid in Cheapside* notably reworks the standard of acquiescent cuckoldry advocated by Ovid's *Amores* 3.4, Ben Jonson's *Volpone* (1605–1606) offers a similarly remarkable embellishment upon the jealous cuckoldry encouraged in *Amores* 2.19. In the case of *Volpone,* moreover, the debt to Ovid is manifest and deliberate, perhaps most obviously so in Volpone's proposal that he and Celia should "in changed shapes, act OVIDS tales" (3.7.221) while cuckolding Celia's husband, Corvino. But it is Corvino himself who embodies the mocking attitude toward husbandly jealousy projected by *Amores* 2.19. Taken together, Allwit and Corvino thus refigure the opposing horns of the Ovidian cuckold's dilemma; the former abdicates his manhood by surrendering his sexual identity, whereas the latter clings so tightly to his masculine prerogatives that those prerogatives themselves prove his undoing.

In part, at least, Corvino's problem arises from the fact that his masculine prerogatives are themselves fundamentally contradictory, and one of Jonson's great achievements in *Volpone* is arguably that he has recognized the nature and extent of this contradiction. On one level, the conflict is purely libidinal; as Katharine Maus has observed, "The cuckold is entranced by the scene of his own betrayal" (566), which constitutes both a titillating enactment of voyeuristic fantasy and a humiliating displacement from the sexual scene. Corvino is a classic case in point; on one hand, his character displays a positively febrile interest in the "sports" his wife might enjoy behind his back, an interest that even leads him, in a court of law and before a tribunal of judges, to fabricate the details of a cuckoldry that never occurs:

> This woman (please your father-hoods) is a whore,
> Of most hot exercise. . . .
>   I may say, these eyes
> Haue seene her glew'd vnto that peece of cedar,
> That fine well-timber'd gallant: and . . . here,
> The letters may be read, thorough the horne,
> That make the story perfect. (4.5.117–126)

On the other hand, however, Corvino's erotic fascination with his own cuckoldry is counterbalanced by rampant jealousy. Thus, after the famous scene in which Volpone impersonates a mountebank in order to get a glimpse of Celia from her bedroom window, and in which Celia encourages his attentions by dropping her handkerchief as a favor, Corvino promises to shackle his wife within a windowless room:

> First, I will haue this bawdy light dam'd up;
> . . . .
> Then, here's a locke, which I will hang vpon thee;
> And, now I thinke on't, I will keep thee backe-wards;
> Thy lodging shall be backe-wards; thy walkes back-wards;
> Thy prospect—all be backe-wards; and no pleasure,
> That thou shalt know, but backe-wards. (2.5.50–61)

Since Corvino's jealousy is a function of his sexual anxieties, it is no accident that his jealous fantasy of physical confinement should culminate in a thinly veiled threat of anal penetration; in Corvino's character, erotic excitement gives birth to jealous fear, which in turn generates more erotic excitement.

This contradictory libidinal investment, in turn, is paralleled by broader contradictions in Corvino's exercise of husbandly and paternal authority. Celia is not only an erotic object for him; she is also a member of his family—a word *Volpone* employs in its Latin legal sense of "household" or "estate"[12]—and to this extent she is the most notable part of her husband's "fortune" (1.5.81). Libidinal and economic investments merge, for Corvino, in the figure of his wife, who therefore becomes a test case for his ability to control his estate in general. When told that a certain physician has offered his daughter to Volpone in an attempt to revive the supposed invalid, Corvino himself frames the matter as a challenge to his own authority: "Wherefore should not I / As well command my bloud, and my affections, / As this dull Doctor?" (2.6.70–72). Just as, on the erotic level, Corvino is both fascinated with and horrified by the prospect of his own cuckoldry, on the domestic level he seeks to control his wife both by keeping her entirely for himself and by putting her to public use. Thus, while pushing her into Volpone's bedroom, he can exhort her, "If you bee / Loyall, and mine, be wonne, respect my venture" (3.7.36–37).

In a sense, Corvino's plight is the *reductio ad absurdum* of paternal absolutism. Pursuing an unattainable ideal of complete control over his estate, he is forced into a conundrum: Can a husband prostitute his wife's chastity without making himself a cuckold? This paradox—of the can-God-make-a-boulder-too-big-for-God-to-lift variety—generates growing anxiety in Corvino, who therefore casts about uneasily for reassurance: "The thing, in't selfe, / I know, is nothing" (2.6.69–70);

"There is no shame in this, now, is there?" (4.5.127). Moreover, as a final irony, Corvino himself has been told that the ideal he is pursuing is unattainable: that there is no such thing as *absolute* husbandly authority. He confesses as much to his own wife, in words that take *Amores* 3.4.6 ("*Nec custodiri, ne velit, ulla potest*") as their *locus classicus:* "Doe not I know, if women haue a will, / They'll doe 'gainst all the watches, o' the world? / And that the fiercest spies, are tam'd with gold?" (2.7.8–10). Corvino, of course, is his own "fiercest spie," unmindful of the extent to which he himself has been "tam'd with gold" through the offer of Volpone's inheritance. This lack of self-awareness, in turn, signals the extent to which the wisdom Corvino quotes remains unassimilated to his character; it is inert matter, irrelevant to the operations of his own jealousy and greed.

In other words, Corvino has never really learned the lesson that Ovid seeks to impress upon the addressee of *Amores* 3.4: that in the end, a wife's reproductivity is beyond her husband's governance. Instead, Corvino remains steadfastly in the position that Ovid urges upon the husband of *Amores* 2.19. Bricking up windows and purchasing chastity belts, Corvino pursues a vision of husbandly security that simply does not exist, and in pursuing this vision he displays his own folly for the entertainment and enrichment of others. He too, like Allwit in *A Chaste Maid in Cheapside,* must watch his pretensions to independent manhood vanish, absorbed into a femininity that both encompasses and escapes it. To this extent, the figures of Corvino and Allwit recapitulate and enlarge disparate patterns of masculine anxiety explored by Ovid in the *Amores.*

5. Different Lies to Different Husbands

Although Ovid's *Amores* dwell consistently upon the themes of love and adultery, they do not in fact have a single, continuous narrative line. *Amores* 2.19 and 3.4 offer a case in point; although they deal with the same general subject—how a husband should behave when his wife is being seduced—they give entirely different advice and therefore presuppose different audiences and situations. Indeed, some of their humor may derive from this discontinuity; as readers move from *Amores* 2.19 to 3.4, they may appreciate the cynical opportunism with which the poems' central consciousness modifies his language and strategies. In effect, the poet-narrator of the *Amores* tells different lies to different husbands. He encourages the husband of Elegy 2.19 in the specious fantasy that wifely fidelity can be manufactured by physical constraint—that if one can only guard one's wife closely and jealously enough, one can transform her into the paragon of women and oneself into the happiest of men. To the husband of *Amores* 3.4, however, Ovid offers a different untruth: the notion that his wife's sexual behavior is of no consequence whatever to his identity and reputation, except insofar as her infidelity may secure him the occasional dinner invitation.

These two lies in turn are both attractive because, despite their extreme dissimilarity of circumstance, they hold out the same promise. They both operate as fantasies of independence, in which an injured husband can recover his sense of self-sufficiency either through acts of discipline and surveillance or through parallel gestures of indifference and escape. In constructing the figures of Corvino and Allwit, Jonson and Middleton explore these two fantasies and suggest the extent to which they may be equally unattainable. Thus it is perhaps inevitable that Jonson and Middleton should both revise Ovid by taking the advice given in *Amores* 2.19 and 3.4, respectively, to its apparent extreme. For Jonson's Corvino, the fantasy of total husbandly control collapses into a self-discrediting conundrum, because any husbandly authority that is really total will sooner or later be called upon to transgress its own logic and limits. For Middleton's Allwit, likewise, the idea that a husband can hold himself aloof from his wife's infidelity is equally untenable, given the social grounding of marriage, masculinity, and what one might call the genealogical ego.

Finally, if one is interested in asking why the Renaissance cuckold-motif bestializes its victims as it does, an explanation may lie in the distance that separates Jonson's and Middleton's characters from their classical antecedents. For a condition that Ovid considers particular and degrading has, at the hands of his Renaissance successors, evolved into a broad figuration of the impossibility of manhood in general. To this extent, the cuckoldry motif can serve as a marker of relative anthropocentrism turned against itself; it serves as a fantasy not about the failure of particular individuals, but of the broader discursive order that generates them. Whereas Ovid consistently assumes that husbands are conflicted and dependent, and uses this insight as the basis for offering tongue-in-cheek advice on how to deal with wifely infidelity, Jonson and Middleton, on the other hand, construct dramatic characters who take Ovid's advice in deadly earnest, and who thus carry it to extremes not imagined in Ovid's own verse. In the process, these characters act out an anxiety that the central consciousness of the *Amores* exists to deny: the anxiety that masculinity itself might be an unattainable fantasy, an ideal of self-containment and self-control of which the indices—wifely chastity and masculine libido—are always beyond one's management. Hence the horns of the cuckold, which paradoxically mark their recipient with the stigmata both of sexual complaisancy and of impotence, while simultaneously subjecting him to an outrage and contempt that should logically be reserved for the man who has wronged him; if he deserves such treatment, it is because he has made poor forked animals of us all. In short, Jonson and Middleton suggest that the cuckold's dilemma is not at all unique: that it is, in its broadest and simplest terms, the dilemma of being a man.

CHAPTER THREE

DEAD PARROT SKETCH

Are you going to extend the limits of prejudice to include the flora and fauna of this island?

—*Derek Walcott*, Pantomime

1. APPROPRIATING THE EXOTIC

The subject of this chapter—the growing popularity of pet parrots in early modern England and its consequences for literary representation—may seem inauspiciously trivial, to put the matter kindly. However, I believe this subject is important because of the way it is *rendered* trivial in the sixteenth and seventeenth centuries. In any case, the early European explorers of the New World considered parrots neither silly nor inconsequential. In the journals of Christopher Columbus, for instance, virtually no other animal gets as much attention as does the parrot; and for Columbus, the birds were an object of wonder and speculation. When he first made landfall in the New World, he encountered "no animals of any kind . . . except parrots" (1492; see *Journal of the First Voyage* 1990, 31); the first islanders he met "swam out to the ships' boats . . . and brought parrots and balls of cotton thread . . . and they bartered with us" (29); and on October 21, 1492, he observed "flocks of parrots that darken the sun, and birds of so many kinds so different from our own that it is a marvel" (51).

Other explorers, too, pay close attention to parrots, and the literature of New World discovery conducts something like an extended conversation with itself about the birds, a conversation in which the explorers consider how to put these remarkable creatures to the best possible use. On one hand, for instance, they seem to be a promising source of food. Peter Martyr notes that certain Caribbean islanders fatten parrots for their table "as we bringe up capons and hennes" (1552, sig. B2r); and Martin Fernandez de Enciso takes the hint, including, in a list of American "bestes of good mete and savour," such "grete plentie of foules as popingais of dyvers sortes, gret partriches, pecockys, duckys and herings and dyvers other straunge byrdes" (1519; see *A Brief Summe of Geographie* 1932, 153). However, the European newcomers do not usually value parrots for their culinary potential; the survivors of Sir John Hawkins's unfortunate Indies mission of 1567 to 1568 are typical in lamenting that they had to eat "cats and dogs, mice, rats, parrats and munkies" (Hakluyt 1904, 9:408). But the birds do prove serviceable in other ways. Amerigo Vespucci noted that the American tribes' "riches consist" among other things "of variegated birds' feathers," and that one tribe he encountered presented him with "feathers of very great value, . . . many bows and arrows, and . . . numberless parrots of different colors" (1505–1506; see *The Four Voyages of Amerigo Vespucci* 1966, 98, 109). Peter Martyr and Joseph Acosta also mention the value of the feathers collected by the inhabitants of Central America (Martyr sig. 2G1v; Purchas 1965, 15:135). And in 1570, John Chilton could observe that the people of Chiapas "pay their tribute to the king [of Spain] all in Cotton wooll and Feathers" (Hakluyt 9:369).

However, it is as pets that the parrots of the New World prove most commercially useful in Europe, and—as this chapter argues—their growing popularity as pets leads to their appropriation by writers to license various kinds of social and political subordination. The subject of this chapter, in other words, is the shifting symbolic status of a particular variety of exotic bird, which gradually, between the twelfth and seventeenth centuries, ceases to be a marker of the wondrous and instead becomes an emblem of the subaltern. This shift manifests itself in a wide range of cultural products, and it involves a gradual but dramatic shift from the discursive register of anthropomorphism to that of relative anthropocentrism. But most immediately, it expresses itself in and through European encounters with the New World. From very early on, parrots afford a signal instance of the Old World's acquisition of the New. By 1526, for instance, when Gonzalo Fernandez de Oviedo publishes his *General and Natural History of the Indies* (see *Natural History of the West Indies*, 1959), he can already dismiss parrots from his discussion of the local fauna. His

reason? They are all over Europe, and have thus been effectively removed from the purview of Oviedo's work: "There are so many
species of parrot that it would be a long task to describe them. They
are better subjects for the painter's brush than for words. Since so
many species have been carried to Spain, it is hardly worth while to
take time to describe them here" (65). For Oviedo, one of the most
ubiquitous and varied families of New World avifauna has been spir-
ited out of the Americas altogether, transformed into the literal and
conceptual property of Europe.[1] By the eighteenth century this gesture has become commonplace, so that in 1714 Alexander Pope can
contemptuously describe "Men, Monkeys, Lap-dogs, [and] Parrots"
as the mindless denizens of a lady's drawing-room ("Rape of the
Lock" 1993, 4.120).

These dismissive references to parrots form part of a larger discursive pattern that the present chapter seeks to describe, a pattern developing out of the culture of early modern exploration. Among the
distinctive features of this larger discourse are the association of parrots with painting, as in the foregoing quotation from Oviedo, and
the association of parrots with subordinate and ostensibly inferior
men, as in the barb from Pope. Moreover, these two bonds of association are interrelated. Not only do parrots become popular objects
of painterly display, but artists regularly elide them with servants,
children, and decorative trinkets of various kinds, while sometimes
presenting them, in the process, as ornamental backdrops or coun-
terpoints to the portraiture of aristocratic subjects. Flemish and
Dutch painting of the seventeenth century seems particularly rich in
such depictions of the birds, and some examples may illustrate their
progressive iconographic association with luxury consumables and,
eventually, with socially subordinate human beings. Given the powerful influence of art from the Low Countries upon the visual culture
of seventeenth-century England, the paintings in question are particularly appropriate to the present analysis.

Jan Davidszoon de Heem's *Elaborate Tabletop Still-Life with Foodstuffs, Exotic Animals, and Precious Objects* (late 1640s; see Figure
3.1) provides a lush example of how parrots could be situated, in
seventeenth-century painting, amongst the worldly goods of a newly
expanding colonial and mercantile culture. De Heem's painting, itself a luxury item, depicts a glut of other luxury items, the whole as-
semblage rendered visually overpowering by its studied disarray. Nor
does the composition merely assault the sense of sight. The culinary
objects that are depicted—oysters, boiled lobster, half a dozen varieties of ripe fruit—make a concerted appeal to the sense of taste; a

glass of wine and a peeled lemon introduce an element of olfactory experience; and the textures of de Heem's inedible objects, from soft, hanging fabrics to ornately wrought precious metals, engage the viewer's tactile responses as well. The breadth of this sensory appeal is characteristic of de Heem's work, which has long been appreciated for its "ability to capture the full range of one's sensual experiences" (Wheelock 1995, 103).

Surmounting this mingle-mangle as the only two living beings in a throng of inanimate objects, two parrots confront one another in the painting's upper left-hand corner. The uppermost of these two, an African gray, stands on a suspended perch and regards the other bird with suspicion while holding a piece of fruit in its beak. Beneath and to the left of its convoluted form, a green-winged macaw reaches up covetously for the fruit, its beak open in an apparent growl that is the painting's sole appeal to the viewer's sense of hearing. A bird of Central and South America, the macaw contrasts implicitly with the African gray, the two between them representing the exotica of the New and Old Worlds, respectively. And thus, despite their lively interaction, the painting remains avowedly a still life; the curvature of the African gray's body in the upper left-hand corner parallels that of the whelk shells in the lower right-hand corner; the red of the macaw's feathers picks up that of the boiled lobster and the table-cloth upon which it rests, and points upward, in turn, to the red of the African gray's tail. The birds, like everything else in de Heem's painting, are objects: extraordinarily colorful, striking, and mobile objects, but objects nonetheless. Serving on one level as "a compilation of the beauties of God's creations" (Wheelock 104), the subject matter of de Heem's still life thus also embodies a sheer delight in material acquisition, an impulse to collect and to own. At the apex of the geometrical composition that lends expression to this impulse, one encounters de Heem's birds.

This placement effectively installs the parrots at the supreme point in a composition that reflects the great chain of lower being, itself articulated as a progression from inert matter through flowers and fruit, mollusks and crustaceans, to the birds in question. But if parrots can thus be objectified as elements of the brute creation, they can also be imported, by virtue of their intelligence and articulacy, into the human order as well. That is what happens in Jan Steen's great allegorical panel *The Effects of Intemperance* (Figure 3.2). Steen's theme is manifestly "the havoc wrought on the proper conduct of the family and of society as a whole by self-indulgence" (Brown 1984, 88), in particular the alcoholic variety, and he illus-

Figure 3.1: Jan Davidszoon de Heem, *Elaborate Tabletop Still-Life with Foodstuffs, Exotic Animals, and Precious Objects* (Bequest of John Ringling, Collection of The John and Mable Ringling Museum of Art, the State Art Museum of Florida, Sarasota, FL)

trates that havoc with a circular arrangement of figures that lends visual expression to the interdependence of kin. Dominating the left side of his composition is the slumped figure of the family's mother, insensate with drink, an overturned wine pitcher at her feet to render

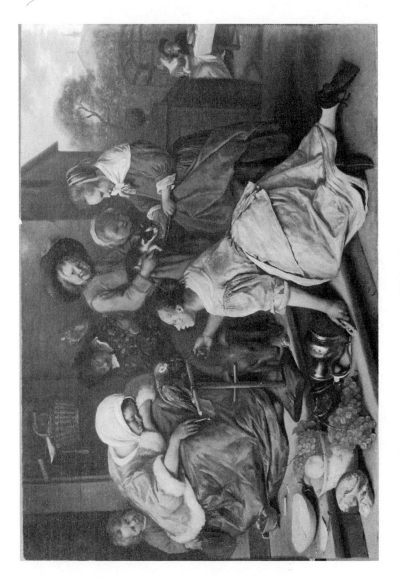

Figure 3.2: Jan Steen, *The Effects of Intemperance* (National Gallery, London)

explicit the cause of her stupor. Spiraling out from her sleeping form are the family's children, all gleefully engaged in various misdemeanors; one stealthily picks the mother's pocket, another encourages a pig to eat scraps of food from the floor, and another holds the family cat while two accomplices feed it a meat pie. Completing the geometrical circuit back to the sleeping mother, the eldest daughter sprawls on her knees across the bottom center of the panel, her right arm upraised, feeding a glass of wine to an African gray parrot. The drunken mother and the drinking parrot slouch and perch side by side in obvious parallelism.

As for the precise nature of this parallelism, it is worth considering from seemingly opposed standpoints. First, of course, the parrot's drinking mimics the mother's drunkenness, "perverting the emulation and instruction on which the household regimen should be based" by "imitating vice rather than virtue" (Schama 1988, 209–210). In a domestic hierarchy whose governing figure succumbs to such laxity, laxity itself becomes a governing principle, communicating itself downward through the entire household order. But this view of matters may also be reversed; the prominent presence of animals—not just the parrot, but also a cat and a swine, the last of these snuffling at the mother's feet—in Steen's painting suggests the bestial character of the mother's behavior, which reverses the normal hierarchical pattern whereby inferiors imitate their superiors. These two patterns of moral emulation, taken together, help to explain the circular arrangement of Steen's figures, for those figures present the viewer with a parrot-and-egg dilemma; does degeneracy propagate itself from above or from below, through emulation of the better sort by the meaner sort, or vice versa?

The juxtaposition of parrot and mother particularly foregrounds this question by bringing together the extreme registers of the family hierarchy in such a way that it is not wholly clear who is mirroring whom. True, the bird is learning to drink, whereas the mother has clearly already conned her lesson, but the mother's slumped form exactly repeats the natural contours of the parrot on its perch, suggesting reversion to a prior bestial condition for which the bird in question supplies the proximate example. The ambivalent interchange thus figured between woman and parrot gains further resonance from the painting's general theme, which draws—as scholars regularly note (Schama 209, Brown 88)—upon the text of Proverbs 20.1: "Wine is a mocker." In a sense, of course, the parrot mocks its owner, parodying the consumption of wine that has rendered her contemptible; however, the woman has also in a sense become a mockery of herself (and of the parrot) by allowing her fondness for strong drink to compromise her humanity. The parrot, whose startling articulacy renders it anomalously anthropomorphic, provides an ideal vehicle for the representation of this mockery; as the mother aspires to bestiality, so the bird aspires to humanity. To this extent, the figural parallelism that Steen establishes between the bird and the woman serves as a visual counterpart to the parrot's ability to mimic the human voice. The bird becomes a caricature of, and is in turn caricatured by, the people who surround it.

If we turn from genre painting to portraiture, we encounter something similar. Here again, parrots appear in association with inferior or subordinate individuals, individuals who are in some way—for instance by virtue of their age or their race or their gender—apparently incomplete. (Michiel Janszoon van Miereveldt's *Child with a Parrot*, for a brief instance, is drawn as a "highly stylized piece of pattern" [S. C. Smith 1929, 44], with the ornate lace and red ribbons of the child's apparel offset by the red head and lores of the bird. The painting is a stunning trinket, depicting two stunning trifles.) Through such patterns of association, parrots likewise gain ethnic significance as an item of visual representation more or less equivalent to the "black slaves" who, according to Peter Fryer, were fast becoming "the smart thing for titled and propertied families in England to have," and who thus recur in aristocratic portraits like those recently surveyed by Kim Hall (Fryer 9; Hall 226–253). In most cases, parrots and ethnic servants do not occupy the same painterly space, although a trip to any good gallery will yield examples of portraiture involving one or the other. It is as if there were only room for one exotic toy in any painting. However, Anthony Van Dyck supplies an exception that helps prove the rule.[2]

Van Dyck's portrait of William Fielding, first Earl of Denbigh (now in the National Gallery in London; see Figure 3.3) commits a noteworthy geographical solecism by juxtaposing servants and parrots.[3] Denbigh, who had visited Persia and India from 1631 to 1633, commissioned Van Dyck to commemorate the trip by painting him in Asian dress, on a hunting expedition, and accompanied by a dark-skinned page. As Denbigh strides forward, bearing a flintlock or fowling-piece in his right hand, he "makes a gesture of mild surprise as [the] servant . . . points to a parrot perched in a palm tree" (Millar 56). But the bird itself is profoundly out of place; a green-winged macaw, native to the New World, it bears no resemblance to any species of parrot indigenous to the Middle East.[4] The general composition of Van Dyck's painting is triangular in nature;

Figure 3.3: Anthony Van Dyck, *Portrait of William Fielding, First Earl of Denbigh* (National Gallery, London)

Denbigh himself, rifle in hand, forms one corner of the arrangement, and the line of gaze from the ethnic servant to him supplies a graded base for the overall figure grouping. But within the triangle of Denbigh, servant, and parrot, the latter two figures mirror each other with particular intimacy. The servant looks to Denbigh while gesturing aloft, with curved arm and hand, toward the bird; as Richard Wendorf has noted, "the guide's lips, like the parrot's jaws, are slightly parted" (1990, 102);[5] the bird, its body arced in a way that mimics the curvature of the servant's hand, stares down at Denbigh, reversing the path of visual attention invoked by the gesturing attendant and likewise paralleling the attendant's own line of gaze. Together, parrot and servant form something like a pair of parentheses or quotation marks, embracing Denbigh from above and below. Given the orientalist theme of Van Dyck's painting, the choice of bird here may be strikingly wrong, but taken together with the dark-skinned servant it marks out the space of the foreign and subsumes that space within the domestic.

2. "A MYNYON TO WAYT VPPON A QUENE"

The association of parrots with servants may seem accidental in the instance of Van Dyck's portrait, but in other cases it assuredly is not. In 1536, for instance, the President of the Spanish Council of the Indies and personal confessor to Emperor Charles V, Cardinal Garcia de Loaisa, issued a directive that empowered Spanish captains "to enslave Indians at their will" (qtd. in Hanke 1937, 84). When friar Bernardino de Minaya, a Spanish missionary in the New World and an advocate of Indian rights, learned of the decree, he returned to Spain and appealed to the cardinal on behalf of the Indians, arguing that they were human beings, capable of speech and understanding, and deserving of humane treatment. For his part, Loaisa justified his decree by countering that "the Indians were no more than parrots" (Greenblatt 1991, 99).[6] Loaisa's point is simple—perhaps even stupid—but nonetheless far-reaching; if, for parrots, there is no connection between speech and understanding, then they may be employed as a model for the treatment of other articulate but subordinate creatures. As Keith Thomas has observed, "the story of religious persecution in the early modern period makes it abundantly clear that, for those who committed acts of bloody atrocity, the dehumanization of their victims by reclassifying them as animals was often a necessary mental preliminary" (1983, 48), and the same point could easily be made about ethnic persecution as well. In any case, when it came to the Indians who worked their mines, Spaniards like Loaisa had an obvious political stake in the idea that human speech could be dissociated from human intellect.

Thus, to turn from historical to belletristic material, it may be no coincidence that one of the most famous parrots in English literature, *Robinson Crusoe*'s Poll, is described increasingly in terms of anthropomorphized subordination. When the castaway first encounters birds on his island, they are an undifferentiated mass of "innumerable number of fowls . . . , making a confused screaming, and crying every one according to his usual note" (Defoe 1719/1961, 56); eventually Crusoe captures one parrot, then others, teaches them to speak, and in the process even mistakes their language for that of another human being (141); finally, thus, he can describe himself in the following terms: "There was my majesty, the prince and lord of the whole island: I had the lives of all my subjects at my absolute command. . . . Then to see how like a king I dined, too, all alone, attended by my servants; Poll, as if he had been my favourite, was the only person permitted to talk to me" (147). In effect, the history of Crusoe's involvement with parrots is the history of a twofold transformation; as Crusoe takes on the character of a monarch, he turns Poll into a "servant"—a "person" who mirrors and confirms his own self-announced sovereignty. This metamorphosis, in turn, prepares for and leads almost naturally into Crusoe's later acquisition of a human servant. On the levels of theme and narrative, that is, Poll functions as a kind of Man Friday with feathers.

But *Robinson Crusoe* stands late in the process of cultural development this chapter seeks to document. The principal literary texts I wish to discuss here date from the sixteenth and seventeenth centuries, when parrots are still a fairly prominent novelty in early modern English society, and when their unprecedented abundance entails a fairly rapid, dramatic shift in their symbolic value. The shift in question is well documented by the OED, and it occurs on two levels more or less simultaneously. First, there is a process of lexical substitution whereby the standard medieval term for "parrot," "popinjay," is rendered archaic and replaced by the newer word. As for the new word itself, which first appears in English "c. 1525," the OED is not wholly certain how it originates but conjectures it to be from the French "*Perrot:* 'a man's proper name, being a diminutive or derivative of Pierre'" (OED sb. "Parrot").[7] One should not overemphasize a conjectural derivation, but in any case the appearance of the new substantive "parrot" in sixteenth-century English is paralleled by a second shift, this time on the level of social metaphor. On one hand, the OED notes that in medieval usage parrots are frequently evoked "in a eulogistic sense in allusion to the beauty and rarity of the bird" (sb. "Popinjay" 4.a.), but in sixteenth-century discourse, the same birds begin to be taken instead as "a type of vanity or empty conceit" (sb. "Popinjay" 4.b.). The change is considerable, and it occurs roughly within a century. Thus, around 1450, Thomas Lydgate can extol the Virgin Mary as a "popiniay, plumed with all clennesse" (77); in similar fashion, Richard de Holland's beast-fable *The Buke of the Howlat* can represent the "Pacocke of pryce" as the Pope of birds, and "the proper Pape Iaye, provde in his apparale," as the Pope's chamberlain (ca. 1450; in *Scottish Alliterative Poems* 1897, 90, 125). Vittore Crivelli's *Enthroned Virgin and Child, with Angels* (ca. 1481) offers a fine painterly instance of this association, placing an alexandrine ring-necked parakeet in the company of the blessed, to the left of Mary's throne (see Figure 3.4). However, by 1528 William Tyndale can charge that Catholic priests "playe the popengay with Credo say ye: volo saye ye and baptismum saye ye" (89b), and by 1596 Thomas Nashe can complain that Gabriel Harvey "would do nothing but crake and parret it in Print, in how manie Noble-mens fauours he was" (1958, 3:136).[8]

For a specifically visual confirmation of this semiotic shift, cartographic records prove most helpful. From classical times until the late fifteenth century, of course, parrots were associated specifically with Asia, and it is in this capacity that one first appears on a European map: the Ebstorf map of circa 1235, attributed to Gervase of Tilbury (see Figures 3.5 and 3.6; original destroyed in World War II). In a fashion typical of pre-Columbian cartography, the Ebstorf map divides the earth into three sections—Europe (bottom left), Africa (bottom right), and Asia (top)—all supermposed upon a drawing of the body of Christ. Again in typical fashion, it includes elaborate illustrations of cities, rivers, peoples, flora, fauna, and so on. The parrot—an alexandrine ring-necked parakeet—appears here in the upper right-hand section of the map, at the base of Christ's head, as a native of India; more generally, it takes up residence alongside a host of mythic and marvelous creatures derived from the bestiary tradition and, ultimately, from Pliny. Africa contains not only an elephant, leopard, and hyena, but also a mirmicaleon, camelopardalis, and tarandrius; Europe hosts not only the more familiar lion, tiger, and bear, but also the more exotic aurochs, bonacus, and gryphe; Asia harbors not only the parrot but also the antdog, saiga antelope, and chameleon, along with an inscription attesting also to the presence of unicorns,

Figure 3.4: Vittore Crivelli, *Enthroned Virgin and Child, with Angels* (Philadelphia Museum of Art: Purchased with the W. P. Wilstach Fund, 1896).

Figure 3.5: The Ebstorf map of the world, ca. 1235, from the Miller reproduction
(Photo: AKG London)

ibexes, manticora, and so on (see George 1969, 29–30). In this
context, the parrot is clearly still a wonder among wonders, and
clearly still associated with the fabulous East.

Indeed, this identification of the parrot with Asia encouraged early
explorers like Columbus to conclude, when they arrived in the New
World and encountered flocks of the birds there, that they had in fact
reached the Indies (see, e.g., Martyr, sig. A3v). Somewhat later, after
this misconception gave way, the parrot quickly became associated
even more with the New World than the East. When Pedro Cabral
discovered Brazil in 1500, the large flocks of macaws he encountered
there seem to have struck him as the "greatest novelty" of the region
(Greenlee 1938, 26, n. 1), and he promptly christened the "new
land . . . that of the parrots [*papaga*], because some are found there
which are an arm and a half in length, of various colors" (Greenlee

Figure 3.6: Detail of the Ebstorf map of the world, ca. 1235, from the Miller reproduction (Photo: AKG London). The earliest appearance of parrots on a European map is to be found in the upper right-hand corner, directly below the head of Christ.

120). For the time being the name stuck, and for the next 20 years or so parrots became the most prominent of wonders to find their way onto maps of the New World. The Portuguese manuscript map called the Cantino planisphere, named after its maker Alberto Cantino, who produced it in 1502, provides an outstanding case in point (see Figure 3.7). Whereas Cantino's handwritten note alongside the coast of Brazil describes the region's human inhabitants in some detail, it is the psittacine natives that receive most prominent visual representation on the map itself. Moreover, since he was aware of the existence of different species of parrot both in Brazil and in West Africa, Cantino has carefully differentiated between the kinds; his illustrations of the large, long-tailed Brazilian macaws, in red, blue, and yellow, contrast sharply with the smaller Senegal and African gray parrots occupying the

African portion of the map (George 57–60). This attention to geographical detail would not survive the cultural and historical developments separating Cantino's map from Van Dyck's portrait of the Earl of Denbigh one hundred and thirty years later.

However, Cantino's cartographic attention to New World parrots is by no means unique in the early sixteenth century; one can locate similar interest in contemporary maps by Nicolo de Caveri and Martin Waldseemuller, among others (George 60). The famous Piri Reis map of 1513, named after its compiler, Muhiddin Piri, typifies the association between parrots and indigenous peoples in this cartographic tradition. The Piri Reis map was compiled, as Piri himself observes in the accompanying notes, from a variety of sources, apparently including a map of Columbus's second voyage to the New World (McIntosh 2000, 135–136). If this is indeed the case, the Piri Reis map has the distinction of being the sole surviving copy of Columbus's own charts; in any case, it features rather rudimentary drawings of parrots upon a number of Caribbean islands, together with a lengthy note that devotes attention to the birds. For Piri, moreover, the birds were of particular interest in terms of their significance to local peoples. As his note on them remarks, "there are four kinds of parrots—white, red, green, and black. The people eat the flesh of parrots and their headdress is made entirely of parrots' wool [i.e., feathers]" (qtd. in McIntosh 11). This observation—which echoes similar statements by European explorers—may have been drawn in part from the comments of a Spanish mariner, captured by Reis, who claimed to have accompanied Columbus on three of his voyages to the west. But provenance notwithstanding, Piri's note certainly parallels the interest in parrots recorded in Columbus's surviving journal, and, like Columbus and other explorers of his day, Piri juxtaposes the avicultural and ethnographic marvels of the New World in a way that will outlast the initial wonder elicited by both.

Indeed, within fifty years of the Piri Reis map, parrots have already been divested of their symbolic value for cartographers of the New World. By the late sixteenth century they seldom appear at all on maps of the region; and in the meantime they undergo a swift process of trivialization and displacement that removes them from the position of centrality they once occupied in cartographic representations of the Americas. Diego Gutierrez's New World map of 1562, designed for Philip II of Spain and engraved by Hieronymus Cock, offers a good closing instance of this trend (see Figure 3.8). Here South America is still richly illustrated with indigenous wonders of various sorts. Brazil, the space occupied so prominently by macaws

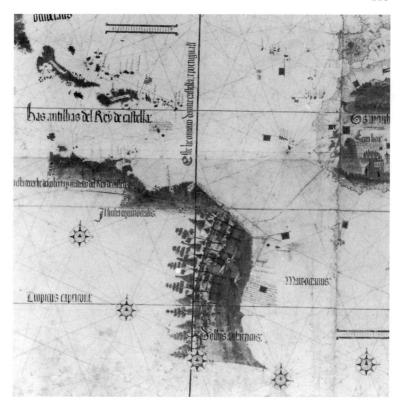

Figure 3.7: Detail of the Cantino planisphere, depicting parrots in Brazil and on the coast of West Africa (Biblioteca Estense, Modena—Su concessione del Ministero per i Beni e le Attivà Culturali)

on the Cantino planisphere of 60 years earlier, is here marked out with a series of detailed and lurid engravings of native cannibalism (see Figure 3.9);[9] Patagonia is occupied by giants (Figure 3.10); Mexico is given an erupting volcano; and the surrounding oceans abound with tritons, sea monsters, and galleons. But the only beast remaining in South America is a wild dog, who stands guard over Peru. Indeed, the two species of animal arguably most representative of the New world—the parrot and the monkey—have been removed from their native ground and imported to the bottom left-hand corner of the map, where they adorn its colophon (see Figure 3.11). Abstracted from their original habitat, the parrots here are less a geographical marvel than an item of marginal decoration, appropriate to the map's subject matter but wholly incidental to its concerns.

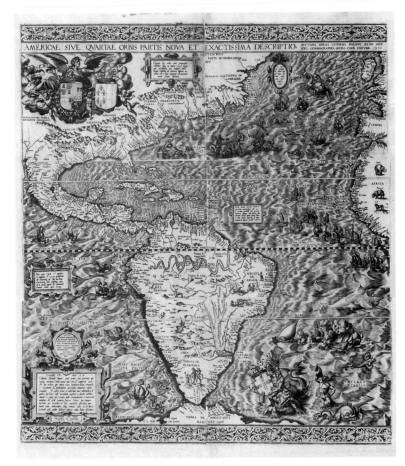

Figure 3.8: The 1562 New World map of Diego Gutierrez (Library of Congress, Washington, DC)

This displacement and relegation to the sphere of ornament are typical of the general treatment that parrots undergo in sixteenth- and seventeenth-century European representation.

Of course, this semiotic shift does not occur in a completely straightforward manner. Particularly in the sixteenth century, parrots may serve both as marvels and as trivia, as figures of praise and as objects of ridicule. As late as mid-century, Conrad Gesner thus insists that "The parrot surpasses other birds in cleverness and understanding, because it has a large head and it is born into India from the gen-

Figure 3.9: Detail from the 1562 New World map of Diego Gutierrez, depicting cannibals in Brazil (Library of Congress, Washington, DC)

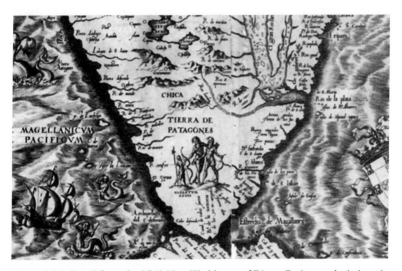

Figure 3.10: Detail from the 1562 New World map of Diego Gutierrez, depicting giants in Patagonia (Library of Congress, Washington, DC)

uine heavens, whence it has learned not only how to speak but even how to think" ("Psittacus inter aves ingenio sagacitateq[ue] praestat, quod grandi sit capite atq[ue] in India caelo syncero nascatur: unde etiam didicit non solum loqui, sed meditari" [1604, 723; sig. 2P1r]).

Figure 3.11: The colophon of the Diego Gutierrez map, adorned with parrots and monkeys (Library of Congress, Washington, DC)

Gesner's ideas here may be traced back as far as Aelian's *On The Characteristics of Animals* (ca. 200 A.D./1959), where we are told that in India "Parrots are kept and crowd around the king. But no Indian eats a Parrot in spite of their great numbers, the reason being that the Brahmins regard them as sacred and even place them above all other birds" (13.18). This tradition receives intermediary support from Boccaccio's *Genealogia Deorum* (1494/1976) as well:

> Psittacus was the son of Deucalion and Pyrrha . . . : having been imbued with the learning of his grandfather Prometheus, he travelled among the Ethiopians, where he was held in the greatest veneration when he had passed a very long time there. He then prayed to the gods that he be withdrawn from human matters, and, moved by his prayers, the gods easily transformed him into the bird of his name. I

believe the cause of this tale to be the fame of his strength and name, which endured in his perpetual green color; these birds are generally green. There are some people who believe this to have been the Psittacus who was said to have been one of the seven wise men.

[Psytacus Deucalionis & Pyrrhae filius . . . : Promethei aui sui imbutus ad aethiopas abiit: ubi in maxima ueneratione habitus cum in longissimum euasisset aeuum: orauit ut rebus subtraheretur humanis. cuius precibus dii faciles eum in auem sui nominis mutauere. Huius ego fictionis causam credo sui nominis & uirtutis phamam: quae eo cano mortuo uiriditate durauit perpetua: uti sunt uirides aues illae. Fuere q[ui] crederent hunc Psittacum eum fuisse: q[ui] unus ex septe[m] sapientibus dictus e[st].] (4.49)

Similarly, Boccaccio's fifth eclogue elaborates a pastoral allegory in which the city of Naples, prior to the flight of Queen Joan and Louis of Taranto in 1348, figures as a garden of Eden distinguished by the presence of miraculous and precious fowl:

> Here the bright birds made their nests;
> The parrot, much enraptured with the land,
> Came all the way here from her dried-up fields;
> And so did the supremely gorgeous phoenix. (5.43–46)

Such traditions, still available in the sixteenth century although by then in decline, invest the title figure of John Skelton's *Speke, Parrot* (ca. 1525; see *The Poetical Works of John Skelton*, 1965), a bird that combines both the medieval tendency to view parrots as emblems of excellence and the emerging modern inclination to associate them with satirical discourse. In keeping with the former tendency, the psittacine narrator of Skelton's poem introduces himself in terms similar to those employed by Gesner and Boccaccio:

> My name is Parrot, a byrd of paradyse,
>   By nature devysed of a wondrous kynde,
> Dyentely dyeted with dyuers dylycate spyce,
>   Tyl Euphrates, that flode, dryueth me into Inde;
>   Where men of that country by fortune me fynd. (1–5)

Skelton's parrot, born and raised in paradise, functions according to Arthur Kinney "as if [it] were a prophet or Christ," conveying divine revelation to its hearers (1987, 16). Likewise, it also bears the marks of rarity and social distinction:

With my becke bent, my lyttyl wanton eye,
  My fedders fresh as is the emrawde grene,
About my neck a cyrculet lyke the ryche rubye,
  My lyttyl leggys, my feet both fete and clene,
  I am a mynyon to wayt vppon a quene. (17–21)

Here too, as later in *Robinson Crusoe,* is the figure of parrot as servant, but in this case the servitude is dignified with references to
gemstones, to paradisiacal origins, to dainty diets of spice, and so on.
Finally, added to these other marks of distinction, is a macaronic articulacy of breathtaking scope:

Lyke your pus cate, Parrot can mute and cry
  In Lattyn, in Ebrew, Araby, and Caldey;
    In Greke tong Parrot can bothe speke and say,
  As Percyus, that poet, doth reporte of me,
  Quis expedivit psittaco suum chaire? (26–30)

A remarkable bird, this, and so far it is grounded largely in a medieval tradition of eulogistic metaphor whereby parrots function as
emblems of virtue, value, wonder, and even wisdom. But Skelton's
parrot is also something of a transitional figure; as Stanley Fish has
observed, it also participates in "the more conventional image"—
presumably more conventional because more familiar to modernity—
"of mimic-fool," an image that "contradicts" the paradisiacal origins
described above (1965, 136). In short, Skelton's parrot exhibits peculiarities that associate it with satirical invective and intellectual
vacuity, and it prefigures ways of thinking about parrots that would
become current in the next two centuries. Thus *Speke, Parrot* develops a trenchant and remarkably obscure anti-Wolsey diatribe, in
which Skelton's bird accuses the prelate of everything from corruption of the criminal justice system ("So many thevys hangyd, and
thevys never the lesse" [470]) to the unethical sale of pardons ("So
many bullys of pardon puplysshyd and shewyd" [508]). To this extent, Skelton's parrot is indeed a satirical beast, but it serves as a vehicle rather than an object of satirical representation. In addition,
however, the bird also behaves in ways that impugn its own good
sense; indeed, for most of the poem one may doubt whether the parrot is in its right mind at all. As the bird itself remarks, one should
pursue nothing—not even sanity—to excess:

Moderata juvant, but *toto* doth excede;
  Dyscressyon is moder of noble vertues all;

Myden agan in Greke tonge we rede;
. . . .
In mesure is tresure, *cum sensu maturato;*
Ne tropo sanno, ne tropo mato. (52–65)

While the parrot advises against extremes, even of moderation, its language assumes what one commentator has described as an "offensively polyglot" character (Pollet 1971, 121), modulating from Latin to English to Greek to English to Latin to Italian and in the process exhibiting no "dyscressyon" whatsoever. Such speech comes close to an emergent model of empty, labile, and mechanical articulacy that will be firmly associated with parrots within 50 years after the composition of Skelton's poem.

3. A GROAT A QUART

Indeed, within fifty years of Skelton's poem, parrots underwent a massive change of sociocultural status in early modern Europe. As Keith Thomas observes, "commercial bird-dealers" first appeared in England "in Tudor times, and in the late seventeenth century there was a large London market in singing-birds, some caught at home by professional bird-catchers, others exotics imported from the tropics" (111); moreover, the birds thus available were increasingly marketed as pets rather than as edible fowl or breeders. This pattern of development helps explain why, in the early modern period, parrots begin to lose the exalted mythic status granted them by Boccaccio, Skelton, and others. Also, the increasing availability of parrots as pets may help explain their increased availability as objects of literary fun, too. In general, parrots lose the quasi-mythical status they enjoyed in medieval culture, which accounted for them largely through the anthropomorphic category of the marvelous beast, and are resituated in a more humble discursive station through the standard representational tropes of relative anthropocentrism. Parrot jokes, for instance, begin to appear in sixteenth- and seventeenth-century jestbooks and related texts; moreover, these jokes generally associate psittacine articulacy with intellectual emptiness. The parrots of early modern jestbooks make no claims to have been born in paradise, or to be able both to speak and to think, or to have mastered all tongues; these birds are much humbler creatures than the narrator of *Speke, Parrot*. But their articulacy persists, now as a marker not of rarity or excellence or wisdom, but rather as the emblem of an amusing ontological inferiority.

For instance, the *Banquet of Jests*—a seventeenth-century compendium of witticisms attributed to Archie Armstrong, court fool to James I and Charles I—contains a lengthy tale about a talkative parrot. The bird in question belonged to a wine merchant, whence it had learned to repeat the phrase "A groat a quart, a groat a quart" (1640; see *A Nest of Ninnies* 1970, 163). When the merchant raised his prices, the parrot continued its chatter unchanged, with the result that customers accused the merchant of double-dealing. The merchant, incensed by the trouble thus created, threw the bird "in a great rage into the kennel—from whence she crawled forth, being nothing all over but dirt" (*A Nest of Ninnies* 163). Meanwhile, as the bird pulled itself out of the muck, "by chance, came by a Sow which had been wallowing in the mire and was in a most beastly pickle, which the Parrot spying, . . . said, 'Alas, poor Sow, hast thou cried wine for a groat a quart, too?'" (*Nest of Ninnies* 163).

It is worth noting that the parrot in this joke is, at least, still capable of something like thought. But its cognitive capacities are clearly limited. It can't seem to grasp the mechanics of consumer-price inflation, for instance, and, although it properly relates cause to effect in the case of its chatter and subsequent predicament, it then mistakenly identifies its own situation with the unrelated case of a bemucked sow. In fact, the bird's mental limitations are the key to this joke's humor, such as it is; the parrot stands in for the various numbskulls and nitwits who wander through early modern jestbooks like Robert Armin's *Nest of Ninnies* (1607), and who generally function as the butt of the jestbooks' comedy.

Gesner relates a similar joke in his *Historia Animalium* (1551–1558):

> Recently a certain friend told us a pleasant story of a parrot, which he said fell out of the palace of Henry VIII, at London in England, into the river Thames flowing nearby. It cried out, "A boat, a boat, for twenty pound!" which it had heard uttered very often, and which it had then memorized very easily, its voice accustomed to those who call the ferryman from the opposite bank by price (as if they were placed in some danger, or others even in jest). A certain ferryman, thus aroused, rowed out hastily and picked up the bird and returned it to the king (to whom he recognized it to belong) in hopes of just so much of a reward as the bird had promised. The king agreed that he would settle on whatever reward the bird named when again asked. The bird responded, "Give the knave a groat."

[Nuper amicus quidam recitavit nobis iucundum de psittaco historiam quem aiebat Londini in Anglia a palatio regis Henrici octavi in preaterlabentem fluvium Thamesim decidisse, & voce consueta iis qui quantocunq[ue] pretio (ut in periculo aliquo constatii, aut alii etiam ioco) portitorem ex opposita ripa vocant, *a bot a bot for twenty pound*... , quam saepissime enunciari audierate, & tum commodissime meminerate, exclamasse. Ea excitatem portitorem quendam, propere adnavigasse & sustulisse avem, & regi (ad quem pertinere agnoscebat) reddidisse, tantum mercedis sperantem, quantum avis promiserat. Rex pactus est ut quam avis interrogata denuo mercedem dixisset, acciperat. Respondit avis, Gibe *the knabe a grotte.*] (724; sig. 2P1v)

Here the humor arises from the juxtaposition of parrot and ferryman, and from uncertainty as to which is cleverer. The ferryman, intent upon earning an easy 20 pounds, fails to reckon on the possibility that the parrot has learned to name any smaller sum; the parrot, on the other hand, may or may not have outsmarted his savior intentionally. If the intent is there, the ferryman must suffer the distinct indignity of having been duped by a bird; if the intent is absent, the ferryman has duped himself. In either case, the bird's articulacy provides the occasion for a duel of cunning between unarmed combatants.

Again, John Locke's *Essay Concerning Human Understanding* (1690/1961) reproduces a lengthy and humorous parrot anecdote from Sir William Temple's *Memoirs* (1686) in order to illustrate the view that "it is not the *idea* of a thinking or rational being alone that makes the *idea* of a man in most people's sense, but of a body so and so shaped, joined to it" (1:280):

I had a mind to know from ... Prince *Maurice's* ... own mouth ... of an old *parrot* he had in *Brazil* during his government there, that spoke and asked and answered common questions like a reasonable creature.... He told me ... he had so much curiosity as to send for it ...; and when it came first into the room where the Prince was, with a great many *Dutchmen* about him, it said presently: *What a company of white men are here?* They asked it what he thought that man was, pointing to the Prince. It answered, *some general or other.* When they brought it close to him, he asked it: *D'ou venez-vous?* It answered: *De Marinnan.* The Prince: *A qui etes-vous?* The parrot: *A un Portugais.* Prince: *Que fais-tu la?* Parrot: *Je garde les poules.* The Prince laughed and said: *Vous gardez les poules?* The parrot answered: *Oui, moi, & je sais bien faire,* and made the chuck four or five times that people use to make to chickens when they call them. (1:279)

For Locke, the bird in this tale serves as a well-nigh "incredible" (1:280), practically "ridiculous" (1:280), but nonetheless radically downsized version of the miraculous parrots one encounters in Boccaccio, Skelton, and the like. Nor is it sufficient for Locke to have reduced the marvelous capacities of the medieval parrot to the ability to tend chickens and sustain a child's conversation. Even these abilities are rendered suspect, and are invoked merely as an outrageous case that, despite its outrageousness, still does not successfully call into question distinctions among species:

> The Prince . . . and our author . . . both . . . call this talker a *parrot;*
> and I ask anyone else who thinks such a story fit to be told, whether,
> if this *parrot* and all of its kind had always talked, . . . they would not
> have passed for a race of *rational animals;* but yet for all that they
> would have been allowed to be men and not *parrots?* (1:280)

With Locke, in other words, the parrot's inability to reason is taken for granted, and the story of a rational bird is invoked merely as a fantasy that, for all its popularity amongst the credulous, would still change nothing about the order of creation even in the unlikely event that it were somehow true.

This contemptuous view of avian speech achieves its *reductio ad absurdum* in another tale of a talking bird—albeit not, this time, a parrot. In his jestbook *Wit and Mirth* (1630/1967), John Taylor the Water Poet tells several jokes about "A Wealthy *Monsieur* in *France* (hauing profound reuenues, and a shallow braine)" (179; sig. 2Qr). Among this worthy's exploits is his purchase of an expensive jackdaw, a bird supposedly able to speak "*French, Italian, Spanish, Dutch,* and *Latin*" (179; sig. 2Q2r). Unfortunately, in buying the bird the French gentleman falls prey to false advertising:

> Iack-Daw (after a moneth or fiue weekes time) neuer spake otherwise
> then his fathers speech *Kaw, Kaw:* whereat the Monsieur said, that the
> Knaue had cozened him of his money: but it is no great matter . . . :
> for, quoth he, though my Daw does not speak, yet I am in good hope
> that he thinkes the more. (179–180; sigs. 2Q2r-v)

Here again a fool and a talking bird are juxtaposed so that their use of language sheds light upon their mutual idiocy; the stupidity of the man in question is thrown into relief by the silence of the bird. This bond of association between articulate birds and dim-witted or otherwise inferior men emerges from early modern jestbooks as one more instance of the general discursive pattern this chapter addresses, nor do I wish to deny the occasional humor of such discourse. Rather than employing the fearsome powers of literary criticism to condemn people who make jokes about parrots, I wish simply to note that these jokes arise from and contribute to a particular set of cultural arrangements, and that the arrangements in question use the inferiority of articulate birds as a template for the construction of various kinds of social inferiority. In some cases—for instance that of an empty-headed gentleman and his (non-)talking jackdaw—this parallelism may be perfectly appropriate and amusing and more or less socioeconomically innocent. In other cases—for instance that of an empty-headed *French* gentleman and his talking bird—we may be confronted with something more, or less, than good clean fun.

3. Pestered With a Popingay

In any case, by Shakespeare's day parrots had become a standard object of ridicule in English literary discourse. Shakespeare himself helps illustrate the pejorative symbolic uses that early modern English culture had begun to find for parrots; he mentions the birds ten times in his works, in consistently satirical fashion, consistently in association with ideas of social inferiority and witlessness. Salerio in *The Merchant of Venice* (ca. 1594–1598) talks abstractly of "strange fellows" who "laugh like parrots" at the somber tones of a bagpipe (1.2.50–53); later in the same play, when Launcelot Gobbo has rung the changes on a typically atrocious pun ("It is much that the Moor should be more than reason; but if she be less than an honest woman, she is indeed more than I took her for" [3.5.40–42]), Lorenzo likens such wordplay to the chatter of birds: "I think the best grace of wit will shortly turn into silence, and discourse grow commendable in none only but parrots" (3.5.44–46). In *1 Henry IV* (ca. 1596–1598), Prince Hall mocks the taciturn assurances of the inn-drawer Francis ("Anon, anon, sir" [2.4.97]) by marveling "that ever this fellow should have fewer words than a parrot, and yet the son of a woman" (2.4.98–99). Again, in *1 Henry IV,* Hotspur describes the king's messenger sent for the prisoners from the battle of Holmedon as a "popingay" who "pestered" him with "many holiday and lady terms" (1.3.50, 46). In *Othello* (ca. 1605) Cassio laments that his drunkenness has caused him to "speak parrot," to "squabble," "swagger," "swear," and "discourse fustian with [his] own shadow" (2.3.279–281). In *Much Ado About Nothing* (ca. 1598–1599), Benedick mocks Beatrice's repetitive insults by calling her "a rare parrot-teacher" (1.1.138).

In almost every such case, parrots gain value as a social marker because they embody processes of mechanical and therefore imperfect linguistic imitation. This emphasis upon psittacine articulacy helps clarify the association, already documented in this chapter, of parrots with servants. As parrots grow more common, their ability to talk grows less miraculous and thus becomes a tool for the imposition of hegemonic social relations; hence the tendency in early modern Europe is to configure psittacine articulacy as an index of mindlessness and inferiority. The case of Francis the drawer in *1 Henry 4* is both representative and particularly interesting in this respect. Like a parrot, Francis has a limited vocabulary that he employs indiscriminately; one good way to insult the poor fellow, therefore, is to identify him with creatures lower than he on the great chain of being. But to make this identification is also to call into question the distinctions that lend meaning to the chain of being itself; that is why Prince Hal can think it remarkable that Francis should "yet [be] the son of a woman." To use parrots as the basis for an invidious *social* discrimination is, at least by analogy, to admit them into the sphere of culture. And to identify even a base-born human being with such a bird is, by the same token, to risk reconstituting humanity *tout court* under the sign of the natural. Hal recognizes this fact and tries to compensate for it by expressing disbelief when he sees the markers of nature and culture coalesce. In doing so, he also tacitly registers the potential conflict between an absolute anthropocentrism that would regard Francis as human and a relative anthropocentrism that would consider his humanity as impaired.

In effect, Prince Hal's parrot analogy institutes social discriminations similar to those described by Gail Paster in her recent work on gender and humoral medicine. For Paster, humoral medicine organizes tropes of bodily uncontrol—specifically urinary, lacteal, and menstrual incontinence (1993, 23–63; 163–280)—in ways that disparage feminine identity while associating masculinity with "an emergent ideology of bodily refinement and exquisite self-control" (14). Prince Hal's parrot reference, and the others like it, also serve as a vehicle for the representation of incontinence. For them, however, the incontinence in question is not somatic but linguistic, and the discriminations they institute are primarily related to social rank rather than gender. Francis squawks one word over and over, irrespective of the circumstances; Launcelot Gobbo's inane puns make even the prattle of a parrot seem sensible, and they prompt Lorenzo to locate true "wit," the genuine capacity for signification, in "silence"; Benedick characterizes Beatrice's wit as empty and repetitious, like the speech of a parrot. In each of these cases, the bird analogy serves to identify a human subject's inability either a) to control language sensibly and economically or b) to choose the second-best alternative and shut up altogether. The person in question tries to use language, but language ends up using him or her instead.

That is also the point of Ben Jonson's epigram "On Court-Parrat" (Epigram 71, 1612–1613): "To plucke downe mine, POLL sets up new wits still, / Still, 'tis his lucke to praise me 'gainst his will." Poll seeks to dispraise the speaker of the poem by indirection, by commending others at the speaker's expense. Hence the formal balance between the two hemistichs of the epigram's first line: the critical act of plucking down is opposed to that of setting up, the speaker is poised against the new wits being applauded in his stead, and Court-Parrat's own name, "POLL," sits astride the line's caesura, marking the spot from which the critical distinctions described by the line supposedly emanate. But the irony is that they don't. As line two begins by parroting the first line's rhyme-word, it nonetheless also marks a moment at which the adverbial "still" of line one, referring to Court-Parrat's incessant chatter, metamorphoses into the adversative "still" of line two: a sign that the chatter in question has in fact changed nothing at all. Hence the poem's conclusion: Poll praises the author against his will because his attempts at dispraise, inept as they are, prove that Poll cannot control his own capacity for signification.

Indeed, it is Jonson, not Shakespeare, who elevates this standard emblematic use of parrots to its most enduring literary form. I refer, of course, to the figure of Sir Politic Would-Be, who translates the foibles of Francis the drawer into an extended dramatic motif. Sir Pol is the principle of mechanical repetition incarnate, and he sees such repetition as pregnant with meaning. Thus he makes a fine tool for a playwright who—as critics have often noted[10]—is inherently fond of *enumeratio*. As Anne Barton has observed, *Volpone* is full of catalogues, and Sir Politic Would-Be, in particular, seems to be constantly "rummaging through the contents of some gothic lumber-room of the imagination, turning out toothpicks and baboons, oranges, muskmelons, apricots, porpoises and lion-whelps, tinderboxes, onions, sprats, frayed stockings and Selsey cockles" (1986, 109). This enumeration reaches its peak when Peregrine reads aloud from Sir Pol's diary and finds it to be an ongoing list of trivialities:

Notandum,
A rat had gnawne my spurre-lethers; notwithstanding,
I put on new, and did goe forth: but, first,

> I threw three beanes ouer the threshold. *Item,*
> I went, and bought two tooth-pickes, whereof one
> I burst, immediatly, in a discourse
> With a *dutch* merchant, 'bout *ragion del stato.*
> From him I went, and payd a *moccinigo,*
> For peecing my silke stockings; by the way
> I cheapen'd sprats: and at St MARKES I vrin'd.
>   (4.1.135–144)

Here is the motif of psittacine repetition in its apotheosis; Sir Politic, unable to distinguish between significant and insignificant detail, generates a language that has been almost completely divested of its referential value. It is what Shakespeare's Cassio would elsewhere call "speaking parrot."

Moreover, Sir Pol's vacuous talk not only signals his intellectual and moral inferiority; it also associates that inferiority with ethnic difference. By now this association should be familiar. John Taylor's French Monsieur, for instance, confirms anti-French prejudices by his assumption that talk—even a jackdaw's—invariably betokens intelligence, and that the absence of talk betokens even more intelligence; for Cardinal Loaisa, by the same measure, the inhabitants of the New World seem to advertise their racial inferiority through the imperfection of their efforts to learn Spanish, efforts that recall those of a talking bird; Skelton's Parrot brings his own wit into question through his aggressive and often inappropriate glossolalia; and so on. For his part, Sir Politic Would-Be quickly reveals himself to be a fake Italian of the sort denounced by Roger Ascham in the famous adage "*Inglese Italianato e un diabolo incarnato*" (1570/1966, 65). A self-conscious Machiavel whose ineptitude alone places him beyond Ascham's serious censure, Sir Pol has visited Venice in obedience to "a peculiar humour of [his] wiues, / . . . to obserue, / To quote, to learne the language, and so forth" (2.1.11–13). His admiration of "Italian mountebanks" (2.2.4) leads him to view them—contrary to the common sense of Peregrine—as "the onely languag'd-men, of all the world" (2.2.13). And this desire to "learne the language" of Italy—common to both Sir Pol and his wife—culminates in Lady Would-Be's ostentatious familiarity with Italian verse:

> VOLPONE: The Poet,
>   As old in time, as PLATO, and as knowing,
>   Say's that your highest female grace is silence.
> LADY WOULD-BE: Which o' your Poets? PETRARCH? or TASSO?'
>   or DANTE?

GVERRINI? ARIOSTO? ARETINE?
CIECO *di Hadria?* I have read them all. (3.4.76–81)

In sum, Sir Politic Would-Be and his wife signify their fundamental baseness of character through the ease with which they are colonized by the language of others, particularly ethnic others. In this respect, of course, they suffer by comparison to the true traveling bird of Jonson's play, the unassailably English—and appropriately laconic—Peregrine. Indeed, the Would-Bes' efforts to "quote" the language and customs of Venice may be viewed as a reversal of the processes of "colonial quotation" recently documented by Barbara Fuchs (1997, 50), processes whereby a colonizing power reads its current imperialist ventures in terms of past historical experiences that may be taken to license the ongoing project of nation building. Sir Politic and his wife are in no position to engage in such strenuous representational activity, for they have no experience of their own to project onto the imperialist scene. Instead, the vacuum of their minds invites colonization by others, and the minutiae of Venetian culture assemble willy-nilly to make up the deficit in the Would-Bes' own intellectual and moral resources. The result is a pair of dramatic characters who seem to be drowning in irrelevant detail, who are so impressionable that everything is of equal importance to them, and who are thus forever doomed to miss the point of action and conversation. Susceptibility to influence, inability to make intellectual distinctions, and a concomitant failure to make sense of the world in general: these are the outstanding features of Sir Politic and Lady Would-Be as dramatic characters, features also found in emerging early modern notions of psittacine articulacy.

5. THINKING WITH PARROTS

Thus Shakespeare and Jonson, along with other of their contemporaries, help redefine the significance of psittacine articulacy within English-speaking culture. They help inaugurate a new way of thinking about parrots—or more precisely, to borrow a phrase from Peter Stallybrass and Allon White (1986, 44), a new way of thinking *with* parrots.[11] In a sense, this new way of thinking may simply be a transcontinental illustration of the adage that familiarity breeds contempt; as parrots grow increasingly subject to European acquisition and domestication, English writers work systematically to divest them of what Stephen Greenblatt has called "the marvelous" (1991, 25 and passim). However, the contempt thus generated is neither culturally arbitrary nor economically neutral. In the end, pet parrots are no more insignificant to the social world of early modern England than are the other, homologous and equally trivial "particles of cultural wealth and show" recently documented by Patricia Fumerton (1991, 1). This discussion began by noting that early explorers of the New World seem interested in determining how to use parrots in the best possible way. What European cultures discover, I think, is that the best use for the birds is a symbolic one: the identification of psittacine articulacy with an intellectual inferiority that can then be used to reinforce various hegemonic social and ethnic relations. The consequences of this identification extend well beyond the scope of the present study; on one hand, for instance, parrots survive as a resonant motif in colonial and postcolonial literature, while on the other hand they help constitute a model of the carefully limited articulacy that colonial educators have often sought to reproduce among subject peoples.

Thus it is perhaps appropriate in this chapter to review two quick examples of the common fate accorded to parrots and servants in the later literature of European colonialism. I draw these instances from a wide range of possibilities, including the immolated parrot Coco of Jean Rhys's *Wide Sargasso Sea;* the Sappho-quoting bordello parrot of Isak Dinesen's *Out of Africa;* the Garcimarquesian parrots of *One Hundred Years of Solitude* and *Love in the Time of Cholera;* and Derek Walcott's revision of Robinson Crusoe's Poll in *Pantomime.*[12] Each of these works offers a fascinating juxtaposition of servants with pet birds, but there is no space to deal with them all here; instead, I will confine myself to two other texts of a related nature.

First, there is Conrad's *Nostromo* (1904/1963), in which Charles Gould and his wife occupy a palatial residence described as follows:

> Subdued voices ascended in the early mornings from the paved well of the quadrangle. . . . Barefooted servants passed to and fro, issuing from dark, low doorways below; two laundry girls with baskets of washed linen; the baker with the tray of bread made for the day; Leonarda, [Mrs. Gould's] own *camerista.* . . . Then the old porter would hobble in, sweeping the flagstones, and the house was ready for the day. . . . [A] cluster of *flor de nochebuena* blazed in great masses before the open glass doors of the reception rooms. A big green parrot, brilliant like an emerald in a cage that flashed like gold, screamed out ferociously, "*Viva Costaguana!*," then called twice mellifluously, "Leonarda! Leonarda!," in imitation of Mrs. Gould's voice, and suddenly took refuge in immobility and silence. (68–69)

On the metonymic axis, this passage elides servants with pets; the catalogue of laundry girls, bakers, chambermaids, and porters culminates in its vision of Mrs. Gould's parrot, speaking to the other
domestics in imitation of its mistress. On the axis of metaphor, by the
same token, the bird constitutes a typically pessimistic Conradian
joke: an ironic caricature of the Costaguanan *vox populi*, mindlessly
squawking the patriotic slogan of the moment. It is a joke rendered
all the more sardonic because in this case the slogan in question
means "Long live the Birdshit Coast!"

In George Orwell's *Burmese Days* (1934/1963), on the other
hand, there is no pet bird to provide a model for the behavior of
household servants, and at least one Englishman seems to feel this
absence acutely. Hence his frustration in the following exchange:

> "Butler!"
> "Yes, master?"
> "How much ice have we got left?"
> "'Bout twenty pounds, master. Will only last to-day, I think. I find it
> very difficult to keep ice cool now."
> "Don't talk like that, damn you—'I find it very difficult!' Have you
> swallowed a dictionary? 'Please, master, can't keeping ice cool'—
> that's how you ought to talk. We shall have to sack this fellow if he
> gets to talk English too well. I can't stick servants who talk Eng-
> lish." (24–25)

Orwell's *pukka sahib* aspires to a state of affairs similar to that displayed in *Nostromo:* one characterized by the unambiguous subordination of the domestic help, one in which servants and parrots are
conceptually—and conversationally—interchangeable. To be a
source of material profit, after all, the servant must be able to speak
the master's tongue, but the servant's inferior social status requires
that she or he not speak it too well.[13]

Psittacine articulacy, as conceived by early modern writers, provides
an ideal model of this arrangement. In effect, both the bird and the
servant are most useful if kept in a carefully managed state of semicoherence, and this state seems first to have become thinkable in England in the sixteenth and seventeenth centuries. Indeed, it is probably
inevitable that semicoherence should become a recurrent object of literary representation, for literary representation takes language—its fe-
licities and idiosyncrasies, its social instrumentality and cultural
significance—as a fundamental stock-in-trade. To this extent, literature helps do the work of conceptualizing social and ethnic differences
through language; and in the case of the materials surveyed here, the

English literary tradition seems determined to equate such differences with difference of species. The result is a closed, self-referential semiotic in which the exploitation of wildlife licenses the exploitation of human beings and vice versa, and in which the categories of literary thought serve to render both forms of exploitation inevitable, commonplace, and therefore trivial. It was in the construction of just such a semiotic that early modern European culture found its best most enduring use for the New World's marvelous birds.

CHAPTER FOUR

ANIMAL FUN FOR EVERYONE

1. NEVER WORK WITH CHILDREN OR ANIMALS

I draw the title of this chapter from a television jingle used recently to promote a private petting zoo in South Georgia. The heading for this opening section of the chapter, in turn, is a famous piece of show-business advice popularly attributed to W. C. Fields. I begin with these two lines not only because of the temporal distance that separates them from my immediate subject, but also because of their undeniable relevance to that subject. I am concerned here with animals *as* animals: how people understand beasts in themselves; how people distinguish between the human and bestial orders without the mutual overcoding that is such an ubiquitous feature of our attitudes toward nature; and, of course, most specifically, how beasts might function as beasts on the early English stage.

The petting-zoo jingle addresses these issues as they impinge upon life in late-twentieth-century America, where the difference inherent to animal nature is regularly sentimentalized in ways that allow for certain forms of popular entertainment: not only the petting (and nonpetting) zoo, but also the circus, the theme park, the regional fair, the summer camp hayride, the local nature trail, and by extension, perhaps, novels like the popular British import *All Things Bright and Beautiful* and films like *Babe*. While these products of our culture exhibit varying degrees of sophistication and even (in the case of *Babe*) a certain direness of vision, they concur in presenting nature in general, and the animal world in particular, as a source of wholesome family entertainment—as offering pastimes appropriate to children, and therefore doubly appropriate for parents to share with their children.

This is very largely an infantilizing vision of the natural world, which figures within it primarily as an object of wonder for the young, and which the adult world accommodates as an index of its commitment to parental nurturance. To this extent, the very concept of "animal fun" as family entertainment, while superficially inclusive (being something that adults and children are expected to participate in together), also performs on a slightly deeper level an elaborate segregation of parent from child, for the entertainment plays to the child more directly and overtly, and often in very different ways, than to the accompanying grownup. In effect, the idea of "animal fun for everyone" associates children with animals within a carefully maintained zone of adult supervision, and presents this association as a good thing.

It is an association that W. C. Fields, in his curmudgeonly way, repeats. In his view, children and animals are conjoined in an ungodly alliance against the adult world. As he remarks elsewhere, "Anyone who hates children and dogs can't be all bad"; and elsewhere still, he reduces this same sentiment to its aphoristic essence: "Your kid looks like a monkey." This evil confederacy, in turn, affects him most acutely in his chosen trade, for the refusal of children and animals to act predictably leads to the ever-present threat that they will upstage, confuse, and embarrass an adult performer committed to his script; hence, in another witticism, he reminds a child actor that "Your line is 'Goo, goo.' Don't blow it." For Fields, the best thing to do with children and animals is to send them someplace where they can do as little damage as possible, presumably as far away from him as possible. Again we confront the association of children with animals, again in simultaneous conjunction and contradistinction to adults. The only difference is that Fields foregrounds the contradistinction to a degree that the petting-zoo jingle does not. His attitude is not far different from that of the harried middle-aged parents who pack their sons and daughters off to summer camp with relief, signing a fat check in the process and feeling virtuous for having provided their children with a wholesome, natural environment, blessedly under *someone else's* adult supervision.

On the surface, at least, this general identification of children with animals may seem merely to repeat patterns of relation that we have already observed within early modern and premodern discourse. As I noted in the introduction to this work, for instance, Renaissance authors regularly identified schoolchildren with colts, and in doing this they themselves were repeating an already venerable literary habit. But the social function of contemporary identification is very different from that of its predecessors, which conflate children with animals in order to license parallel disciplinary regimens for both, and to confirm absolute patriarchal authority over both in the process. The late twentieth-century association of children with animals, on the contrary, marks them as objects not of discipline but of protection; it confers upon parents (rather than only fathers) the signs not so much of authority as of responsibility, and locates within both child and animal a brand of innocence that eventuates in privilege, a physical and mental and emotional vulnerability that renders them in a sense sacred, blessed with the inviolable blessedness of the meek. There is no question of W. C. Fields beating the child actor who upstages him. On the contrary, he must be protected *from* the child, because in his world children have become a separate and privileged form of life. As historians of childhood have shown, the medieval and early modern tendency was to view children largely as miniature adults,[1] a tendency that is reflected in the early English drama by the "general precociousness" (Snyder 1999, 2) of Shakespeare's children and their counterparts in such non-Shakespearean plays as Webster's *White Devil* (1612). On the contrary, the association of children with animals in the twentieth century tends to mark children off from adults, and in the process to sentimentalize and ennoble both childhood and the animal world, in a way that it does not in the early modern period.

And if early modern cultural practice tended to associate children with animals in a manner that postmodern practice does not, the theatrical results of this difference are registered not only in the way early modern authors drew the characters of children for onstage presentation, but also in the way authors and players treated the actual children who inhabited the world of the theater itself. Here again, W. C. Fields' remarks about children and animals are useful, for they draw attention to a profound disagreement between his theatrical sensibility and that of early modern dramatists like Shakespeare. The early modern dramatists, after all, worked with children on a regular basis; in the celebrated case of the children's acting companies, they went so far as to work with nothing *but* child actors; and when a Shakespearean character complains about unpredictable behavior disrupting stage business, it is the behavior not of child actors but of adult comics: "And let those that be your clowns speak no more than is set down for them, for there be of them that will themselves laugh to set on some quantity of barren spectators to laugh too, though in the mean time some necessary question of the play be then to be consider'd" (*Hamlet* 3.2.38–43). Yet paradoxically, the early dramatists seem to have shared Fields's feelings about animals. The appearance of animals onstage in the early theater was a rare thing, and the comparable use of animals in other forms of popular entertainment (most particularly bull- and bear-baiting, but also cock-fighting, bear-dancing, and other trained-animal performances), is often derided by early English writers as base and contemptible.

So the late-twentieth-century alliance between children and animals breaks down entirely if we try to apply it to the recorded practices of the early modern stage. Instead of identifying child performers with animals, the world of early modern entertainment seems to have associated children with men, while banishing beasts to a separate, and markedly inferior, sphere of activity. Of course, bear-baiting, cock-fighting, and the like did have their advocates, and we will examine some of their work in the following pages. As a rule—and counterintuitively, given the brutality of the behavior in question—that work is distinguished by anthropomorphic tropes and expressions that place animals and human beings together within a single circle of society. But in general, the supporters of bloodsports convey the impression of arguing against the current of received high-cultural opinion, and they convey this impression despite the fact that animal-baitings and similar entertainments were patronized at all levels of society, up to and including the crown. Within certain limits, in fact, the cultural status of bloodsports and other animal divertissements in early modern England was arguably comparable to that of pornography in postmodern Europe and America. On one hand, the sports were clearly profitable, widespread, and even taken as broadly representative of national character and identity. Yet at the same time, they were uneasily tolerated, vigorously attacked by religious zealots, and openly disparaged within the circles of polite, informed society—many of whose members nonetheless contributed individually, in some way or other, to the activities they denounced.

In addressing the role of animals in early modern English dramatic entertainment, this chapter also examines the attitudes that such entertainment promotes with regard to the animal world. In doing this, my discussion begins with a general review of what we know about the early English bloodsports and their relation to the theater, and proceeds from there to a more detailed analysis of a less lurid and popular subject: the role played by animals on the early modern English public stage itself. This analysis inevitably centers upon notions of theatrical imitation, for it is in terms of their mimetic ability—or disability—that animals are often presented to early modern audiences. Indeed there is a widespread tendency, among early modern English proponents of animal entertainment, to legitimize the entertainment by attributing mimetic and therefore didactic qualities to the entertainers themselves. Ironically, the idioms of anthropomorphism thus come to license a particularly nasty sort of exploitation of animals. Yet when it comes to the early English public stage, we shall see that prevailing attitudes toward animals and their ability to perform run in a contrary direction, and that in the rare cases in which dramatists like Jonson and Shakespeare bring animals onstage, they present the beasts as exempt from the governing logic of theatrical imitation. To this extent—and again, perhaps, ironically—the early theater emerges as a bastion of absolute anthropocentrism, eliding children to the category of adulthood and exempting the bestial from theatrical activity *tout court*. This exemption, in turn, I take as central to early modern constructions of the animal world: an exemption not from the baseline ability to mimic human behavior or human language (which animals obviously do all the time), but an exemption, instead, from the broad patterns of expectation and obligation within which such mimicry takes on social meaning.

2. PARIS GARDEN, ETC.

I have claimed that animal entertainments were generally disparaged by Tudor and early Stuart intellectuals, and I would like to start my discussion of these entertainments with three cases in point. The first, and earliest, of these appears among the epigrams of Sir John Davies (1594), where Davies satirizes a law student with a taste for low entertainment:

> Publius [a] student at the Common-law,
> Oft leaves his Bookes, and for his recreation,
> To Paris-garden doth himselfe withdrawe;
> Where he is rauisht with such delectation,
> As downe among the beares and dogges he goes;
> Where, whilst he skipping cries "to head to head,"
> His satten doublet and his veluet hose
> Are all with spittle from aboue be-spread:
> When he is like his father's countrey Hall,
> Stinking with dogges and muted all with haukes;
> And rightly too on him this filth doth fall,
> Which for such filthy sports his bookes forsakes;
> Leaving old Ployden, Dyer, Brooke alone,
> To see old Harry Hunkes and Sacarson. ("In Publium")

The contempt here manifests itself in a variety of ways worth noting. First, there is Publius's status as a student of law; for whatever reason, literary references to bear-baiting repeatedly figure the sport in relation to legal activity, and this association may be worth considering in its own right. (Davies himself might still have been a law student when he wrote this epigram.) Second, the epigram is structured around a prominent metamorphic and devolutionary theme, whereby Publius, abandoning the inns of court for Paris Garden, adopts in the process the mannerisms of the bear-garden's most prominent denizens. "As down among the bears and dogs he goes" (this description itself suggesting both moral and physical descent), he enters into a mimetic relation that takes bears and dogs as its model; his doublet and hose, flecked with spittle and dung ("muted" means "beshitten"), attest to his transformation from man to beast. And third, this transformation is also figured through another sort of mimesis entirely: not that of physical gesture but of literary expression. Thus Davies's final couplet frames Publius's degeneration as an exchange of authority figures; Publius abandons the seminal figures of the common law—Plowden, Dyer, and so on—for their counterparts in the bear-ring, the most famous fighting bears of their day, Harry Hunks and Sackerson. Yet this exchange is not just of authority figures but of relations to authority as well, for Plowden, Dyer, and Brooke were never available to Publius *in propria persona*. Their names, unlike those of Harry Hunks and Sackerson, function metonymically to denominate the texts that bear (so to speak) their identity. In short, Publius has not just traded one set of heroes for another; he has traded a model of articulate imitation for a model of inarticulate imitation, and in so doing he has betrayed his own nature.

A rather similar moment of satire occurs in Shakespeare's *Merry Wives of Windsor* (ca. 1597–1601), where the nitwit Slender woos Anne Page by extolling his own character as an aficionado of bear-baiting:

> *Slen.* Why do your dogs bark so? be there bears i' th' town?
> *Anne.* I think there are, sir, I heard them talk'd of.
> *Slen.* I love the sport well, but I shall as soon quarrel at it as any man in England. You are afraid if you see the bear loose, are you not?
> *Anne.* Ay indeed, sir.
> *Slen.* That's meat and drink to me, now. I have seen Sackerson loose twenty times, and have taken him by the chain; but (I warrant you) the women have so cried and shriek'd at it, that it pass'd. But women, indeed, cannot abide 'em, they are very ill-favor'd rough things. (1.1.286–299)

Slender, like Publius before him, is associated with the legal profession; his uncle, Justice Shallow, accompanies him virtually every time he appears onstage, and even goes so far as to speak for him when he has further occasion for courtship (3.4.36–53). Like Publius again, Slender finds himself torn between competing pastimes—in this case courtship and bear-baiting—and Slender, like Publius, clearly prefers the latter. Moreover, in Slender's case as in that of Publius, this preference signals a degeneracy of mind that renders him unworthy of human company. Elsewhere, to be sure, Shakespeare alludes to bear-baiting in more or less neutral terms (see, e.g., the famous metaphors in *Macbeth* 5.7.1–2 and *King Lear* 3.7.53–54),[2] but nowhere else in his work does he use the sport as an extended element of character construction, and in Slender's case the fondness for bear-baiting is clearly symptomatic of congenital idiocy. It is only one final irony that Slender should fail to understand this fact, and should seek to impress Anne with his passion for the sport. As he parades his familiarity with bears and dogs, he also reveals his hopeless incompetence as a conversationalist. Like Publius again, he has chosen inarticulate beasts over articulate people, and this choice has rendered him unequal to the demands of conjugal society.

The induction to Ben Jonson's *Bartholomew Fair* (1614), in turn, expresses a pointed aversion to bear-baiting as a consequence of the circumstances in which the play itself was originally produced. First acted at the Hope Theater on Bankside, *Bartholomew Fair* was written for a venue intentionally designed to host both plays and bear-baitings on alternate days. This architectural peculiarity of the Hope seems to have stung Jonson, for he draws attention to it in the prefatory stage business with which his comedy (in standard Jonsonian fashion) opens. There the audience is confronted with three members of the acting company's backstage crew—the Stage-Keeper, Book-Holder (or prompter), and Scrivener (or company scribe)—who between them debate the merits of the upcoming play. Of the three, the Stage-Keeper takes Jonson to task for setting his play in a fairground without featuring all of the customary fairground activities, including the spectacle of performing animals: "Hee has ne'er . . . a Iugler with a wel-educated Ape to come ouer the chaine, for the *King of England,* and backe againe for the *Prince,* and sit still on his arse for the *Pope,* and the *King of Spaine!*" (Induction 13–20). Yet the Book-Holder counters this criticism on the author's behalf by associating the Stage-Keeper with even commoner, and less savory, kinds of animal fun:

Booke. What's the business?

Sta. Nothing, but the vnderstanding Gentlemen o' the ground here, ask'd my iudgement.

Booke. Your iudgement, Rascall? for what? sweeping the *Stage?* or gathering vp the broken Apples for the beares within? Away Rogue, it's come to a fine degree in these *spectacles* when such a youth as you pretend to a iudgement. (Induction 48–54)

Thus the induction to *Bartholomew Fair* figures the relation between Jonson and his detractors through the opposition of Book-Holder to Stage-Keeper, who in turn figure their difference from one another through their attitude toward animal entertainments. Note also that this opposition once more engages issues of literacy and linguistic mimesis. The author's representative in this little critical debate is, after all, the *Book*-Holder, and he impugns the Stage-Keeper's "iudgement" by associating him with inarticulate, unscripted pastimes such as bear-baiting, in contradistinction to the literate "spectacles" produced by the author. Finally, then, the dispute between Stage-Keeper and Book-Holder is resolved by the company Scrivener, who composes a legal contract to settle their differences, and one of the clauses of this agreement speaks straight to the Stage-Keeper's claim that Jonson has not accurately copied the atmosphere of the fairground: "And though the *Fayre* be not kept in the same Region, that some here, perhaps, would haue it, yet thinke, that therein the *Author* hath obseru'd a speciall *Decorum,* the place being as durty as *Smithfield,* and as stinking euery whit" (Induction.156–160). With this the Scrivener's contract concludes, returning us to the issue with which the Stage-Keeper's attack upon Jonson had begun, and apparently sealing a compromise between Stage-Keeper and Book-Holder. If the audience will tolerate a certain deviation from the precise elements of the fairground, the author will endeavor to keep the general character of the fair intact, and to this end he will rely upon the stench and filth of the bear-garden. Thus the Scrivener's contract—yet another allusion to bear-baiting within a legal context—simultaneously claims credit to the author for the unseemliness of his play's venue, and yet also distances the author from that venue, which emerges as the defining locale of his unlettered detractors.

There is no shortage of other, similarly disparaging references to animal-baiting in early modern letters. John Tatham, in the Prologue to *Fancies Theater* "spoken upon removing of the late Fortune Players to the Bull" (1640), complains that by expelling the actors the Fortune

has t'ane
A course to banish Modesty, and retaine
More dinn, and *incivility* than hath been
Known in the *Bearwards Court,* the *Beargarden.* (Prologue
    7–10)

John Weever's epigram "In Caluum" (1599; see *Epigrammes* 1911)
jocularly suggests that Calvus, whose charactonymic baldness is actually a product of syphilis, "lost his haire, / By *Paris* garden bayting a
white beare" (1–2), and while the joke here is none too obvious, it is
clearly no compliment to either Calvus or bear-baiting. And of course
there are numerous Puritans who, like Philip Stubbes, denounce the
sport as a "filthie, stinkyng, and ... perilous exercise ..., [not]
meete for any Christian" (1583, sig. Q5v).[3] Even John Taylor the
Water-Poet, a staunch admirer of bloodsports and a virulent anti-
Puritan, adopts an ironic tone toward the bears, who, he says, "do
please the hearing and the sight, / And sure their sent will any man
invite" (*Bull, Beare, and Horse,* sig. D5v). On the whole, the animals
appear to have struck a nerve with early modern audiences; bear-baiting is a guilty pleasure, eliciting strong reactions both of condemnation and delight, and marking individuals indelibly through the
particular reaction they evince. As a rule, the condemnation seems to
have been associated with professionals, literary intellectuals, and religious activists, while the delight was more typical of apprentices, laborers, and country dwellers.

   As for the proponents of bloodsport, they do not present a terri-
bly consistent or coordinated defense of the activity, but some of
what they say does speak directly to the attitudes expressed above. In
particular, where Davies, Shakespeare, Jonson, and others depict
bear-baiting as a degrading activity whose inarticulacy and brutish-
ness compromise human standards of reason and dignity, the de-
fenders of blood pastimes reply that these pastimes are in fact a
rational didactic instrument. Thus, for instance, George Wilson's
Commendation of Cockes, and Cock-fighting (1607), records how

   Themistocles, that worthy valiant and time-eternized Conqueror ...
   commanded that two Cockes of the kind, should bee brought unto
   him, and be set downe to fight before him, in the open view of all his
   valiant souldiers ... : which bloody battell was no sooner ended, but
   Themistocles commanding silence, began this Oration. . . . As your Director I advise you, as your Captaine I counsell you, and as your friend
   & fellow souldier I instantly exhort you, to call to mind the invincible
   courage of these unreasonable creatures. . . . Let not us I say, shew

more cowardize and fainthearted timorousnesse, then these silly
fowles. (sig. B1v-B2v)

John Taylor says much the same thing of bull- and bear-baiting:

> As for the Game I boldly dare relate,
> 'Tis not for Boys, or fooles effeminate,
> For whoso'ere comes thither, most and least,
> May see and learne some courage from a Beast. (*Bull, Beare,*
>   *and Horse,* sig. D7r)

And when Richard Laneham concludes his well-known account of
the bear-baiting staged for Queen Elizabeth at Kenilworth Castle in
1575 by Robert Dudley, he refers to the pleasure of the entertainment in a way that once again suggests respect and appreciation of
the animals' valor:

> It was a sport very pleazaunt of theez beastz; to see the Bear with his
> pink nyez lering after hiz enmiez approch, the nimblness and wayt of
> the Dog to take avauntage, and the fors and experiens of the Bear agayn
> to avoyd the assauts: If he wear bitten in one place, hoow he woold
> pynch in an oother to get free: that if he wear taken onez, then what
> shyft, with byting, with clawying, with roring, tossing and tumbling, he
> woold work to wynd himself from them: and when he was lose, to
> shake his ears twyse or thryse with the blud and the slaver aboout his
> fiznamy, was a matter of goodly releef. (in Nichols 1788, 1:16)

For bloodsport enthusiasts like Wilson, Taylor, and Laneham, the
events seem to have offered instruction by example, demonstrating
and communicating to onlookers the true character of physical
courage.

In other words, for such enthusiasts bloodsport is an exceptionally
earnest sort of morality play, instructing its auditors in virtue through
a performance that requires supreme commitment and sacrifice from
its principals. Laneham thus devotes most of his description of bear-
baiting to the development of an elaborate juridical metaphor
whereby dogs and bears become plaintiffs and defendants in a
toughly debated lawsuit:

> Well, Syr, the Bearz wear brought foorth intoo the court, the Dogs set
> too them, too argu the points even face to face; they had learned
> Coounsel also a both parts. . . . If the Dog in pleadyng would pluck
> the Bear by the throt, the Bear with travers woould claw him again by

the scalp; confess and a list, but avoyd a coold not that waz bound to the bar. (in Nichols 1788, 1:15–16)

To appreciate this description as an exercise in courtroom drama, we scarcely need recall that acting was regarded as a species of oratory during the Renaissance (Orgel 1975, 16–17). And George Wilson, for his part, makes the theatrical parallel explicit in his account of a fighting-cock named after one of Elizabethan England's most famous comic actors:

> No longer agoe, than the 4 day of May 1602, at a Cock-fighting in the Citie of Norwich aforesayd, a cocke called *Tarleton* (who was so intit-uled, because he alwayes came to the fight like a Drummer, making a thundering noyse with his winges) which Cocke having there fought may [sic] battels, with mightie and fierce Adversaries: and being both wearied with long fighting, and also verie hardly matched, at the length he had his eyes both of them beaten out of his head, his spurres broken off, and his bill brused, and rigorously rent from off his face, so that there remained no hope of him, but that he should be instantly killed, . . . yet behold a rare and miraculous wonder, a most admirable seldome or never seene accident; for all this he fought still most stoutly with his Adversary, and would never shrinke from him, or give him over, until he had . . . most couragiously slaine him. Oh inestimable stoutnesse! (sig. D4r-v)

Here the cock's juxtaposition to theatrical entertainment is signaled not only by its name (this in turn a product of the similarity between the drumming of its wings and that associated with the jigs of the co-median Tarleton), but also by the sheer character of the cock's per-formance as an edifying and delightful spectacle of courage. Such testimony suggests that the spatial imbrication of acting and blood-sports—the placement of bear-baiting arenas in theaters and of act-ing companies in cockpits—exerted a significant influence upon the way in which these juxtaposed pastimes, and their performers, could be understood.

In short, the physical contiguity and conceptual equivalency of theaters and animal arenas threatens to produce what René Girard has called a "crisis of distinctions" (1957, 52), a crisis rendered all the more severe because, in extra-occupational ways, there are dis-tinctions aplenty between actors and animals. For playwrights like Ben Jonson, who was famously interested in defining the theater as a bastion of legitimate high culture founded upon the classical tra-dition, the bulls, bears, and horses of Paris Garden could obviously be a source of embarrassment. Yet Jonson's appeal to high-cultural antiquity was complicated by the fact that there was also a long-standing tradition that associated the English theater with animal entertainments. In his *Survey of London* (1598), John Stow thus relates the two activities by matter-of-fact juxtaposition: "Of late times . . . have been vsed Comedies, Tragedies, Enterludes, and Histories, both true and fained: for the acting whereof, certaine publike places have been erected. Also Cockes of the game are yet cherished by divers men for their pleasure" (sig. H2v). Likewise, bull- and bear-baiting were venerable pastimes, described as early as 1174 in William Fitzstephen's *Descriptio Londinae* (qtd. in Lee 1916, 435–436), and associated with the London theaters by the German traveler Paul Hentzner in 1598:

> Further outside London there are several theaters, in which English actors perform comedies and tragedies almost every day, to a great assembly of people. . . . There is also moreover another place having the form of a theater, appointed for the exercise of bulls and bears, which, being chained by the hinder part, are wonderfully attacked by those large English hunting-dogs that they call mastiffs in the vernacular.

> [Sunt porro Londini extra Urbem *Theatra* aliquot, in quibus Histriones Angli Comoedias & Tragoedias singulis fere diebus, in magna hominum frequentia agunt. . . . Est & alius postea *locus* Theatri quoq[ue] formam habens, *Ursorum et Taurorum venationibus destinatus,* qui a postica parte alligati a magnis illis canibus & molossis Anglicis, quos lingua verbacula Dockem appellant, mire exagitantur. (sig. R3v)]

And this casual association of bloodsport with acting continues, of course, even beyond the closing of the theaters, as evidenced by Edmund Gayton's *Pleasant Notes Upon Don Quixote* (1654):

> I have known upon one of the *Festivals* . . . where the Players have been, notwithstanding their bills to the contrary, to act what a major part of the company had a mind to. . . . And unless this were done, and the popular humour satisfied, . . . the Benches, the tiles, the laths, the stones, Oranges, Apples, Nuts, flew about most liberally. . . . Nothing but noise and tumult fills the house, until a cogg take 'um, and then to the Bawdy houses, and reforme them; and instantly to the Banks side, where the poor Beares must conclude the riot, and fight twenty dogs at a time. (qtd. in Bentley 1941, 2:691)

But none of this is news: the juxtaposition—both spatial and conceptual—of bear-garden to theater is perhaps the most obvious peculiarity of early modern English bloodsport. I review it here not to urge it as a novelty, but to note its consequences for the issue of theatrical legitimacy and, beyond that, for the theater's status with regard to the opposition between nature and culture. As I have already noted, early English dramatists (as well as nondramatic authors) took some pains to distance themselves from the very animal entertainments with which they shared the Bankside. As for the theater companies in general, they seem to have behaved likewise, granting as little space and time as possible to their animal colleagues:

> A Privy Council letter of 1591 [insists that] the players . . . lie idle upon Thursdays and leave that day free for bear-baitings and similar pastimes, which were "always accustomed and practized upon it." . . . Nor does it seem that the attempt to give a special protection to the royal "game" permanently maintained itself. The Admiral's Men, despite Edward Alleyn's interest in the Bear Garden [secured by him and his father-in-law Philip Henslowe in 1594], certainly did not yield the Thursdays from 1594 to 1597, and when about 1614 Henslowe and Jacob Meade had occasion to combine playing and baiting in the Hope, they had to insert special stipulations in their agreements with the actors, in order to secure one day a fortnight for the bears. (Chambers 1923, 1:316)

Of course, this grudging behavior on the part of the players is a function of economic interest as much as of principle. But even so, economic interest and principle seem to coalesce in the theatrical opposition to bear-baiting. One expects to hear antitheatrical Puritans condemn the bears; one is perhaps a bit more surprised to encounter similar intolerance among dramatists and actors. Yet there it is, and the principle of it reappears when the dramatists and actors work with animals onstage. Don't mistake these animals for actors, the playwrights seem to be saying. Don't mistake their actions for acting.

3. ANIMALS ON PARADE

Ben Jonson's *Every Man Out of His Humour* (1599) thus takes pains to stage an animal performance that is rendered most conspicuous by its lack of performativity. *Every Man Out* is a great beached whale of a play, as long as a short novel, practically devoid of plot action, and instead replete with a bewilderingly large cast of characters whose every other line is an Elizabethan in-joke. Postmodern readers—even those with an interest in early modern literature—can find the play both tedious and baffling. Amidst its general welter of inactivity, the character of Puntarvolo, wandering aimlessly through his scenes accompanied everywhere by his dog, typifies the work's character-grounded, context-specific comedy. He is a particularly evanescent and refined sort of joke.

In this respect Puntarvolo participates in his play's overall dramatic strategy, which is grounded upon the exposure of affectation rather than the achievement of goals. Or more precisely, the goal that *Every Man Out* seeks to achieve *is* the exposure of affectation; within Jonson's comedy, this deflation holds the climactic place reserved for weddings in Shakespearean romantic comedy and family reunions in Fletcherian romance. Thus, with very few exceptions, the characters of *Every Man Out* are distinguished by some form or other of social pretence—a particular "humor" for self-promotion and self-dramatization—that is displayed to the top of its bent and then violently, humiliatingly deflated. As for the kinds of pretence in question, they are of course inevitably age- and place-specific. The companions Clove and Orange adopt a ridiculous Latinate vocabulary to convince others of their literary attainments. The wretched farmer Sordido hoards his grain against poor harvests so as to sell dear and catapult his family into gentility by sending his son to the Inns of Court. The son, Fungoso, neglects his studies and squanders his father's money on rich apparel, whereby he seeks to imitate the magnificence of the courtier Fastidius Brisk. Brisk, for his part, squanders his estate on clothing so as to deflect attention from his miserable poverty of wit. Sordido's brother Sogliardo, another country clown, comes to the city with money so as to learn how to be a gentleman, and the con man Shift is more than happy to accept Sordido's cash in return for the requisite lessons in how to strut, swear, and take tobacco. The citizen's wife Fallace demonstrates her quality by heaping scorn upon her husband and doting instead upon the vacuous courtier Brisk, who in turn dotes upon the court lady Saviolina, who in turn heaps scorn upon everyone. And so forth.

Amidst this parade of affectation, the character of Puntarvolo can be distinguished by three attributes. First, he is fond of acting out tableaux in which he presents himself to his own wife as a knight-errant in need of shelter, craves admission to her imagined castle, and courts her "as shee were a stranger neuer encounter'd before" (2.1.139–140). Second, he is addicted to the Elizabethan practice of dealing upon returns: that is, of traveling abroad while lending sums of money to speculators at home, who are pledged to refund the money with interest upon his safe return. And third, he is inordinately attached to his household animals, and foremost among them to his dog. These three qualities, while seemingly disparate (the fantasy of knight-errantry, for instance, is illustrated in Act 2 of Jonson's comedy and then dropped entirely for the rest of the play), in fact all display roughly the same tendency to a particular—and particularly ludicrous—sort of self-promotion, a self-promotion grounded upon the shifting significance of travel in early modern English society.

The game of knight-errantry offers the simplest case in point, and therefore Jonson is right to use it as an introductory device, thus sketching in Puntarvolo's character before allowing it scope for more excessive and improbable behavior. In effect, this game seeks to render the humdrum exotic by assigning to it the trappings of courtly romance. When Puntarvolo presents himself (to his wife) as "a poore knight errant . . . that hunting in the adjacent forrest, was by aduenture in the pursuit of a hart, brought to this place; which hart . . . escaped by enchantment" (2.3.47–50), he positions himself unwittingly as an English Don Quixote, investing ordinary people and places with a ridiculously inflated significance drawn from a past that never was, but that figures mythically as an emblem of Puntarvolo's own aspirations. It is an additional irony that in the very same passage, Puntarvolo gestures toward one of the most tired and predictable of Petrarchan motifs: the heart as hart, escaping from the hapless lover as in Petrarch's *Rime* 190 and innumerable imitations.[4] While Puntarvolo strives to render the quotidian exotic, his formulations of the exotic are themselves mired in banality. The aura of silliness that surrounds such antics might find a partial postmodern counterpart in the behavior of *Star Trek* enthusiasts such as those depicted in the recent documentary film "Trekkies"—individuals so committed to an anachronistic fiction that they impose the forms of that fiction upon their relations with the immediate world. However, in the case of Puntarvolo the fiction in question is not just silly; in Jonson's play it becomes positively harmful, for it involves an element of social masquerade—a tendency to tamper with accepted social standards and discriminations—that one cannot reproduce at present by wearing a Starfleet uniform in public.

This element of social transgression in Puntarvolo's fantasy, in turn, becomes clearer if we think of errantry—that is, travel—as a marker of personal distinction. The typical wanderings of chivalric romance, on one hand, serve as both a test of personal mettle and a confirmation of the wanderer's nobility of purpose; such wandering exposes the knight-errant to solitude, difficulty, and peril in service of some higher end commensurate with the notion of chivalric honor. In 1599, on the other hand, travel was becoming increasingly meaningful in a variety of other capacities: as an exploratory and/or colonial venture presenting great risks and equally great possibilities of reward; as a profitable commercial enterprise; as a vehicle for the entertainment and education of a privileged few; and as what we might best call a publicity gimmick of sorts. These separate forms of early modern travel, in turn, were closely and even inextricably intertwined. Exploratory and colonial travel, for instance, is well illustrated in the heroic pages of Richard Hakluyt and Samuel Purchas, yet most Renaissance exploration, in turn, was driven by the desire to establish regular and convenient trade routes for purposes of commercial travel. (Late in 1599, the year of *Every Man Out*'s original performance, the English Company and Fellowship of Merchant Adventurers for the Discovery of Unknown Lands was preparing the first of its naval forays into Asia, forays that would lead in turn to the foundation of the British East India Company in 1657.)[5] As for leisure and educational travel, these obviously become more feasible as commercial bonds between nations are regularized to enable the transfer of bills of credit, the reliable exchange of currency, and other related services that had been significantly improved in Europe during the sixteenth century.[6] (Thus the idea of the Grand Tour was growing popular in the late 1500s—the young John Milton would embark upon one in 1638—and Jonson himself would spend 1612 and 1613 in France as tutor to the son of Sir Walter Raleigh.) In such cases a high semiotic register that describes travel as a noble or heroic or privileged pursuit obviously coexists with a lower discursive register in which travel is conjoined with merchandising and profit and bourgeois culture. But with the institution of travel as a publicity mechanism, this intermingling of discourses achieves a new intensity, and it seems to be precisely this sort of self-promotional travel, with its concomitant intermixture of social vocabularies, that Puntarvolo exists to caricature.

There is, for instance, his fondness for dealing upon returns. This popular Elizabethan practice seems to have combined some of the attractions of gambling (the traveler bets that he can make it back home in the prescribed time and manner necessary to collect his investment) with those of itinerant self-advertising. This latter practice, in turn, had begun to achieve a fair level of visibility in late Elizabethan England, perhaps as a partial result of the popular excitement generated by bands of wandering players, minstrels, and the like and, far less regularly, by royal progresses and similar noble recreations.[7] In any case, in 1600 the comedian Will Kemp made such self-promotion immortal by laying out money three to one and leaving the Lord Chamberlain's Men to dance a morris from London to Norwich, where he hung up his shoes "in the Guild-hall . . . , equally deuided, nailde on the wall" (sig. D1r-v); in the very same year, as Jonson readied *Every Man Out* for the printer, he apparently inserted an allusion to this stunt where the character Carlo Buffone wishes godspeed to Puntarvolo by saying "Would I had one of *Kemps* shoes to throw after you" (4.8.145–146).[8] The joke here only becomes apparent when we grasp that, by dealing upon returns, Puntarvolo has made a public spectacle of himself akin to that created by Kemp in his itinerant morris, and that the railer Carlo Buffone is exploiting this fact for dramatic irony. For Buffone bestows his blessing upon Puntarvolo, not—as one might expect—when the latter is about to embark upon a lengthy voyage but when he is hastening by boat from London to Whitehall in order to witness a practical joke to be played upon the lady Saviolina. For all his talk about travel to exotic lands (and he is constantly talking about it), this is as far abroad as Puntarvolo ever gets.

Later in his career, Jonson himself becomes deeply and rather ambivalently involved in various self-promotional travel schemes. He contributes prefatory prose and verse to Thomas Coryate's *Crudities* (1611), a massive account of Coryate's picaresque tour of France, Italy, and Germany in 1608, published with copious mock-heroic front matter as a kind of coterie joke. When Coryate then sets out on another journey, this time to India, he includes Jonson among the gentlemen to whom he addresses his *Greeting from the Court of the Great Mogul* (1616; sig. G3r), a lengthy open letter that makes its way into print as a means of keeping its author visible in London while pursuing his oddball journey. In 1618 to 1619 Jonson himself takes to the road in a much-publicized walking tour to Scotland and back, a tour that enables him to leave the court at Whitehall during a delicate time in his career and to boost his authorial stock in the process.[9] And, apparently to the poet's annoyance, he promptly discovers that this walking tour, routed up the east coast of Britain, has spawned an imitation; in the same year, John Taylor the Water Poet travels north along the west coast and writes an account of his own journey in verse and prose.

Taylor in fact presents an excellent instance both of the popularity of such travel in early modern England and of the plebeian associations to which it could be subject. A former Thames ferryman with a flair for impromptu versifying, Taylor left his original trade to set up as a popular poet, pamphleteer, and—for want of a better term—performance artist. He did much to make a spectacle of himself, for instance by challenging other poets to extemporaneous

rhyming contests and by contributing, late in his career, to the virulent anti-Puritan satire of the Caroline period; however, one of his
most popular sorts of undertaking—exemplified by the walking
tour to Scotland—involved the announcement of a journey, always
idiosyncratic, of which he promised, upon its completion, to compose a written account. He solicited subscriptions for the travel-
ogue, thereby assuring his work of a paying audience, and his travel
in turn widened his sphere of acquaintance while presenting him as
a curiosity to an audience beyond that of London itself. In the case
of his *Penniless Pilgrimage* to Scotland, Taylor had undertaken not
only to walk to Scotland and back, but to do so "not carrying any
Money to or fro, neither Begging, Borrowing, or Asking Meate,
Drinke or Lodging" (1619; see *Works of John Taylor* 1967, sig.
M1v). Taylor brought his own distinctive persona to this trip, as to
all of his many others, presenting himself as a bluff, cheerful man of
the people, loyal to his sovereign, ignorant of Latin and proud of it,
possessed of a shrewd working-class wit and lacking in formal education. And this kind of popular, humble conservatism served him
fairly well; Ben Jonson, while in the midst of his own Scottish trip
in the winter of 1619, could thus complain to William Drummond
of Hawthornden that "The King said Sir P. Sidney was no poet neither did he see ever any verses in England to ye Scullors [i.e., Taylor's]" (Drummond 1925–1952, 371–372).

One can perhaps understand the peevishness of this remark if
one considers how much Taylor's career looks like an overdrawn
copy of Jonson's own. Both men had worked at humble occupa-
tions; both were intimately associated with London; both were
drawn to literary pursuits by their native inclination and talent;
both received the praise and favor of King James I; both were ardent supporters of the monarchy and vehement anti-Puritans; and
now, in 1619, both were taking the same trip. Indeed, one of the
crucial points distinguishing the two men—Jonson's ardent neo-
classicism—in a way merely underscored their similarities, for
Jonson's grand literary aspirations always contrasted uneasily with
his modest origins, and Taylor's very existence drew attention to
the latter. Like a sort of bumbling doppelganger, Taylor enacted a
parodic version of Jonson's own self-promotional travel project,
and in the process he made that project look thoroughly inappropriate for a canonized representative of high literary culture. Small
marvel, then, that Taylor begins his *Penniless Pilgrimage* by insist-
ing that he did not "*undergoe this proiect, either in malice, or mock-*

age of Master Benjamin Ionson" (sig. M1r). One may wonder whether this is the declaration of a fool or a knave, or both; in any case, it simply aggravates Jonson's potential embarrassment by pointing out that there is indeed cause for embarrassment.

The character of Puntarvolo in *Every Man Out*, in turn, demonstrates just how deep-seated that cause for embarrassment could actually be. For Puntarvolo's interest in self-promotional travel predates Taylor's by some two decades, and Taylor's (as we have seen) parodies Jonson's own. The unfortunate result of this imitative sequence is that the older Jonson, on his Scottish journey, can look dangerously like a caricature of one of his own satirical characterizations. Of course, this aspect of matters is not yet visible in 1599, when *Every Man Out* is first being performed; but later developments nonetheless underscore the particular kind of social condemnation to which Jonson exposes Puntarvolo, for his is a character simultaneously invested in the most grandiose of travel fictions drawn from courtly romance and in the cheesiest of popular self-promotional gimmicks. And finally, this strange combination of qualities— this concurrent fondness for knight-errantry and buffoonery—also helps to explain Puntarvolo's fondness for his dog.

On one hand, the connection of dogs with knight-errantry derives from their identity as hunting animals. When Puntarvolo first appears onstage, he is fresh from hunting and the first thing he does is to make provision for his hounds, reserving his favorite as a personal companion: "Forrester, giue winde to thy horne. . . . Depart, leaue the dogge, and take with thee what thou hast deseru'd" (2.2.1–4). The growing popularity of hunting dogs in Elizabethan and Jacobean England—like their association with the gentle social ranks— is well attested in the literature of the day. As Keith Thomas has nicely put it, "Then, as now, the passion for unnecessary dogs started with the royal family" (102); thus, when presented during a visit to Cambridge with a copy of John Caius's *De Antiquitate Cantabridgiae*, James I could reportedly complain, "What shall I do with this book? Give me rather Dr. Caius's *De Canibus*" (Fuller 1952, 421). For a character like Puntarvolo, with pretensions to courtliness, gentility, and knight-errantry, the dog might seem an essential accoutrement. Yet it is also increasingly a bourgeois accessory; to quote from Thomas again, "Pet-keeping had been fashionable among the well-to-do in the Middle Ages. . . . But it was in the sixteenth and seventeenth centuries that pets seemed to have really established themselves as a normal feature of the middle-class household" (110).

The vast majority of those pets, of course, were dogs, and to this extent Puntarvolo's own animal companion reflects a threatened degradation of the markers of rank and privilege in Elizabethan society. This is a degradation to which Puntarvolo also contributes, as we have seen, when he encourages a confusion of the practices of courtly and self-promotional travel.

Again, Puntarvolo's dog is not only confusing in terms of the social significance he confers upon his owner; the dog's own purpose in life is hard to identify. On one hand, he appears to be a hunting dog, as I have noted. Thus Fastidius Brisk, introducing Puntarvolo via the eternal hunting triangle of man, hound, and horse, can observe that he "has dialogues, and discourses betweene his horse, himselfe, and his dogge" (2.1.137–138); and Puntarvolo himself appears shortly thereafter, fresh from his horse, ushered in by "*A cry of hounds*" (2.1.172 s.d.), in the company of his favorite dog. But thenceforth the dog's status as a hunting animal is little in evidence. On the contrary, he seems to be a confused kind of lapdog; Puntarvolo carries him everywhere, even to court, and when it becomes clear that he cannot convey the beast into the presence-chamber, he fusses over him ludicrously: "But stay, I take thought how to bestow my dogge, he is no competent attendant for the presence" (5.1.3–5); and again, to an unfortunate groom, "My honest friend, may I commit the tuition of this dogge to thy prudent care?" (5.1.17–19); and a few lines later, explaining why he has not made even greater trouble over the animal, "There were no policie in that: that were to let [the groom] know the value of the gemme he holds, and so, to tempt fraile nature against her disposition" (5.1.26–28); and so on. It may not be accidental that in this last passage Puntarvolo refers to his dog as a "gemme"; when, in *Two Gentlemen of Verona* (ca. 1594), Proteus seeks to bestow a lapdog upon Sylvia as a token of his love, he calls the beast his "little jewel" (4.4.47), and such terms of endearment seem more appropriate to the household pet than to the hunting animal. Coming from Puntarvolo, such a mode of expression further underscores the confusion fundamental to his character, which apparently cannot distinguish between knight-errantry and the traveling sideshow, or between hunting hound and lapdog.

These two parallel forms of confusion, in turn, are conflated by the precise terms of Puntarvolo's self-promotional travel scheme. As he originally conceives it, this scheme is to "put forth some fiue thousand pound, to be paid me, fiue for one, vpon the returne of my selfe, my wife, and my dog, from the *Turkes* court in *Constan-*

tinople. If all, or either of vs miscarry in the iourney, 'tis gone: if we be successefull, why, there will be fiue and twenty thousand pound" (2.3.245–250). (Later, when Puntarvolo's wife decides not to undertake the journey, he replaces her with his cat.) These terms, obviously designed to draw attention to the voyage, don't simply juxtapose Puntarvolo's confusion about animals with his confusion about travel. They also invert one of the principal functions of exploratory travel in the sixteenth and seventeenth centuries: the documentation and acquisition of exotic fauna. The development and maintenance of menageries had become something of a princely mania in the early years of Renaissance exploration, a mania driven by the explorers themselves as they returned to port laden with gold, silver, silks, spices, botanicals, and strange beasts of every imaginable kind. Attention has been recently drawn, for instance, to the private zoo established by Pope Leo X upon his elevation to the papacy in 1513.[10] This collection was stocked in part by princely gifts, including leopards, parrots, parrakeets, Indian fowl, Indian dogs, a cheetah, an elephant, and a rhinoceros (which actually died while in transport); these gifts, in turn, had come to the Pope's temporal brethren through the efforts of their explorers and had in some cases already formed part of the temporal sovereigns' own menageries. Nor were the English slow to develop their own collections of exotic animals. Beginning in 1604, James I went so far as to vary the original sport of bear-baiting by replacing the bears with lions drawn from his personal pride (Nichols, *James* 1:320; 1:516; 2:307; 2:259). Likewise, James's Secretary of State, Robert Cecil, Earl of Salisbury, was so passionate about his own menagerie that he instructed an English East India fleet in 1607 to "bring . . . some parrots, monkeys, marmasetts, or other strange beasts and fowls that you esteeme rare and delightful" from India for his personal use (qtd. in Giles Milton 146).

In any event, this interest in collecting strange animals could easily intersect with the parallel interest of early ethnography in documenting and collecting strange races. That is the point of Trinculo's wonderment in *The Tempest* upon his discovery of Caliban:

> What have we here? a man or a fish? dead or alive? A fish, he smells like a fish. . . . A strange fish! Were I in England now (as once I was) and had but this fish painted, not a holiday fool there but would give a piece of silver. There would this monster make a man; any strange beast there makes a man. When they will not give a doit to relieve a lame beggar, they will lay out ten to see a dead Indian. (2.2.24–33)

Trinculo's words emphasize the equivalence of the exotic beast and the exotic person—dead fish and dead Indian—as objects of curiosity and collection, display and profit. Nor is it coincidental to this train of association that the very ships to bring back strange animals often brought back strange people as well; the fleet that received Robert Cecil's request for exotic beasts, for instance, returned to port with a very homesick native South African as part of its cargo (Giles Milton 1999, 146–148). For the adventurers and public of early modern England, the animal and human wonders of the world could easily become interchangeable.

For Puntarvolo, busily planning his journey to Istanbul, such associations and equivalencies function as an indictment of personal character. First of all, his journey to exotic lands seeks not to convey riches back to England, but rather to generate wealth at home, out of nothing, as it were. Second, this same journey counterintuitively posits the English man and his domestic animal as objects of display; instead of returning to London with "parrots, monkeys, marmasetts," and so on, Puntarvolo would transport his own humdrum pets to the land of the Turks as a kind of traveling sideshow of Englishness. And in seeking to make this unfortunate spectacle of himself, he also renders English man and English dog equivalent in a way that undermines the ascendancy of (English) culture over (foreign) nature. As the scurrilous railer Carlo Buffone explains to the bumpkin Sogliardo, who wishes to visit a London ordinary to see the "gallants" there, "the fashion is, when any stranger comes in among'st 'hem, they all stand vp and stare at him, as he were some vnknowne beast, brought out of *Affrick:* but that'll bee help't with a good aduenturous face" (3.6.175–179). This passage, of course, speaks to the rudeness of Jonson's fellow Londoners and the simplicity of a rustic character who might view them as the height of fashion; however, it also casts its shadow upon Puntarvolo's grander pretensions to travel. In journeying to the Ottoman court, Puntarvolo, his dog, and the cat who replaces his wife would acquire parallel status as a sort of animals on parade.

Finally, this tendency to degrade people to the status of animals also entails a complementary tendency to promote animals to the status of people, and Puntarvolo's character is distinguished by just such a humor. From our point of view, this may be the most recognizably silly and simultaneously most endearing of Puntarvolo's character traits; in his undiscriminating and unstinting fondness for his dog and other animals, he foreshadows our own sentimental attachment to our pets. But in a social context in which the idea of the house-pet itself is a relative novelty, and in which the very word "pet" has not yet acquired currency as standard English,[11] Puntarvolo's fixation upon his dog becomes an object of contempt and ridicule, a reprehensible failure to differentiate between beasts and people. The other characters in Jonson's comedy make regular fun of Puntarvolo by drawing attention to his emotional bond with his favorite animal. Fastidius Brisk introduces him by noting derisively that he talks to his dog (2.1.137–138); later Brisk mockingly salutes Puntarvolo with the line "You are right well encounter'd, sir, how do's your faire dog?" (3.4.92–93). The con man Shift, who is busy teaching Sogliardo how to smoke a pipe, boasts, "I can make this dogge take as many *whiffes* as I list, and hee shall retaine, or effume them, at my pleasure" (3.6.162–163)—a claim Puntarvolo takes so seriously that he considers Shift a threat to the dog's character. The pretentious Saviolina, hearing that Puntarvolo has brought the dog to court but left his cat at home, exclaims in mock wonderment, "How dare you trust her behind you, sir?," to which Puntarvolo responds, "Troth, madame, shee hath sore eyes, and shee doth keepe her chamber" (5.2.9–12). And so forth.

It is this particular aspect of Puntarvolo's behavior—his tendency to treat animals as if they were people—that the play chooses to discipline most sternly. Thus, in the array of punishments with which Jonson concludes his comedy, he arranges to have Puntarvolo's dog fall into the hands of the splenetic satirist Macilente, who poisons it. Macilente and his fellow railer Carlo Buffone share a joke about "the passionate knight . . . shedding funerall teares ouer his departed dogge" (5.5.16–17); and when Puntarvolo makes his final appearance onstage, these same characters taunt him gleefully:

> CARL. 'Fore god, sir PVNTARVOLO, I am sorry for your heauiness: body a me, a shrewd mischance! why, had you no vnicornes horne, nor bezoars stone about you? ha?
> . . . .
> PVNT. Sir, I would request you, be silent.
> MACI. Nay, to him againe.
> CARL. Take comfort, good knight, if your cat ha' recouered her catarrhe, fear nothing; your dogges mischance may be holpen.
> (5.5.80–5.6.5)

To the late-twentieth-century ear, these lines may exemplify Jonson at his cruelest and most unsympathetic. After all, ours is a society steeped in Puntarvolo's humor, and when dead pets appear on the contemporary stage or screen they are usually an object of horror rather than of fun. But the disciplinary character of Macilente's gesture is clear; it is an effort to reestablish boundaries—between the aristocratic and the base, the marvelous and the banal, the exotic and the mundane, culture and nature—that Puntarvolo violates with almost every breath he draws. Macilente, like the play of which he is part, is deeply opposed to the idea that animals should occupy the same conceptual space as people.

4. THE DOG IS HIMSELF

Few of Shakespeare's works are so generally disparaged as is *The Two Gentlemen of Verona* (ca. 1594). Clifford Leech has summarized the opinions of Shakespeare's early editors by declaring that the play "has been the recipient of indulgence rather than praise" (1969, liii); more recently, Anne Barton's *Riverside* preface to *Two Gentlemen* begins by calling it "the least loved and least regarded of Shakespeare's comedies" (*Riverside Shakespeare* 1997, 177); and more recently still, Harold Bloom has described it as "the weakest of all of Shakespeare's comedies" (1998, 36). I have neither the ability nor the will to reverse this imposing tradition of condemnation; however, I would like to make one modest claim for the play's unsurpassed excellence. For in *Two Gentlemen of Verona,* Shakespeare produced the most perfect dramatic role that he ever composed for a dog. To this extent, the figure of Crab must be ranked alongside such masterpieces of dramatic characterization as Hamlet, Othello, Shylock, Falstaff, Desdemona, and Viola; it is the very best of its kind that Shakespeare ever created.

Crab's success as a theatrical character, in turn, speaks directly to another distinctive feature of *Two Gentlemen of Verona:* It is perhaps the earliest of Shakespeare's surviving plays to manifest the sustained metatheatrical awareness that will become such a dominant motif in the poet's later works. In this regard, *Two Gentlemen* helps to pioneer one of the signature characteristics of Shakespeare's mature style; the play is constantly calling attention, in various ways, to its own status as a thing to be acted. Of course, most of what is acted in *Two Gentlemen* is in one way or another badly done. Indeed, not only is the play itself defective, if considered from the standpoint of its critical reception; it is also *about* the defects of playing. In effect, it is a dramatic failure that dramatizes dramatic failures, and among the failures in question, those of Crab and his hapless owner, the servant Launce, take pride of place.

Much of *Two Gentlemen*'s metadrama is clearly calculated, and calculated to draw attention to the inherent theatricality of the courtship (and friendship) behavior that is the play's principal subject. As Jeffrey Masten has remarked, the language of *Two Gentlemen* "resonates with the gentlemanly conduct books" (1997, 38); from start to finish, the play's characters all woo by the book, and their dialogue tends to deflate this practice, often through the ironic commentary of servants and women. When Proteus promises the departing Valentine, "Upon some book I love I'll pray for thee," Valentine is ready with a derisive response based upon his low opinion of Proteus's literary tastes: "That's on some shallow story of deep love, / How young Leander cross'd the Hellespont" (1.1.21–22). When Valentine then falls in love himself, Speed mocks him for acting like Proteus, who in turn is acting a role made silly by its similarity to a series of undignified real-life referents: "You have learn'd, like Sir Proteus, to wreathe your arms, like a malcontent; to relish a love-song, like a robin-redbreast; to walk alone, like one that had the pestilence; to sigh, like a schoolboy that had lost his ABC" (2.1.18–23). In this sequence of comparisons, Valentine's love becomes an imitation of Proteus's imitation of a delinquent schoolboy who has lost his book. It therefore seems doubly ironic later on when the Duke of Milan, suspicious of Valentine's designs upon his daughter Silvia, draws the young man out by asking him to be his "tutor" in courtship:

> There is a lady in Milano here
> Whom I affect, but she is nice and coy,
> And nought esteems my aged eloquence.
> Now therefore would I have thee to my tutor
> . . . .
> How and which way I may bestow myself
> To be regarded in her sun-bright eye. (3.1.81–88)

But the Duke, whose request in this case is insincere and rightly calculated to betray Valentine's own love intrigue, himself proves no great scholar when it comes to affairs of the heart. Instead he and Thurio, his chosen suitor for Silvia, ingenuously seek courtship advice from Proteus, whose own secret passion for the Duke's daughter leads him to misdirect them in cynical fashion:

> Write till your ink be dry, and with your tears
> Moist it again, and frame some feeling line

> That may discover such integrity. . . .
> . . . .
> After your dire-lamenting elegies,
> Visit by night your lady's chamber-window
> With some sweet consort; to their instruments
> Tune a deploring dump—the night's dead silence
> Will well become such sweet-complaining grievance.
>   (3.2.74–85)

Knowing what he is about, Proteus frames his advice so as to render Thurio doubly obnoxious to Silvia if he follows it. Stalk her, Proteus tells him; hound her by day and night, with letters and with songs; be constantly "complaining." But it is just one more of *Two Gentlemen*'s many ironies that Valentine has already given virtually this same counsel to the Duke in good faith:

> A woman sometimes scorns what best contents her. . . .
> Take no repulse, what ever she doth say;
> For "get you gone," she doth not mean "away!"
> Flatter and praise, commend, extol their graces;
> Though ne'er so black, say they have angels' faces.
> That man that hath a tongue, I say is no man.
> If with his tongue he cannot win a woman. (3.1.93–105)

Through such juxtapositions, *Two Gentleman* presents its courtship behavior as an inept sort of playacting, the rote performance of a bad script that has little relation to the living circumstances within which it is played out. In this respect Shakespeare's characters in *Two Gentlemen* are all too clearly *charactered;* they aspire not to independent life, but rather to insertion within a discourse by Castiglione or Capellanus.

This concern with the literary character of lovemaking, in turn, resurfaces in another one of *Two Gentlemen*'s principal themes: a fascination with literal acts of reading and writing. Lovemaking in this play may be the performance of precomposed scripts, but it is a performance that itself entails the further production of further scripts; as Jonathan Goldberg has observed, "Bearers of the letter, characters themselves and in relation to others . . . are *impressed* with the letter" in Shakespeare's play (79). Thus missives fly thick and fast in *Two Gentlemen of Verona,* always in ways that deal with love and courtship, always in ways that are confused or inaccurate or inept.[12] Proteus sends a love letter to Julia, and it winds up instead in the hands of Julia's maid, Lucetta (1.2.37–38), and then gets torn to pieces (1.2.96). When Julia responds to Proteus with a letter of her own and Proteus's father, Antonio, catches him reading it, Proteus pretends the missive comes from Valentine instead, thus opening the way for Antonio to inform him that he is to be packed off to Milan (1.3.45–71). Silvia enjoins the smitten Valentine to compose a letter on her behalf for the man she adores, and when she then returns the letter to him, Valentine is too stupid to recognize this as a declaration of love (2.1.87–170). The Duke frustrates Valentine's plan to elope with Silvia when he discovers a note in which Valentine has appointed the time for the deed (3.1.140–151). When asked for advice on how to woo a woman, the first thing Proteus recommends is that one write a sonnet (3.2.69–70). Even the clown Launce enumerates the qualities of his beloved in a "love-letter" (3.1.381) that he and his fellow-servant Speed read aloud (3.1.263–381). Surrounded by such events, Julia's transvestite disguise as the page Sebastian acquires a thoroughly preconditioned quality; we may call it the performance of lovemaking (in the pursuit of Proteus) according to a preordained pattern (the traditionally scripted behavior of masculinity) to which it alludes self-consciously in the act of performance:

> At Pentecost,
> When all our pageants of delight were play'd,
> Our youth got me to play the woman's part,
> And I was trimm'd in Madam Julia's gown,
> Which serv'd me as fit, by all men's judgments,
> As if the garment had been made for me. (4.4.158–163)

For Julia/Sebastian, as for virtually every other character in *Two Gentlemen of Verona,* courtship involves acting, which involves reading, which involves writing, which is itself—as Kenneth Burke once famously noted—an act of courtship.[13]

This is the context within which Launce's relationship with his dog Crab acquires its particular metadramatic resonance. Jeffrey Masten has argued that the vocabularies of heteroerotic courtship and homoerotic courtiership shadow one another in this play, so that "male friendship and Petrarchan love . . . speak a remarkably similar language" (39). My point, in turn, is that Launce and Crab parallel various conjunctions of friends and lovers in *Two Gentlemen* while simultaneously frustrating the mutual scripting that makes those other conjunctions possible. Thus the dyad of Launce and Crab seems deliberately constructed to draw attention to the subject of performance, for not only do these characters emphasize the importance of other pairs—paired characters and even, as Patricia Parker has pointed out, linguistic "doublets" (Parker 1987, 69–71)—in the play; they also undercut the very parallelism they embody, for they are most imperfectly joined to the work of which they are a part. In effect, both characters enact a breakdown of theatrical mimesis in the very mechanisms that convey them onstage. In the case of Launce, this breakdown occurs in Act 1, Scene 1, when his master Proteus posts a love letter to Julia. Launce would be the obvious courier for this message, but instead Proteus uses his friend Valentine's servant, Speed, as if Launce didn't exist; then, when Speed does the job in an unsatisfactory way, Proteus complains, "I must go send some better messenger" (1.1.151), again as if he did not have his own candidate ready to hand. Likewise, the conveyance of the letter itself is inconsistent, since Speed claims he gave it to Julia (1.1.94–98), whereas in the next scene we learn that he has actually handed it to Lucetta (1.2.38–40). As for Crab, a similar inconsistency mars his role, too; on one hand, Julia learns that the dog is to become "a present" to Proteus's "lady" Silvia (4.2.78–80); yet two scenes later we discover that Proteus never wanted to send Crab to Silvia at all, and that Launce gave the dog to her only after having lost another dog, a "little jewel" that was actually Proteus's intended present to his lady (4.4.45–61). It is as if Launce and Crab were deliberately constructed to serve as theatrical anomalies: central failures in a play about the failures of playing.

Of course, plot inconsistencies of the sort I have just described are probably not intentional. But if they were not intended, they should have been, for they nicely anticipate the principal function of Launce and Crab within this play. In brief, that function is to create expectations of theatrical mimesis that they then repeatedly, comically frustrate. It has recently been observed that "the stage dog seems to hover uncertainly between the illusory realm of the play, and the audience's world of everyday reality" (Beadle 1994, 21); for his part, Crab seems designed to draw nonstop attention to his failure to fit into the dramatic world within which he finds himself. Thus time and again, Launce and Crab invite the audience to see them in a doubling relation to the play's other characters, and to extract from that doubling a particular message or moral that is commensurate with the play's broader social and ethical investments. Yet every time the audience accepts this invitation it is immediately retracted, for Launce and Crab remind us again and again that in an important way they aren't acting at all. Far from being their comedy's paradigmatic role-players, Launce and Crab serve as a kind of theatrical black hole: a spot in the play where all role-playing stops.

In performing this function, Launce and Crab complement each other well. It is Launce's job to invite the audience to recognize a metadramatic parallel, and it is left to Crab to deflate the expectation thus created; Launce sets the viewers up, and Crab then brings them crashing to the ground. Together, the two characters are given very limited stage exposure; Launce appears in only four scenes in *Two Gentlemen of Verona,* and Crab is with him in only three of those. Yet even in this restricted compass, Launce manages to suggest a wide range of ways in which he and Crab may echo their play's broader thematic concerns. There is, for instance, the famous set speech in which Launce, having lost the little lapdog he was supposed to convey from Proteus to Silvia as a love token, and having substituted Crab for the dog thus lost, describes the resulting mayhem:

> O, 'tis a foul thing when a cur canot keep himself in all companies! . . .
> You shall judge: he thrusts me himself into the company of three or
> four gentleman-like dogs, under the Duke's table. He had not been
> there (bless the mark!) a pissing-while, but all the chamber smelt him.
> "Out with the dog," says one. "What cur is that?" says another. "Whip
> him out," says the third. "Hang him up," say the Duke. (4.4.9–22)

Launce's narrative, like much comic writing before and since, discovers that there is good fun to be had by exploiting the similarities between dogs and their owners, and in this case, the similarity in question is one of social rank. In the company of the Duke and the Duke's dogs, both Launce and Crab are out of their element, a connection perhaps signaled by the redundant accusative "thrusts me himself," and unquestionably brought home by the reference to "gentleman-like dogs." Thus one expects the dog's behavior to reflect upon its master's manners, and certainly Crab's lack of intestinal discretion betrays a concomitant lack of gentility. As Crab farts in company, the audience is encouraged to read this gesture—in the manner of countless Renaissance conduct books—as expressive of the low breeding that the dog shares with its humble master. This parallelism is then seemingly reinforced by the fact that Launce takes Crab's offense upon himself and undergoes punishment for it in place of the dog (4.4.22–29). Yet this very act of substitution, whereby an innocent man voluntarily takes on the sins of a guilty dog, disrupts the relationship the narrative invites us to discern, for if dog and owner truly paralleled one another, their behavior would be of a piece, and it clearly is not. The substitution of Launce for

Crab gains dramatic force from the incommensurability of the figures being interchanged.

Again, when Launce and Crab make their first appearance onstage, they solicit another sort of comparison with other characters in the play, only to frustrate once more the comparison thus provoked. Here the scene is Verona, where Proteus, his servant, and his servant's dog are preparing to leave for Milan. Proteus has just said farewell to his beloved Julia, and the parting has been brief and muted, leading Proteus to exclaim, "Julia, farewell! What, gone without a word? / Ay, so true love should do: it cannot speak" (2.2.16–17). This, then, is immediately followed by Launce's appearance with his dog, in the wake of an equally unsatisfactory leavetaking:

> I have receiv'd my proportion, like the prodigious son, and am going with Sir Proteus to the Imperial's court. I think Crab my dog be the sourest-natur'd dog that lives: my mother weeping, my father wailing, my sister crying, our maid howling, our cat wringing its hands, and all our house in a great perplexity, yet did not this cruel-hearted cur shed one tear. He is a stone, a very pibble-stone, and has no more pity in him than a dog. (2.3.3–11)

Here the play encourages its audience not only to observe a structural parallelism between two juxtaposed scenes of departure, but also to trace correspondences of character between the scenes. And the obvious correspondences to be traced in this case are between Crab and Julia and Launce and Proteus, respectively. Crab is following Launce to Milan, just as Julia will eventually follow Proteus. Crab and Julia both remain silent, refusing the opportunity to participate in predictable displays of emotion. Launce and Proteus, on the other hand, not only participate in those very displays but also express dismay when their partners refuse to follow suit.

As for Crab's role in this scene of lachrymose leavetaking: it gestures toward literary parallelisms that exceed the bounds of the leavetaking scene itself. In the most recent and thorough critical examination of Crab's historical antecedents, Richard Beadle has documented the existence of a lengthy tradition, in medieval and classical literature, of dramatic and nondramatic "dogs which howl or weep for their sufferings" (25; see 21–28). As Beadle argues, Crab "is ultimately descended from the solo mime's performing dog, best known in dramatic tradition from the erotic farce of 'The Weeping Bitch'" (30). However, it is precisely Crab's *refusal* to weep that focuses an audience's attention, which in effect is thus brought to bear

upon Crab's disengagement from the conventions of canine performance and affectivity that his own existence presupposes.

Likewise, anyone who is inclined to read Julia and Crab as parallel characters will be confused by the play's further developments,
particularly as those developments are represented by Proteus's gift
of Crab to Silvia. In structural terms, this gift produces some of the
most artful comic doubling to be found in *Two Gentlemen of
Verona*. Whereas the play has already offered us a plot grounded in
cross-wooing (as Proteus abandons his beloved Julia in order to
pursue Valentine's Silvia) and cross-dressing (as Julia adopts the
persona of Sebastian the page so as to follow Proteus to Milan), it
now gives us a comic instance of what can only be called cross-
petting, as Proteus attempts to send his little lapdog to Silvia as a
gift, only to have it replaced by Crab with disastrous results. Most
immediately, this confusion reinforces the social discriminations
elaborated elsewhere in the play; Crab is no "little jewel" of a lapdog (4.4.47), any more than he is one of the Duke's "gentleman-
like dogs," and once again the contrast between kinds of dogs
encourages a similar contrast between the kinds of people with
whom the dogs are associated. Thus when Launce confesses that,
like his master, he is in love, he frames his confession in terms not
of lapdogs but of a different class of cur entirely:

> I am in love. . . . She hath more qualities than a water-spaniel, which
> is much in a bare Christian. Here is the cate-log of her condition. "*In-
> primis*, She can fetch and carry." Why, a horse can do no more; nay, a
> horse cannot fetch, but only carry, therefore she is better than a jade.
> (3.1.266–277)

To this extent, Crab's misadventures with Silvia seem designed not
to encourage an association of the dog either with her or with Julia,
but rather to draw attention to the extreme inappropriateness of any
such association. Instead, the gift episode implicates Crab in another
pattern of association entirely, one developed at length in an influential essay by Harold Brooks (1963):

> I do not think it extravagant, provided that one is not too serious
> about it, to see reflected in Crab, comically and a little pathetically, the
> transgressor in Proteus. The want of sensibility to old ties and to his
> friend Launce's feelings which Crab is alleged to show at parting from
> home, is ominous as a parallel to Proteus' parting from Julia and im-
> pending reunion with Valentine. As a present for Silvia, Crab resem-
> bles the love that Proteus proffers her. He is a sorry changeling for the

true love gift Proteus meant to bestow. He is unfit for Silvia (perse-
cuting her with most objectionable attentions!), and offensive where
true courtliness should rule. Like Proteus, he gets his friend into trouble. And as Crab is only saved by Launce's quixotic, self-sacrificial af-
fection, so Proteus is only saved by the extremes to which Valentine is
ready to carry his friendship and Julia her love. (99)

Of the numerous doublings and interrelations that scholars have
been tempted to discern between the figure of Crab and the other
characters in *Two Gentlemen,* this is perhaps the most elaborate and
convincing. Yet for that very reason, it risks missing a most important
point about Crab, a point that Shakespeare's play makes whenever
possible: the dog simply isn't acting.

This may seem a rather bald and obvious observation, but it carries with it certain important consequences. First off, the refusal to
act sits oddly at the center of a play in which practically everyone is
performing: reading from scripts, writing new scripts, coaching each
other in wooing techniques, dissembling emotions and affections and
identities, and on and on. Furthermore, it is positively unnerving to
realize that the one card-carrying nonactor in *Two Gentlemen* is also
the focal point for the play's metadramatic parallelisms; Crab shadows the play's other characters as a street-mime shadows an oblivious
passerby, with rich comic results. Yet the shadowing function is emphatically not ascribed to Crab's own mimetic agency. In fact, *Two
Gentlemen* goes out of its way to insist upon the dog's exemption
from the doubling mechanisms intrinsic to language and social display. When Speed asks Launce whether it will be a match between
Proteus and Julia, he responds: "Ask my dog. If he say ay, it will; if
he say no, it will; if he shake his tail and say nothing, it will"
(2.5.35–37)—the point here being, of course, that Crab is so far
from making any answer at all that the answer must be supplied for
him. Elsewhere, this fact frustrates Launce immensely. As he describes his leavetaking in Verona, he concludes, "Now the dog all this
while sheds not a tear, nor speaks a word; but see how I lay the dust
with my tears" (2.3.30–32). And after being whipped from the
Duke's court, he tenders the dog this despairing rebuke: "Did not I
bid thee still mark me, and do as I do? When didst thou see me heave
up my leg and make water against a woman's farthingale? Didst thou
ever see me do such a trick?" (4.4.36–39). Such comments beg for a
response where none will be forthcoming; they insist upon a dialogue
that has never taken place and never will. To this extent, they put
Launce in a position occupied more recently by those critics of *Two*

Gentlemen who would see Crab engaged in comic conversation, elaborating dramatic parallels, parodying the foibles and frustrating the hopes of the other characters in Shakespeare's comedy. In other words, Crab doesn't just make fools of Launce and Julia and Proteus; more importantly, the dog makes fools of the audience.

There are two moments in this play that insist upon this point most vigorously, and they occur in the two long prose set speeches that Launce delivers concerning his dog's misadventures. First, when departing from Verona, Launce attempts to recreate the scene of his family leavetaking, which has occurred offstage, by acting it out for the audience. This inevitably involves a certain amount of impromptu stage direction, and in the course of coaching his actors Launce achieves something like an epiphany:

> This shoe is my father; no, this left shoe is my father; no, no, this left shoe is my mother; nay, that cannot be so neither; yes, it is so, it is so—it hath the worser sole. This shoe, with the hole in it, is my mother, and this my father—a vengeance on't! there 'tis. Now, so, this staff is my sister, for, look you, she is as white as a lily and as small as a wand. This hat is Nan, our maid. I am the dog—no, the dog is himself, and I am the dog—O! the dog is me, and I am myself. (2.3.14–23)

In a bumbling routine that anticipates the histrionic muddle of Bottom and his companions in *A Midsummer Night's Dream,* Launce thoroughly confuses the world of lived experience with that of theatrical imitation. This confusion, in turn, becomes intolerable when Launce seeks an appropriate dramatic stand-in for his dog and concludes that the dog must—no, must not—be "himself." The problem here is that, while the dog clearly "is himself" for all commonplace purposes, to make the dog be "himself" upon the stage is to ask him to participate in patterns of deliberate doubling of which any dog, by virtue of being a dog, is incapable. Crab is certainly himself—no one more contentedly so—but for that very reason Crab is unable to *act* himself, since acting involves an alienation from the persona being adopted, and that alienation, in turn, is a function of language. Being wholly "himself" and nothing other, Crab cannot perform himself, for performance is the province of imitation rather than identity.

This problem reappears with a vengeance during Launce and Crab's unfortunate visit to the Duke's court. Launce's description of this event is one of the most successful speeches in *Two Gentlemen,* and much of its genius lies in the fact that here Launce has put Crab into the position of doing the impossible—being an actor. That, after all, is the whole point of the switch whereby Launce substitutes Crab for Proteus's lost lapdog; in a shift born of desperation, Launce has no choice but to trust his mutt to perform the role of a lady's pet. Recognizing the potential for trouble in this plan, Launce has once again offered his star actor a certain amount of stage direction: "Did I not bid thee still mark me, and do as I do?" (4.4.36–37); and again, "I have taught him, even as one would say precisely, 'Thus I would teach a dog'" (4.4.5–6). The coaching in question can also easily be viewed as instruction in table manners—instruction of a sort quite popular in the Renaissance and surveyed at length in the classic work of Norbert Elias (1935/1978)[14]—and it is utterly, predictably ignored by Crab, who steals Silvia's capon leg without hesitation, breaks wind sourly under the dinner table, then concludes his performance by urinating upon his new mistress's farthingale. "Didst thou ever see me do such a trick?" (4.4.39), Launce asks of the dog, emphasizing, by the by, the element of performance inherent to the entire escapade. The only way to recoup this theatrical failure is through the timely interposition of a more accomplished actor, and Launce rises to the occasion, in effect taking Crab's failures upon himself and atoning for them in the dog's place. Thus what begins as a grotesque carnival performance ends as a passion play.

However, there is one basic difficulty with this reading of the scene, for if the misadventures of Launce and Crab are to be regarded as theater, they are emphatically not performed as such. As with the Verona leavetaking before it, the dinner table scene at the Duke's is transacted entirely offstage, and Launce once again resorts to the narrative function to recreate for the audience a scene to which it is denied immediate access. In a sense, this is a shame, for a scene like that described by Launce would be even more risible when performed than when narrated.[15] However the problem here once again, as with the leavetaking in Verona, is the problem of the dog, whose acting abilities are no more reliable for Shakespeare himself than they are for Launce—although for Shakespeare, the unreliability is of a different order. In Launce's case, the failure of canine trust manifests itself as a consistent refusal to do what is expected and desired; Crab's invincible perversity becomes his defining humor, rather as it is for some of my academic colleagues. He can always be counted upon to do the most exasperating thing possible, and at the most exasperating time; and to this extent Crab himself functions as a carefully drawn dramatic character, endowed with personality, predictable patterns of behavior, and both a place in and a meaning for the social world of Shakespeare's play. Yet this character must exist purely and simply as a function of the dramatic script; to the extent that it relies upon any performative assistance from the dog playing the role of Crab, it risks coming to grief just as does Launce. In short, where Launce cannot trust Crab to behave consistently, Shakespeare cannot trust him to *mis*behave consistently. Thus not only does the dog threaten to frustrate Launce's metatheatrical moments; he also threatens to frustrate Shakespeare's frustration of those moments.

The climactic expression of this dilemma occurs in Crab's climactic moment of comedy: as he concludes his performance before the Duke and Silvia by making water on the latter's farthingale. Part of what makes this funny, after all, is the sheer unselfconsciousness of the gesture; in relieving himself when and where nature prompts him, Crab is simply doing what dogs do. Once again, at the heart of a carefully contrived metatheatrical spectacle, replete with specified roles, rehearsal, and dramatic antecedents, we discover a moment when all the acting stops. With a lift of the hind leg, Crab propels us beyond theatrical representation. Yet by the same token, Shakespeare's script tacitly acknowledges its inability to stage this very moment of nontheater. Instead, it gives us a staged narrative representation of the failure of dramatic representation; and in doing this, *Two Gentlemen of Verona* arguably uncovers the signal failure that is dramatic activity's enabling condition: the inability to progress from imitation to identity, to *become* the character being played.

Perhaps, oddly enough, this is why actors counsel us, four hundred years after Shakespeare, never to work with animals: because in a basic way, animals remain exempt from the linguistic alienation that makes drama a fit analogue for human life. For even if we could imagine a dog so perfectly trained to play the role of Crab that he might be trusted to act out the dinner table scene onstage, with the proper intestinal and urinary gestures supplied properly and consistently on cue, we would not have the natural and spontaneous nonacting to which Shakespeare alludes; at best, we would simply have a bestial representation of a human representation of the failure of representation. That is the bad news for Shakespeare and for us: we can't reach Crab from where we are, locked in a sociolinguistic order that takes alienation and role-playing as its fundamental constants. If we are to make sense of such an animal, it is inevitably through the various tropes of anthropomorphism whereby we are slyly, and misleadingly, invited to make sense of Crab onstage; no other method of approach is available. Yet there may also be some good news for us, and for Shakespeare as well, in the theatrical failure that is *Two Gentlemen of Verona*. If so, the good news may be that unlike Crab, we inhabit a world in which we may put ourselves in another's place, however imperfectly; that in doing so we may learn, however imperfectly, to mend our imperfections; and that through this process, however imperfectly, we may learn how to love.

CONCLUSION

SUGGESTED FURTHER READING

This book began with a broad assessment of the discursive uses to which animals could be put in early modern England, and from there it has proceeded to address four particular instances of the literary deployment of animal imagery in highly charged social contexts. Obviously enough, the material covered in these chapters is only a fraction—although, one hopes, a fairly representative fraction—of the general field of study from which it has been drawn. And just as obviously, this field of study has left its mark on contemporary social and political life; animals continue today to be used not simply for material purposes, but also for the ongoing project of defining the human. Thus it is appropriate that this study end with a survey of recent work on the status of animals in Western society. While some of this work is more manifestly engaged with the literature of sixteenth- and seventeenth-century England than is the rest, it is all, to one degree or another, aimed at recovering, extending, preserving, and in some cases correcting social practices and habits of mind that can be encountered in the writing of that period. Any effort to assess the consequences of early modern attitudes toward the natural world must therefore end with contemporary social issues, for it is largely in these issues that the early modern attitudes persist, insofar as they do.

To begin, then, as close to the concerns of this study as possible: from the mid-twentieth century onward, research on the Renaissance drama has displayed a broad and growing interest in early modern formulations of the nature of nature. Audrey Yoder's *Animal Analogy in Shakespeare's Character Portrayal,* first published in 1947 and reprinted in 1975, represents a fairly early attempt to account for Shakespeare's animal references through character analysis. Drawing heavily upon the peculiar strain of anthropomorphic thought that derives from Aesop and Phaedrus,[1] Yoder traces the presence both of direct references to Aesop and of Aesopian character types in Shakespearean drama, and then relates the presence of these character types to the Renaissance tradition of "animal physiognomy" (28). According to Yoder, this tradition, which in Shakespeare's day sought to classify human character by identifying physical resemblances between individual human beings and various species of animal, provided a quasiscientific basis for Shakespeare's portrayal of particular dramatic figures. This connection between Renaissance physiognomy and Shakespearean dramaturgy, in turn, licenses Yoder's traditionally character-centered critical procedure.

However, more recent Renaissance scholarship has tended to dispense with character analysis in favor of a focus upon the literary work's relation to its social, political, and historical context. Working from this vantage point, Annabel Patterson's *Fables of Power* (1991) offers a reappraisal of the beast-fable literature to which Yoder relates Shakespeare's work. Patterson, while a consummate Shakespearean, spends relatively little time on Shakespeare in this particular work, focusing instead upon the political ramifications of the Aesopian fable as it reemerges in postmedieval literature, principally that of the sixteenth and seventeenth centuries. In Patterson's view, the beast fable works as a hitherto underappreciated site of political allegory and ideological contest, offering both conservative and radical political thinkers a literary form that "was not fixed but contestable" (4). Patterson draws a central example of this instability from Shakespeare, who famously appropriates the Aesopian fable of *The Belly and the Members* to his tragedy *Coriolanus* (ca. 1608). As Patterson points out, Shakespeare's reconstruction of this fable alters the fable's terms in such a way as to unfix its political application; the opening scenes of *Coriolanus* transform "a metaphorical rebellion *against* the Belly . . . into a literal rebellion *of* the Belly" (1991, 123). For Patterson, this transformation is representative of the breadth and political lability of the Aesopian tradition.

Within the recent critical dispensation exemplified by Patterson's work, Shakespeare's discursive use of animals becomes more important for its sociopolitical consequences than for its literary antecedents. Proceeding from roughly the same orientation, recent feminist scholars have displayed a particular interest in the symbolic associations between women and animals that populate Shakespeare's work. Jeanne Addison Roberts's *The Shakespearean Wild* (1991), for instance, takes as its starting point the feminist axiom that "woman is to man as nature is to culture" (3),[2] then complicates that position by positing three imbricated subsets of the natural world—a "female Wild," an "animal Wild," and a "barbarian Wild" (5–6)—that serve as concurrent challenges to the various patriarchal regimes represented in Shakespeare's plays. In Roberts's view, the Shakespearean world of nature exists as "the locale for the male's necessary, seductive, and terrifying confrontation with the female" (24). Likewise, the overall trajectory of Shakespeare's career enacts an "increasing suppression and control of the green world" that recapitulates "the typical sequence of male experience" (25) as it progresses through "separation from the . . . maternal Wild" to "consolidation of his position in male Culture," and thence to a return "to the foreign territory . . . to acquire a mate" (25).

Proceeding with a similar feminist focus, Grace Tiffany's *Erotic Beasts and Social Monsters* (1995) examines the plays of Jonson and Shakespeare in terms of their response to a tradition of "mythic androgyny" deriving from Aristophanes's speech in Plato's *Symposium* and positing an originary, undivided, androgynous human nature to which sexual differentiation stands as a subsequent development. In Tiffany's analysis, mythic androgyny aspires to an ideal of erotic interrelation that stages itself not only as a union of male and female, but also as "a human-beast confrontation" (27) nicely embodied— for one instance—in the composite monstrosity of Bottom. For Tiffany, Shakespearean romantic comedy embraces such figures, together with the relatedness and otherness they represent, whereas Jonsonian satirical comedy enacts a suspicion and rejection of such hybrid forms. The result is a series of Jonsonian defensive actions against villains and fools, including Volpone, Mosca, Captain Otter, and Sir John Daw, who are repeatedly stigmatized as part human and part beast, and/or part man and part woman.

A number of briefer studies have recently pursued similar lines of inquiry into the relations between nature and culture in the Shakespearean drama. For instance, in a recent essay on *The Tempest* ("Creature Caliban," 2000), Julia Reinhard Lupton has renewed Tiffany's focus upon treatments of nature and hybridity in the Shakespeare canon, while extracting somewhat different conclusions from her analysis. For Lupton, Caliban embodies mixture in ways that his play cannot tolerate, and thus he enacts a critique of the language of relative anthropocentrism that invests his play. Poised as he is between nature and culture, heaven and earth, the human and the animal, he stages a moment of singularity and particularity that escapes the universalizing tendencies of language. Hence the force with which the play's other characters condemn him: His liminality undermines their own claims to exemplarity. His status as "creature," sui generis, poses a challenge to taxonomies of race.

Also focusing upon Renaissance models of ethnic difference and colonial mastery, Rebecca Ann Bach has discerned a parallelism between the early English enthusiasm for bear-baiting and early formulations of the colonialist project. For Bach, "The logic of dominion reads the material world and its signs, its flora and fauna, as signs of the naturalness of mastery" (1997, 30), and this same interpretive gesture licenses both the exploitation of wildlife (what I have called absolute anthropocentrism) and the exploitation of the racial other (relative anthropocentrism). For Bach, contemporary criticism tacitly endorses this gesture by failing to attend to early modern England's record of environmental degradation and abuse of the animal world, particularly as that record is embodied in the popularity of bull-baiting, cock-fighting, and other blood sports.

In a brief essay entitled "Shakespeare's Dogs" (1998), spun off from her book-length study *Dog Love* (to which I shall return later), Marjorie Garber likewise extends her attention to include not only Shakespeare's work but also Shakespeare's critics. Garber's thesis is that "in the late twentieth century the twin guarantors of 'humanism,' conceived as a set of fast-vanishing values, are . . . Shakespeare and dogs" (293). On this view, Shakespeare's work identifies that holy grail of liberal humanist thought, human nature, most particularly through its references to and treatment of the canine. Scouring twentieth-century popular culture for canine allusions to Shakespeare, Garber discovers them in dog owners' manuals, dog-biscuit advertisements, pop psychology books, television shows, movies, stage plays, and the like. Her conclusion: "All the world's a doghouse, and all the men and women merely spaniels or beagles or bichon frises" (293).

Self-promotion is an ill thing, a vile thing, but at the dawn of the twenty-first century even the meekest and most unworldly of academics must now and then genuflect to the idols of postmodern consumerism. Therefore, with an ethical heaviness of heart made lighter by my guileless lust for glory and lucre, I will draw brief attention to my own additional contributions to the study of animals in early modern English literature. Portions of the present study first saw light as articles (which I have listed on the acknowledgements page); however, I have also published three additional articles that expand in various ways upon material treated in passing within the pages of this book. "Shylock and the Rise of the Household Pet" addresses the prominent use of animal metaphors in *The Merchant of Venice*, thereby elaborating upon the material with which this book begins. This book has also referred in passing to Milton's views on the reasoning capacity of animals, a subject I have taken up at somewhat greater length in an essay entitled "Milton and the Reasoning of Animals: Variations on a Theme by Plutarch." And I have likewise given further attention to *Othello* and the issues of bestiality and disnatured conception in an article entitled "*Othello*'s Monsters," which draws somewhat upon the early teratological discourse to which I have referred elsewhere in these pages.[3]

When we turn away from scholarly work on Shakespeare in particular and Renaissance literature in general, we encounter a similar wealth of material dealing with the more broadly historical character of the relation between nature and culture in early modern England. The definitive study here is Keith Thomas's *Man and the Natural World* (1983), which examines in sustained detail the dominant attitudes toward nature and the animal world in England during the three centuries from 1500 to 1800. The story Thomas tells is one of transition, as a residual medieval set of beliefs, emphasizing anthropocentric privilege and conceiving of the natural environment primarily as an exploitable resource, gradually gave way to a culture of rural nostalgia in which sympathy for the brute elements of God's creation reigned supreme. Yet if, as Thomas maintains, "human civilisation . . . was virtually synonymous with the conquest of nature" in the early modern period (25), he also traces the presence of more sympathetic attitudes toward nature from the very beginning of the period he surveys; and these attitudes gain ground as his narrative moves forward in time, coupled as they are to reforms in education and the treatment of children, abolition of the slave trade, improvement in the social status of women, and other, similar social developments. Thus, while there are important differences between the anthropomorphism examined in the present study and the Romantic reverence for the natural world documented in the final pages of Thomas's book (e.g., 301–302), the latter is in an important sense the lineal descendant of the former.

Thus, as Thomas makes clear, the ideologies of anthropocentrism and anthropomorphism are historically concurrent, albeit not coequal at any given historical moment. Recently, Erica Fudge's *Perceiving Animals* (2000) has examined some of the tensions and ironies resulting from this interrelation. According to Fudge, human and animal nature are not simply paired in early modern thinking: they are interdependent, so much so that formulations of human nature inevitably ground themselves upon a notion of the animal to which they refer, in Derridean fashion, even as they displace it. Drawing her examples from the animals of the bear-garden, whose beastly spectacle enacts various sorts of human social distinction; from Puritan principles of conscience and justification, which associate certain groups of individuals with the brute creation; from humanist education, in which the emphasis on right speaking and right reading aligns inarticulate humanity with the beasts; and from other, similar areas of enquiry, Fudge argues for the enduring instability of the very categories of humanness that Renaissance thought spends much of its energy seeking to manufacture and uphold.

A recent collection of essays entitled *At the Borders of the Human* (1999) and edited by Fudge, Ruth Gilbert, and Susan Wiseman follows this line of argument into a number of context-specific applications. Alan Stewart ("Humanity at a Price" in Fudge et al.), for instance, asserts that the traditionally cerebral, and even spiritual, educational program of Renaissance humanism is in fact "essentially carnal in its orientation" (9). For Stewart, humanism's claim to "place . . . man 'above all the animals'" (10) is subtended by a recurring humanist concern with money, personal affairs, and patronage—a concern that tends to ally humanist scholars with the very elements of residual feudal society against which they sought to define themselves. Bringing similar focus to bear upon the political and anatomical discourse of the seventeenth century, Susan Wiseman discerns within early writing upon the ape-human difference a language "imbued with ideas about socialisation [and] even politics" that reveals the "figurality and potential humanness" of the ape ("Monstrous Perfectibility" in Fudge et al., 215–238). Here again the language of biological difference seems to presuppose an embarrassing sense of the interrelation of human and animal.

Moving beyond studies of the sixteenth and seventeenth centuries, one encounters a variety of historical works dealing with the social significance of animals in other periods as well. Joyce E. Salisbury's *The Beast Within* (1994), for instance, offers a sustained reading of medieval attitudes toward the brute creation as attested to by philosophers and theologians, poets and bestiarists, artists, jurists, and so forth. For Salisbury, the principal feature of these attitudes was a confident assertion of the difference between the human and the bestial, yet by the twelfth century this assumption of difference had to compete with a renewed popularization of "the classical view of animals"—promoted by the genres of myth, animal fable, and bestiary—that construed "animals as metaphors for human behavior" (9). The result is the formation of a late medieval mentality that makes it "increasingly difficult to tell the difference between humans and animals" (101), and that encourages, within the disciplinary language of the high medieval church, a concomitant tendency to focus upon "the bestial that becomes increasingly apparent within humans" (175).

If we move to the nearer end of the chronological period addressed in the present study, two volumes dealing with the nineteenth century deserve particular mention here as well. On one hand, Harriet Ritvo's *The Animal Estate* (1987) engages with the culture of animals in Victorian England and discerns within that culture a mythic reaffirmation of various conservative social fantasies. Thus the newly emerging cult of British beef, with its emphasis on experimental stock breeding by aristocratic amateurs, constituted a "ceremonial reenactment . . . of the traditional rural order" (52). The Victorian rage for dogs likewise "projected an obsessively detailed vision of a stratified order which sorted animals and, by implication, people into snug and appropriate niches" (93). Even the era's interest in exotic beasts enacted a sort of colonial hegemony, since "the use of wild animals as tokens of political submission had ancient roots; for millennia kings and emperors had maintained menageries to symbolize the extent of their sway" (206). Concentrating on the other side of the English Channel, Kathleen Kete's *The Beast in the Boudoir* (1994) discerns similar social imperatives in the pet-keeping culture of nineteenth-century Paris. The Parisian pet reflects its owner's mastery of nature. Unlike the British dog, with its connections to rural pastimes and the traditional, agrarian social order, the Parisian dog was an unmistakably urban creature, and "the concerns of French dog-owners centered around the reconciliation of the dog and the city, of apartment living and animal life" (79). At the same time, Parisian pet-keeping culture formulated itself as a kind of residual *ancien régime* aristocracy, upholding principles of fidelity, order, and cleanliness, for instance, in opposition to the "violent, sexual, and irrational" character of the emergent Parisian working classes (138).

Writing for a broader, less specialized audience than does Ritvo or Kete, Marjorie Garber in her book *Dog Love* has recently traced the history of dog culture in a way that once again locates beasts at the center of efforts to define the human. Garber's eclectic study ranges from classical antiquity to the late twentieth century; in the process it examines the treatment of dogs in the visual arts, literature, cinema, advertising, theater, linguistics, psychoanalysis, anthropology, popular culture, and a wide variety of other media. But if this very broadly conceived work has any particular focus, it is upon the tendency of

dogs to function as a paradigm of human love: to exemplify this traditionally most noble of human sentiments in a way that human beings themselves repeatedly fail to do. As Garber points out, while
surveying recent controversies around the scientific anthropomor-
phization of animals, "paradoxically, the quintessence of the 'human'
is often found in the dog" (34). Within the scientific community, one
result of this displacement has been "the desire to establish a firm
borderline [between human beings and animals] somewhere, any-
where," and a concomitant "scientific gerrymandering, a constant re-
drawing of boundaries to suit the intellectual politics of the time"
(32). On a more general footing, another result of the same displacement is a tendency to see the dog as that "which makes us
human" (42).

Marc Shell's essay "The Family Pet" (1986), a spin-off from his
study of incest in *Measure for Measure* (*The End of Kinship*, 1988),
likewise addresses the specularity of the pet/owner relationship. For
Shell, the institution of pet-keeping represents an innovation within
the essentially "omnivorous" culture of Christianity in that it designates particular animals as inedible (135). This ban on eating pets, in
turn, parallels the ban on sexual intercourse with relatives that informs the incest prohibition in its various articulations. Hence the pet
emerges as a peculiarly liminal and transitional object, simultaneously
blurring the conventional "distinction of which beings are our famil-
ial kin from which are not kin" and the equally fundamental "distinction of which beings are our species kind from which are not our
kind" (121). And pet ownership, which effectively elevates nonhuman animals to the status both of fellow spirits and of family members, thereby reveals the complementarity of the taboos against incest
and bestiality, extreme endogamy and extreme exogamy.

Whereas the work of both Garber and Shell is firmly rooted in their
own experience as Shakespeare scholars, it quickly moves beyond the
limited concerns of early modern English literary history. In doing so,
it engages a variety of recent controversies over the status and proper
treatment of animal life and the environment. Prominent among these
controversies is the contemporary animal rights debate, fueled by ac-
tivist political groups and perhaps best represented on the theoretical
level by the work of ethicist Peter Singer. Singer's groundbreaking
1975 volume *Animal Liberation* makes a forceful case against what he
calls "speciesism": that is, "the sacrifice of the most important interests of members of other species in order to promote the most trivial
interests of our own species" (6). For Singer, such behavior derives its
ultimate, and specious, justification from the view that "we are never

guilty of neglecting the interests of other animals" because "they have no interests" (6). This view, in turn, grounds itself on the further claim that "nonhuman animals have no interests . . . because they are not capable of suffering" (6). Singer's work in *Animal Liberation* aims to debunk both of these assertions while documenting, in appalling detail, the maltreatment of animals in such venues as the research laboratory and the factory farm. More recently, for instance in his introduction to the essay collection *In Defense of Animals* (1985), Singer has sought to provide a theoretical platform for the contemporary animal liberation movement, which, in his formulation, maintains that "where animals and humans have similar interests . . . those interests are to be counted equally, with no automatic discount just because one of the beings is not human" (*Animals* 9).

Political scientists and legal scholars have recently sought to extend such views into the legislative and political arenas, with an increasing measure of visibility. Typical of commentary on these developments is Helena Silverstein's *Unleashing Rights* (1996), which maintains that "the recent extension of rights to animals has fostered reconsideration of the meaning of rights" in general (77); that exponents of the animal rights movement "appear to be highly educated" and that "the connection between [their] philosophical and political activism is strong" (77); and that, since "rights language and judicial decisions provide no determinate outcome" for issues of animal rights, the very indeterminacy of rights language "provides the opportunity to reconstruct legal meaning" so as "to challenge the existing relations of power and the traditional foundations and uses of rights" (224). For Silverstein and legal scholars of her bent, the extension of rights to animals is "hardly shocking," in light of "Western theory's emphasis on natural rights and human rights" (53); indeed, "expanding rights to animals reaffirms human rights in a variety of ways and imbues rights language with a content emphasizing sentience" (33). As for "Western theory's emphasis" on rights and their relation to animals, this has been helpfully exemplified by Paul Clarke and Andrew Linzey's anthology *Political Theory and Animal Rights* (1990), which compactly traces the development of Western thought on the question of animal rights from Plato to contemporary activists like Peter Singer and Tom Regan.

Among scientists, too, there has been a recent tendency to challenge traditional distinctions between nature and culture, the human and the animal, and such challenges often involve that venerable anthropocentric marker of difference, the ability to reason. Recent studies of animal reasoning ability and self-awareness are numerous, and sufficiently removed from this book's immediate focus not to require exhaustive summary.[4] However, Irene Pepperberg's well-known work on avian intelligence bears particular mention in light of my concerns in Chapter 3. For over two decades, Pepperberg has explored the linguistic and rational capacities of African gray parrots, most especially her star research subject, Alex. The results, summarized in her recent book *The Alex Studies,* have been startling, and Alex himself has achieved celebrity status as a result of his extraordinary ability to engage in meaningful conversation. While Pepperberg is reserved in the conclusions she derives from her work with Alex, she notes a marked parallel between psittacine behavior and the abilities of primates (321–322), and she urges a general "reevaluation of animal capacities" (327). She insists that "for far too long, animals in general, and birds in particular, have been denigrated and treated merely as creatures of instinct" (327). On the contrary, she argues, "animals have capacities that are far greater than we were once led to expect" (327–328); for her, as for Milton, they reason not contemptibly.

Pepperberg's work summarizes years of laboratory research that has also produced a number of scholarly articles in respected scientific journals. By way of contrast, Jeffrey Moussaieff Masson and Susan McCarthy's *When Elephants Weep* (1995) addresses a mass audience in a way that is openly critical of standard scientific assumptions and procedures. For Masson and McCarthy, "most people believe . . . that animals can be unhappy and also that they have such primal feelings as happiness, anger, and fear," because most people "have constant evidence of it before their eyes" (xiii); however, "by dint of rigorous training and great efforts of the mind, most modern scientists . . . have succeeded in becoming almost blind to these matters" (xiii). This scientific tendency is encouraged in part by the empirical method's aversion to nonquantifiables, and in part by the heavy financial and professional investment the contemporary scientific community maintains in such practices as animal experimentation. However, it has long been held by evolutionary biologists that at least some emotions perform important survival functions, and may thus not only appear in animals but probably *did* appear in them before the human race ever existed. For Masson and McCarthy, "one should demand no more proof that an animal feels an emotion than would be demanded of a human" (22). Pursuing this line of argument, they cite a broad range of anecdotal evidence that may be used to infer that animals have feelings; prominent among such evidence are the Alex studies, from which Masson and McCarthy extract conclusions to which Pepperberg herself would probably not subscribe.

Thus the status of animals has recently emerged as central to a range of ethical, legal, political, and scientific debates. That being the case, it should be no surprise that animals have also figured significantly in recent debates on questions of gender and sexuality. For instance, amidst the growth in prestige that alternative sexual orientations have enjoyed in literary discourse over the past quarter-century, bestiality has found a leading apologist in Midas Dekkers. In the appropriately entitled *Dearest Pet* (1994), Dekkers broadly surveys the practice of cross-species mating from ancient times to the present day; opposing the traditional and emphatic stigmatization of bestiality as unnatural, he notes that the practice occurs between a wide variety of animal species, both in captivity and in the wild, as well as in a broad range of cultural situations. From classical myth to Asian erotica and the conception of Jesus Christ, Dekkers encounters eroticized representations of beasts at the heart of the faiths that have sustained the most enduring and influential civilizations. Likewise, the historical record encourages Dekkers to maintain that "the mechanisms which break down the barriers between the species . . . are no less natural than the mechanisms which produce them" (73).

However, animals have become more visibly associated with questions of gender and sexuality through the foundation and development, over the past two decades or so, of the ecofeminist movement. Carol J. Adams and Josephine Donovan provide a valuable survey of this movement in their anthology *Animals and Women* (1995), which sets out both to explain why feminism should concern itself with the fate of nonhuman animals and also, in the process, to provide a broad introduction to the major authors currently producing ecofeminist theory. Here, as well as in Adams's *Neither Man Nor Beast* (1994), one encounters a branch of feminist thought that responds to the patriarchal association of women with animals not by denying the association, nor by ignoring it, but rather by extending the feminist critique of political oppression to encompass other forms of life. As Adams summarizes this position, "Ecofeminism posits that the domination of the rest of nature is linked to the domination of women and that both dominations must be eradicated" (*Man Nor Beast* 88). Operating within the same discursive community and obeying the same general commitment, Patrick Murphy's *Literature, Nature, and Other* (1995) proposes to adapt Bakhtin's notion of dialogism to ecofeminist practice so as to achieve "a conceptual framework for being able to critique and affirm without absolutes" (15). The ultimate objective of this effort, for Murphy, is the production of "a livable critical theory, rather than a merely usable one applicable only to literature, language, and thought" (4). With this declaration, Murphy's ecofeminism brings us full circle, back to issues of literary history and literary interpretation such as those with which this survey of further reading began.

Ironically, whereas Murphy's theory aims at being livable, his book is primarily an exercise in academic literary criticism. Indeed, *Literature, Nature, and Other* deals primarily not just with literature, but with a very limited kind of literature. In general, Murphy focuses upon such authors as Patricia Hampl, Joy Harjo, Gary Snyder, and Leslie Marmon Silko: figures well known within a limited circle of professional literary intellectuals, but less visible within the literary marketplace as a whole. Consequently, Murphy's insistence on the broader social instrumentality of his writing may provoke a weary sigh from readers encountering this currently popular academic gesture for the fourth or fifth time. But even writers—indeed, even academic writers—must live their beliefs, and perhaps the fondest of those beliefs is that their writing can in fact affect the world. Hence it should be no surprise that ecofeminism and similar movements within environmentalist thought have produced an increasingly visible counterpart in the realm of literary studies: ecocriticism. In turning to this critical school, we may bring the present summary of further reading to rest once again on the questions of exegesis and hermeneutics, literary scholarship and interpretation, with which it began.

Cheryll Glotfelty and Harold Fromm's *Ecocriticism Reader* (1996) provides an advantageous starting point for study of this new critical movement. Defining ecocriticism broadly as "the study of the relationship between literature and the physical environment" (xviii), Glotfelty and Fromm then subdivide this field into three areas modeled upon Elaine Showalter's tripartite division of feminist literary studies: 1) the study of representations of the environment; 2) the construction of an environmental literary tradition; and 3) the development of an environmental theory that would relate green literary studies to broader environmental commitments such as animal rights, vegetarianism, protection of endangered species, and political activism in general. Within this framework, Glotfelty and Fromm provide excerpts of some of the foundational works of recent green criticism—from Lynn White, Jr.'s historical overview of the habits of mind, consonant with the early "victory of Christianity over paganism" ("The Historical Roots of Our Ecologic Crisis," Glotfelty and Fromm 9), that have contributed to the formation of a late-modern ecological crisis; to Annette Kolodny's classic exploration (in *The Lay of the Land*) of the literary identification of nature with femininity; to

Glen A. Love's call (in "Revaluing Nature") for a literature and criticism that "recognize . . . and dramatize . . . the integration of human with natural cycles of life" (235). Finally, as a supplement to Glotfelty and Fromm's collection, two others prove useful as well. Richard Kerridge and Neil Sammells's *Writing the Environment*, for one, offers a range of recent ecocritical work that complements *The Ecocriticism Reader* by focusing upon British scholarship—including Dominic Head's linkage of green criticism to postmodern theory via a shared deprivileging of the human subject ("The (Im)Possibility of Ecocriticism") and Jonathan Bate's call for a literary bioregionalism that might contrast usefully with such concepts as nationalism and multinational capitalism ("Poetry and Biodiversity"). By contrast, Laurence Coupe's *Green Studies Reader* (2000) takes a diachronic approach to ecocriticism, tracing the movement to roots in the nature writing of Romantics like Coleridge and Wordsworth and following it thence to the recent work of Bate, Kerridge, Glotfelty, Lawrence Buell, and others.

This recent, ecologically motivated and politically alert criticism provides a literary counterpart to contemporary developments in both the hard and social sciences that reconsider humanity's relationship to the other orders of life on earth. Whatever else it may do, ecocriticism represents a fascinating new turn in literary studies, away from the insularity that has often characterized work in the humanities, and equally away from the field's concomitant sense of inferiority *vis-à-vis* the sciences, and toward a sense of the interrelatedness of scientific and humane studies, and toward an increasing sense that the humanities can offer a significant correction to certain tendencies in the sciences that have long gone unchecked. Green literary criticism certainly adds to current interest in interdisciplinary and cultural studies within the arts and humanities, and it may well prove to be one of the major growth areas in the future of literary studies.

In the here and now, the ecocritical project will inevitably, and rightly, inform critical responses to this book. My subject matter is essentially a subset of that with which ecocriticism concerns itself, and like much recent environmentally aware scholarship, this book proceeds from the assumption that nature and culture are mutually constitutive rather than distinct; that the ways in which we think of the natural world are, in a fundamental sense, the ways in which we think of ourselves. If one sets out from this premise, it is hard to evade a broader sense that the critical and the political, the global and the local, the self and the other are inseparably interrelated. Ideally, I would like to have written a book about the nature/culture dyad that remains true to this insight without succumbing, in the process, to the twin pitfalls of self-importance and self-righteousness. But in a more practical sense, I hope this book may encourage readers to dig into the wider body of literature with which I have concluded this study. Ever the academic, I believe that further reading offers the best path to a broad, responsible, and politically engaged reconsideration of how we live in, and with, the world.

NOTES

INTRODUCTION

1. For a survey of recent scholarship on the natural world in Shakespeare's theater, in early modern culture and in contemporary literary and cultural studies, see the concluding section of this book.
Important earlier works on the subject include Emma Phipson's *The
Animal-Lore of Shakespeare's Time*, which catalogues and summarizes
in straightforward fashion Shakespeare's references to various species
of beasts, fish, fowl, reptiles, and insects while viewing these references as evidence of the poet's "sympathy with nature" (3);
Theodore Spencer's *Shakespeare and the Nature of Man*, whose two
opening chapters situate Shakespeare's depiction of nature in a hierarchical world view combining "elements of Aristotelianism, Platon-
ism, Neoplatonism, Stoicism, and Christianity" with "remarkable
unanimity" (1); Audrey Yoder's *Animal Analogy in Shakespeare's
Character Portrayal* (discussed briefly in the conclusion to this
book); John Danby's *Shakespeare's Doctrine of Nature*, which examines *King Lear*, in particular, with reference to Renaissance notions of
nature as "benevolent and orthodox" (31) and, alternatively, as inimical to "the values called human, and the norms called Reason"
(36); Caroline Spurgeon's *Shakespeare's Imagery and What It Tells
Us*, which presents the poet's use of animal imagery as drawn "from
the objects he kn[ew] best" and therefore conveying "definite information about his personality" (12); and Alan Dent's *World of Shakespeare: Animals and Monsters*, which returns to the enumerative
procedure of Phipson and collects a wide range of Shakespearean
beast allusions without relating them to any broader critical thesis.
2. In particular, see Douglas's treatment of the Mosaic dietary laws
(41–57), which outlines a range of ways whereby binary discriminators may be used to distinguish pure from impure foodstuffs, and
which thus offers a broad conceptual model for the opposition of purity to pollution. Similarly, Pierre Bourdieu views ritual as a means of
organizing the universe in terms of normative social practice; thus "a
whole cosmology, an ethic, a metaphysic, a political philosophy" may

be communicated "through injunctions as insignificant as 'stand up straight' or 'don't hold your knife with your left hand'" (94).

3. This distinction is rendered most forthrightly in early treatises on teratology and natural history such as Ambroise Paré's *On Monsters and Marvels* and Ulisse Aldrovandi's *Monstrorum Historia*. In Paré, for instance, "Monsters are things that appear outside the course of Nature (and are usually signs of some forthcoming misfortune)," and the principal causes of monsters are "first . . . the glory of God," and "second, his wrath" (3). In a lengthy and helpful discussion of medieval notions of monstrosity, David Williams has remarked upon the "obvious contradiction" in any attempt (like Paré's) "to create a system of descriptive categories for that which exists to resist and confound systematization." Yet Williams also notes that "the contradiction seems not to have been felt very sharply" in the Middle Ages (107). Recent scholarship has retraced Paré's footsteps by focusing at length upon the mother's role in the creation of monstrous births. Thus, for instance, Phyllis Mack has argued that "a woman's volatile imagination, infused by evil forces, was [considered] sufficient to transform [her] fetus into a monster" (39); Mack thus concludes that "the most potent image of woman's spiritual marginality [in the early modern period] was not the deviant witch brewing potions . . . but the ordinary mother" (35).

4. For a helpful discussion of the interdependence of the social categories of normativity and perversion, see Jonathan Dollimore's *Sexual Dissidence* (103–130), which argues in particular that "perversion [is] a culturally central phenomenon" (103) whose "paradoxical nature endangers the very metaphysic which employs it" (126).

5. I have developed this argument at some length in a separate study that also surveys some of the scholarship dealing with the question of racism in *The Merchant of Venice* ("Shylock" passim).

6. On the question of bee communication, for instance, Emile Benveniste (49–54) argues that while "bees appear to be capable of giving and receiving real messages which contain several data" (52), "the bee's message does not call for any reply" other than a particular behavior (52), and this fact "means that the language of bees lacks the dialogue which is distinctive of human speech" (53). More recently, commenting upon Benveniste's remarks, Gilles Deleuze and Felix Guattari have distinguished bee communication from language insofar as "language is not content to go from a first party to a second party, from one who has seen to one who has not, but necessarily goes from a second party to a third party, neither of whom has seen" (77). For the story of Thomas Mann's daughter and her dog (an autobiographical anecdote that the author claims to have recorded precisely as it occurred), see Paul Auster's recent novel *Timbuktu*, 78–81.

7. The parrot in question, an African gray named Alex, has become something of a cult hero over the past decade, as witnessed by his appearances in the popular press (see, e.g., Stern passim) and his prominent role in a documentary film on parrots that has played repeatedly on the Public Broadcasting System. He has also been the subject of considerable academic publication. For the most recent and thorough account of his exploits see Irene Pepperberg, *The Alex Studies*, passim; in a briefer recent publication ("The African Grey Parrot," passim) Pepperberg has summarized her work with Alex as well as research conducted with a new generation of laboratory parrots, the African Grays Alo and Kyaaro. For a useful review of the classical background to the question of animal communication, see Glidden passim.

8. Michael Neill speaks for many recent scholars when he notes that "any attempt to read back into the early modern period an idea of 'race' based on post-Enlightenment taxonomy is doomed to failure," yet—like such other scholars as Kim Hall and Margo Hendricks—Neill also points out the important role played by early modern cultural artifacts "in the emergence of modern European racial consciousness" (361).

9. For Boemus's immediate impact upon European thought, see Hodgen 111–162. From Boemus, the story of Ham's offspring passes into the history of New World exploration in George Best's *True Discourse of the Three Voyages . . . of Martin Frobisher* (1577), which claims that "the cause of the Ethiopians blacknesse is the curse and naturall infection of blood" because God decreed that Ham and his son "Chus [and] all his posteritie after him should be so blacke and lothsome, that it might remain a spectacle of disobedience to all the worlde" (Hakluyt 7:264). For the position of this tale within the later development of American racism, see Jordan 3–25 and following; for a critique of later theories of scientific racism, see Gould 62–104.

10. Thus, for instance, Mary Janell Metzger has recently pointed out that "Jessica's marriage to Lorenzo would require a Christian audience to conclude either that she is a believer before her marriage or that she is, as she insists, 'sanctified' through her marriage" (56); that "Jessica's marriage reconstitutes her as a body, for according to Christian ecclesiastical and legal authorities, a woman was incorporated into the body of her husband in marriage" (57); and that "becoming one with the body of Christ requires not only her marriage to a Christian but also the conversion of her body in distinctly racial and gendered terms" (57).

11. For useful recent discussion of this pattern of animal identification in Shakespeare's work, see Roberts, esp. 64–68 (in connection primarily with *The Taming of the Shrew*), and Willems passim (with reference to *1 Henry IV* and *Coriolanus*). Also see Lecercle 176–177.

12. For recent studies of the hawking motif in *The Taming of the Shrew*, see Constance Hieatt passim and Margaret Ranald passim.

13. For a detailed study of the judicial punishment of animals in Western Europe, see Evans passim. For a more recent and briefer treatment of the same material from the standpoint of legal theory, see Jamieson passim, esp. 45.

14. For instance, the Deleuzian notion of "becoming-animal" that is outlined in *A Thousand Plateaus* 232–309 may prove congenial to this study. There Deleuze and Guattari proceed from the premises that "one of the main problems of natural history [is] to conceptualize the relationships between animals" (232); that this conceptualization traditionally involves an "analogy of proportionality" whereby "*a* is to *b* as *c* is to *d*" (233); that this logic of proportionality erroneously replaces "the great continuity between nature and culture with a deep rift distributing correspondences without resemblance between the two" (236–237); and that "what needs to be done [instead] is not to compare two organs but to place elements or materials in a relation that uproots the organ from its specificity" (258–259). Thus Deleuze and Guattari opt for a model of relations between the human and animal realms that calls into question the degree to which those realms may actually be constituted as independent entities, and to this extent the present study finds their project highly sympathetic. For helpful commentary upon this aspect of Deleuzian theory, see Canning passim. For a broader discussion of Deleuzian theory that may help to suggest its applicability to the present subject, see Bogue, esp. 88–115.

CHAPTER ONE

1. Jan Kott's early discussion of the play in *Shakespeare Our Contemporary* emphasizes the element of bestiality more than most; yet even for Kott, Titania's bestiality is simply one element of the play's larger focus upon a Brueghelesque "sexual demonology" (220). And while his more recent work in *The Bottom Translation* includes a thorough and suggestive discussion of the relations between bestiality in Apuleius's *Golden Ass* and *A Midsummer Night's Dream* (35–40), it does not attempt to extend that discussion to other elements of the play's structure. Like Kott, J. J. M. Tobin notes the common presence, in Shakespeare and Apuleius, of "an asinine transformation" and "a man so transformed [who] is loved and embraced by a woman" (33); however, he does not develop this observation at length. Deborah Wyrick's remarks about the bestiality parallelism in Shakespeare and Apuleius are perhaps typical of the overall trend in scholarship: "Subliminal erotic perversity notwithstanding, the audience's predominant response to the dalliance between the ass and the

Fairy Queen is one of amusement" (444). And Joseph R. Summers dismisses the issue with an air of finality: "As almost every audience recognizes, the scenes between Bottom and Titania do not descend to nightmarish bestiality" (11).

2. Patterson's revision of this essay in *Shakespeare and the Popular Voice* drops the specific phrase quoted here while retaining the general sense of the passage.

3. See 148–154 for the detail of this argument, which also receives earlier treatment in Dollmore's "Cultural Politics of Perversion" passim.

4. Norman Holland has commented upon the obviously phallic and sexual quality of this dream, describing the serpent image in Erik Erikson's terms as "*intrusive* or *penetrating*" (7) and hence as a figure of "violation" (11). Marjorie Garber has similarly associated the serpent with "violation and betrayal" as well as "male sexuality" and has argued that Hermia "separates Lysander, the beloved, from the serpent with whom she instinctively identifies him"—thus seeking to compensate for her own sexual anxieties (72–73).

5. Harold Brooks has thoroughly catalogued the various sources and analogues of *A Midsummer Night's Dream* (lviii–lxxxviii), and has in the process pointed out that in North's Plutarch—apparently the principal source for the story of Theseus and Hippolyta—the Amazon queen is named Antiope. The name Hippolyta derives instead from Chaucer's *Knight's Tale*. Yet Brooks adds that Seneca's *Hippolytus* stands as a major "neglected source" for Shakespeare's comedy (lxii) and thus could easily have added a classical coloring to Shakespeare's choice of names.

6. Also see 28 Henry VIII, c. 6; 31 Henry VIII, c. 7; 32 Henry VIII, c. 3; 2 and 2 Edward VI, c. 29; 1 Mary, c. 1; and 5 Elizabeth, c. 17.

7. Burke's discussion of pure persuasion in *A Rhetoric of Motives* is of considerable theoretical interest for a reading of such Puritan texts as Beard's *Theatre* and Philip Stubbes's *Anatomy of Abuses*. As Burke explains the term, "Pure persuasion involves the saying of something, not for an extra-verbal advantage to be got by the saying, but because of a satisfaction intrinsic to the saying" (269)—and yet it is a satisfaction, like that of Beard's tales, "always . . . embodied in the 'impurities' of advantage-seeking" (285). This form of persuasion, Burke continues, betrays itself as a principle of "self-interference" (272) or internal contradiction instituted so as to prolong the process of persuasion itself (271). In effect, Burke posits a model of language that contradicts its own acknowledged material aims, and that does so—like Beard's *Theatre*—as a prior condition of its own existence.

8. Such bestial pleasures, of course, later form the basis for Adam and Eve's first experience of fallenness; after their discovery of "Carnal desire" (IX.1013), the first couple falls curiously silent—"as struck'n

mute" (IX.1064). This muteness—testimony to their bestial degradation—stands in specific contrast to the deceptive loquacity of the
serpent, which upsets Eve's ability to distinguish between human and
animal forms: "What may this mean? Language of Man pronounc't
/ By Tongue of Brute, and human sense exprest?" (IX.553–554).
Man and animal have thus traded places, as it were, on the chain of
being; Adam yields his ascendancy over nature (and Eve) by ex-
changing Raphaelic "Wisdom" (whose principal index is speech) for
"foul concupiscence" (IX.1078). Then, as the consequences of his
behavior emerge, Adam responds to them in familiar fashion, seeking
in turn to hand his bestiality on to Eve through the operations of
metaphor: "Out of my sight, thou Serpent, that name best / Befits
thee with him leagu'd, thyself as false / And hateful" (X.867–869).

9. The two most recent authorities on this work, Theresa Kenney and
   Manfred Fleischer, disagree as to the probability of Acidalius's authorship. See Kenney 12–14, Fleischer 110–113.

10. Both Kenney (2–3) and Fleischer (107–108) point out the obvious-
    ness of A New Discourse's attack upon the radical reformed sects. These
    scholars also both point out that the first respondent to this treatise,
    Simon Gedik, was "not blind to the jocular vein in the Disputatio"
    (Fleischer 116), but that he was "definitely not amused" by the work
    because "he [thought] one ought not be amused" (Kenney 9).

11. See Kenney 5–6.

12. Fleischer 117. Des Maizeaux refers to Cujacius's argument in his re-
    vision of Bayle's Dictionnaire (2.2:539[C]), where he claims that,
    like Isaac Vossius before him (writing in the De origine idololatriae
    3.48), he believed Cujacius was merely jesting. I have not consulted
    the work by Vossius, which might conceivably shed a bit more light
    on the subject.

13. For an account of how widely this misinformation circulated at the
    turn of the twentieth century, see Thurston 2–3. I do not know how
    early this claim began to appear in learned circles, but there is at least
    a chance that it could already have been current in the sixteenth cen-
    tury. If so, however, one is surprised not to find reference to it in A
    New Discourse Against Women.

14. Thus Robert Weimann also notes the degree to which A Midsummer
    Night's Dream's aristocratic element is predicated upon "that which
    was naive and down-to-earth in folk mythology" (196). The result,
    he argues, is a play that transforms both high and low rhetoric and
    traditions into "something totally new" (196)—and, we might add,
    totally interconnected.

15. Thus Charles Shattuck (2:71) notes that Augustin Daly's 1888–1896
    productions of A Midsummer Night's Dream "did not include a fat
    and bean-fed horse beguiling a filly foal [sic] with sexy neighing"; this
    passage and others were expurgated in the interest of decency.

16. Also see Orgel's revised version of this essay in *Impersonations* (1996, 10–30, especially 27), where the phrase in question is repeated.

CHAPTER TWO

1. As Katharine Maus notes, "Extraliterary evidence certainly reinforces the view that anxiety about female sexual fidelity ran high in English Renaissance culture; historians report, for instance, that the opprobrious terms cuckold, whore, and whoremaster account for most of the defamation suits brought in sixteenth century church courts" (561–562). Maus bases this assertion, in turn, upon the historical research of Emmison (48–68) and Sharpe (passim).

2. For additional literary-critical discussions of the relation between sexual infidelity, psychology, and social order in early modern England, see Greenblatt 222–254; Fineman passim, esp. 83–100; and Kahn 119–150.

3. See Lacan 1982, 74–85 for a representative, and typically opaque, account of the construction of feminine sexuality. For Lacan, the feminine functions as a marker of wholeness: an emblem of the primordial mother-child dyad from which the subject must be severed as a precondition of its entry into culture. Since, within the social order itself, such wholeness is necessarily an illusion, femininity thus develops in the register of masquerade; as Lacan remarks, with uncharacteristic directness, "It is for what she is not that she expects to be desired as well as loved" (84). In the present chapter, I would extend this notion of masquerade to account for the notions of independent, self-sustaining agency that invest notions of masculine authority; nor is this extension at all in conflict with Lacanian principles, which view both masculine and feminine consciousness as a function of *meconnaissance*.

4. The English translations of Ovid's *Amores* are drawn from Marlowe's *Elegies;* citations of the Latin text are taken from Grant Showerman's Loeb edition. Where the translation and original differ with respect to book, elegy, and line numbers (as most particularly with *Amores* 3.7), the numbers given are those of the Latin text.

5. For two well-known applications of this argument to the early English drama, see Jonathan Dollimore, *Radical Tragedy,* esp. 40–50; and Catherine Belsey, *The Subject of Tragedy,* esp. 149–191. As Belsey summarizes, "The justification of the absolutist definition of marriage is the frailty of women" (168).

6. For one of the numerous media accounts of this recent case of mistaken parental identity, a case in which misguided hospital procedures helped to generate the confusion, see Leehrsen.

7. For early accounts of these flirtations, see Weldon, sig. E6v-I1v; Arthur Wilson, sig. H4r-N1v; Sanderson, sig. 3E4r-3K4r.

8. For discussion of the two so-called precedents, see Cobbett 2:812–813, Somerset 124–125, and Le Comte 101–104. For a concise summary of Abbott's legal objections to the Howards' case, see Welsby 69.

9. Suspicions of Frances Howard's virtue were rife during the annulment proceedings and led to a formal inquest to determine her chastity. Accounts of this inquest can be found in the early historical sources cited in n. 7 above; for modern references, see Somerset 122–123, Snow 57, and Le Comte 101.

10. For a discussion of Ovid's influence upon early modern imperfect-enjoyment poetry, see Boehrer, "Anxiety" passim.

11. OED "Coverture" sv. 9. For a recent application of the legal theory of coverture to the drama of the English Renaissance, see Dolan.

12. *Oxford Latin Dictionary* "Familia" sv. 1 and 6. As Friedrich Engels noted (737), "*Famulus* means a household slave and *familia* signifies the totality of slaves belonging to one individual. Even in the time of Gaius, the *familia, id est patrimonium* (that is, the inheritance) was bequeathed by will." For examples of this usage in *Volpone*, see 1.3.34–35; 1.5.46–49; 5.4.14.

CHAPTER THREE

1. Thus it is perhaps worth noting that Peter Martyr, among others, incorrectly took the discovery of parrots in the New World as evidence that European explorers had reached east Asia (sig. A3v). In doing so, Martyr illustrates a widespread tendency, among explorers and writers of travel narratives, to assimilate parrots to notions of Old World geography.

2. Hall also adduces one more exception: a Wissing portrait, in the National Portrait Gallery, possibly of Charles II's mistress the Duchess of Portsmouth (see Hall 247–249). For a recent study that relates the aristocratic display of ethnic servants to the issue of ethnicity in early modern literary representation, see Margo Hendricks 53–54.

3. See Hall 230–232 for a discussion of the association that this portrait implies between "blackness and valuable goods" (232).

4. The bird's identification as a "Maccaw" dates to the Duke of Hamilton's manuscript *Inventory of the Pictures at Hamilton,* ca. 1698–1712 (qtd. in Martin 55). The bird is clearly a macaw, as indicated by the "bare facial area" that "is the most conspicuous external feature" of parrots belonging to the genera Ara and Anodorhynchus (Forshaw 356). These New World birds "are a very homogeneous group easily distinguishable from Old World parrots" (Forshaw 354).

5. See 101–103 for an extended discussion of the painting in question, a discussion that emphasizes the "triangular" structure of Van Dyck's composition (103) as well as the "inverse relationship" (103) between the figure of Denbigh and its surroundings.

6. Also see Greenblatt's brief reference to the juxtaposition of parrots and islanders in the journals of Columbus (90).

7. According to the OED, "The chief difficulty in this [derivation] is that the sense 'parrot' is not recorded for F. *Perrot* . . . , while *Perrot* does not appear as a man's name in 16th c. Eng., so that points of contact are wanting" (sb. "Parrot").

8. The OED's first instance of the noun "parrot" as a pejorative social metaphor is drawn from J. Bell's *Haddon's Answer to Osorius.* Nashe's reference to Harvey gives the OED its earliest instance of the verb "to parrot" in a similarly derogatory context.

9. For the rise of early cartographic representations of New World cannibalism, and for their occasional conjunction with depictions of parrots, see Susi Colin, "Woodcutters and Cannibals" passim, esp. 176–177.

10. See, e.g., Ann Barton's discussion of *Volpone* in *Ben Jonson, Dramatist,* esp. 108–111, and Jonas Barish's description of Jonson's prose style as "not a logical sequence but 'a series of imaginative moments . . . ,' in which ideas develop out of each other associatively" (51). Alexander Leggatt has also noted that "As a satirist, [Jonson] is more at home with trivia—for example, with the fool who is trying to act well-bred but can produce only a mechanical imitation of breeding" (81). This notion of "mechanical imitation," I believe, is related both to Jonson's fondness for enumeration and to his interest in psittacine repetition.

11. This study is indebted to Stallybrass and White's discussion of the social instrumentality of animal categories (44–59), although that discussion centers upon animal associations that are removed from the developing sixteenth- and seventeenth-century trade in exotic pets.

12. For a recent study of Walcott and Rhys in light of psittacine mimicry and postcolonial theory, see Huggan passim. For Huggan, "the parrot may serve . . . as a reconfirmation of European cultural supremacy; yet . . . it may also serve as a metaphor for the process of colonial mimicry . . . by which . . . postcolonial writers . . . capture Europe's own master narratives and display them . . . as self-imprisoning myths" (658). The present essay, with its earlier historical focus, seeks to trace the processes whereby the "self-imprisoning myth" of "European cultural supremacy" is created in the first place.

13. I cannot depart from this topic without noting the fine gallic twist to which the motif of the semiarticulate servant is subjected by Colette in *Ripening Seed* (*Le ble en herbe*). In that novel the mature seductress Madame Dalleray lures the youth Philippe into her summer home, where

> . . . a red and blue mcaw, on a perch, spread one of its wings with the snap of a fan, to display pink underfeathers, the hue of livid flesh.

"How handsome he is!" Phil said in a hoarse voice.
"All the more handsome for being a non-talker," said Mme.
Dalleray. (44)

CHAPTER FOUR

1. Philippe Ariès's classic *Centuries of Childhood* thus notes "the importance of the seventeenth century in the evolution of the themes of
childhood" (46). It is in this century that "portraits of children on
their own became numerous and commonplace" (46); that "the
child, or at least the child of quality, whether noble or middle-class,
ceased to be dressed like the grown-up" (59); and that adults began
"to avoid any reference, above all any humorous reference, to sexual
matters in the presence of children" (100). Such facts, according to
Aries, help to demonstrate "the non-existence of the modern idea of
childhood at the beginning of the seventeenth century" (100).

2. Further Shakespearean references to bull- and bear-baiting, all brief,
include *Twelfth Night* 1.3.93, *Henry VIII* 5.3.2, *Troilus and Cressida*
5.7.9–12, *2 Henry VI* 5.1.151–154, *Titus Andronicus* 5.1.102, and
The Winter's Tale 5.3.101–102. See Lee 431. None of these passages
involve extended elements of dramatic characterization.

3. For additional Puritan complaints against bear-baiting, see Edward
Hake passim; Stubbes sigs. Q6v-Q7r; John Field passim. Also see
Stow, *Annales,* sigs. 3I1v–3I2r.

4. For the development of this motif in English neo-Petrarchan verse,
see Goldberg, *Echo* 14–37, esp. 19–23; Dubrow 95–104.

5. For a recent discussion of this event and its long-term consequences,
see Giles Milton passim, esp. 66–96.

6. For a useful brief discussion of these developments, see Jardine 98–105.

7. For an account of the Elizabethan royal progresses that emphasizes
their character as public relations spectacles, see Erickson 276–294.

8. For a summary and examination of the scholarship on this point, see
Boehrer, "Shoes" passim.

9. For this view of the trip to Scotland, see David Riggs's account of the
event (254–260), esp. 254–255.

10. For a detailed discussion of the Pope's menagerie, see Bedini passim.
For a description of certain royal gifts to the menagerie, see esp. 19,
28–29, 48, 84.

11. The OED ("Pet" sb. 1) traces the noun "pet" to Scottish and Northern English dialectal sources and gives as its earliest recorded occur-
rence a Scottish usage from 1539. For a brief discussion of the word
and its absorption into standard English usage, see Boehrer, "Shylock" 153–154.

12. For a recent discussion of the function of letter writing in *Two Gentlemen,* see Kiefer passim.

13. See Burke 208 for the claim that all persuasive discourse obeys a "principle of courtship" whose purpose lies in "the transcending of social estrangement."

14. See Elias passim for the definitive study of this body of work. For more recent examinations of the same material, see Whigham passim and Flandrin passim. For recent discussions of *Two Gentlemen* in light of the courtesy book tradition, see Slights passim and Bradbrook passim.

15. It may be worthy of notice that the popular recent film *Shakespeare in Love*, when depicting the performance of *Two Gentlemen* at court, supplies a scene of onstage clownery between Launce and Crab that has no counterpart in the play's surviving text. This late-twentieth-century adaptation of Shakespeare thus supplies the very onstage mis-behavior that is conspicuously absent from Shakespeare's own work.

Conclusion

1. For a brief survey of the animal fable tradition from antiquity through the Middle Ages, see Jill Mann, "Beast Epic and Fable" passim. For the development of this genre in the Renaissance and beyond, see Annabel Patterson, *Fables of Power.*

2. For this argument, see Sherry Ortner, "Is Female to Male as Nature Is to Culture?" passim.

3. For recent scholarly treatment of medieval and early modern terato-logical writing and reproductive discourse, see David Williams, *Deformed Discourse* passim; Erica Fudge, *Perceiving Animals* 115–142; and Thomas Laqueur, *Making Sex* passim, among others.

4. For recent reappraisals of canine intelligence and self-awareness, for instance, see Stanley Coren, *The Intelligence of Dogs,* and Elizabeth Marshall Thomas, *The Hidden Life of Dogs.*

WORKS CITED

PRE-1700

Aelian. *On the Characteristics of Animals.* Trans. A. F. Scholfield. Cambridge, U.S.: Harvard UP, 1959. 3 vols.

Ambrosiaster. *Ambrosiastri qui dicitur Commentarius in Epistulas Paulinas.* Vienna: Hoderl-Pichler-Tempsky, 1968.

Andrewes, Lancelot. *A Patterne of Catachisticall Doctrine.* London, 1630.

Aristophanes. *Aristophanes.* Trans. Benjamin Bickley Rogers. Cambridge, U.S.: Harvard UP, 1924; rpt. 1989. 3 vols.

Aristotle. *The Complete Works of Aristotle.* Ed. Jonathan Barnes. Princeton: Princeton UP, 1984. 3 vols.

Ascham, Roger. *The Scholemaster.* Ed. R. J. Schoeck. Don Mills: J. M. Dent and Sons, 1966.

Aubrey, John. *Aubrey's Brief Lives.* Ed. Oliver Lawson Dick. London: Secker and Warburg, 1949.

Augustine, Saint. *Two Books on Genesis Against the Manichees.* Trans. Roland J. Teske. Washington, DC: Catholic U of America P, 1991.

Bacon, Sir Francis. *The Great Instauration.* In *The Works of Francis Bacon.* Ed. James Spedding. 1870; rpt. New York: Garrett Press, 1968. 4 vols.

Ball, Thomas. *The Life of the Renowned Doctor Preston.* London: Parker and Co., 1885.

Beard, Thomas. *The Theatre of Gods Judgements.* London, 1596.

Best, George. *The Three Voyages of Martin Frobisher in Search of a Passage to Cathay and India . . . , 1576–78.* Ed. Vilhjalmur Stefanasson. London: Argonaut, 1938.

Boccaccio, Giovanni. *Genealogiae.* 1494; rpt. New York: Garland, 1976.

———. *Eclogues.* Trans. Janet Levarie Smarr. New York: Garland, 1987.

[Boemus, Johannes.] *The Fardle of Facions.* London, 1555.

The Book of Beasts. Trans. T. H. White. New York: Dover, 1984.

Bullinger, Heinrich. *The Christen State of Matrimony.* [Trans. Miles Coverdale.] London, 1541.

Castiglione, Baldassare. *The Book of the Courtier.* Trans. Sir Thomas Hoby. New York: AMS, 1967.

Cervantes, Miguel de. *Exemplary Novels.* Trans. John Jones and John Macklin. Warminster: Aris and Phillips, 1992. 4 vols.

Cicero. *De Oratore*. Trans. E. W. Sutton. Cambridge, U.S.: Harvard UP, 1959.

Coke, Edward. *The Third Part of the Institutes of the Laws of England*. London, 1660.

Columbus, Christopher. *Journal of the First Voyage*. Trans. B. W. Ife. Warminster: Aris and Phillips, 1990.

Coryate, Thomas. *Greeting from the Court of the Great Mogul*. 1616; facs. New York: Da Capo, 1968.

Damhoudere, Joost de. *Practica Rerum Criminalium*. Paris, 1557.

Davies, Sir John. *The Complete Poems of Sir John Davies*. Ed. Alexander Grosart. London: Chatto and Windus, 1876.

D'Ewes, Sir Simonds. *The Autobiography and Correspondence of Sir Simonds D'Ewes During the Reigns of James I and Charles I*. London: 1845. 2 vols.

Donne, John. *Selected Prose*. Ed. Helen Gardner and Timothy Healy. Oxford: Clarendon P, 1967.

———. *The Complete English Poems*. Ed. A. J. Smith. Harmondsworth: Penguin, 1971.

Drummond, William. *Informations be Ben Johnston to W. D. when he came to Scotland upon foot*. In C. H. Herford and Percy and Evelyn Simpson, eds., *Ben Jonson*. Vol. 1. Oxford: Clarendon P, 1925–1952. 11 vols.

Enciso, Martin Fernandez de. *A Brief Summe of Geographie*. Trans. Roger Barlow. Ed. E. G. R. Taylor. London: Hakluyt Society, 1932.

Field, John. *A Godly Exhortation*. London, 1583.

Ford, John. *'Tis Pity She's a Whore*. Ed. Derek Roper. Manchester: Manchester UP, 1975.

Fuller, Thomas. *The Worthies of England*. Ed. John Freeman. London: George Allen and Unwin, 1952.

Gesner, Conrad. *Historia Animalium Liber III. Qui Est de Avium Natura*. Frankfurt, 1604.

Gregory of Tours, Saint. *The History of the Franks*. Trans. Lewis Thorpe. Harmondsworth: Penguin, 1974.

Grotius, Hugo. *De Jure Belli et Pacis*. Trans. William Whewell. Cambridge, U.K.: Cambridge UP, 1853. 3 vols.

Hair, Paul, ed. *Before the Bawdy Court: Selections from Church Court and Other Records Relating to the Correction of Moral Offenses in England, Scotland, and New England, 1300–1800*. London: Elek, 1972.

Hake, Edward. *Newes Out of Powles Churchyarde*. London, 1579.

Hakluyt, Richard. *The Principal Navigations Voyages Traffiques and Discoveries of the English Nation*. New York: Macmillan, 1904. 12 vols.

Hentzner, Paul. *Itinerarium Germaniae, Galliae; Angliae; Italiae*. Nurnberg, 1612.

Holland, Richard de. *The Buke of the Howlat*. In F. J. Amours, ed., *Scottish Alliterative Poems in Rhyming Stanzas*. Edinburgh: William Blackwood and Sons, 1897.

Holy Bible. Authorized Version. Cleveland: World Publishing, n.d.

Isocrates. *Isocrates.* Trans. George Norlin. London: William Heinemann, 1929. 3 vols.

Jonson, Ben. *Ben Jonson.* Ed. C. H. Herford and Percy and Evelyn Simpson. Oxford: Clarendon P, 1925–1952. 11 vols.

Kemp, William. *Kemp's Nine Days Wonder.* New York: Johnson Reprint Company, 1972.

Kyd, Thomas. *The First Part of Hieronimo and The Spanish Tragedy.* Ed. Andrew Cairncross. Lincoln: U of Nebraska P, 1967.

Laneham, Robert. *Account of the Queen's Entertainment at Killingworth Castle, 1575.* In John Nichols, *The Progresses and Public Processions of Queen Elizabeth.* London, 1788. 1:1–25.

Locke, John. *An Essay Concerning Human Understanding.* Ed. John Yolton. London: J. M. Dent and Sons, 1961. 2 vols.

Lydgate, Thomas. *Poems.* Ed. John Norton-Smith. Oxford: Clarendon P, 1966.

Lyly, John. *The Complete Works of John Lyly.* Ed. R. Warwick Bond. Oxford: Clarendon P, 1902. 3 vols.

Makin, Bathsua. *An Essay to Revive the Antient Education of Gentlewomen.* Los Angeles: Augustan Reprint Society, 1980.

Mankind. In Joseph Quincy Adams, ed., *Chief Pre-Shakespearean Dramas.* Boston: Houghton Mifflin, 1924.

Markham, Gervase. *Markhams Maister-Peece.* London, 1610.

Marlowe, Christopher. *Hero and Leander.* In Stephen Orgel, ed., *Christopher Marlowe: The Complete Poems and Translations.* New York: Penguin, 1979.

Marston, John. *The Poems of John Marston.* Ed. Arnold Davenport. Liverpool: Liverpool UP, 1961.

Martyr, Peter. *The Decades of the New World or West India.* London, 1555.

Middleton, Thomas. *A Chaste Maid in Cheapside.* Ed. R. B. Parker. London: Methuen, 1969.

Milton, John. *The Riverside Milton.* Ed. Roy Flannagan. Boston: Houghton Mifflin, 1998.

Montaigne, Michel de. *The Essayes of Montaigne.* Trans. John Florio. New York: Modern Library, 1933.

Nashe, Thomas. *The Works of Thomas Nashe.* Ed. R. B. McKerrow. Oxford: Basil Blackwell, 1958. 7 vols.

A Nest of Ninnies and Other English Jestbooks of the Seventeenth Century. Ed. P. M. Zall. Lincoln: U of Nebraska P, 1970.

Niccols, Richard. *The Cuckow.* London, 1607.

The Old English Physiologus. Ed. and Trans. Albert Stanburrough Cook and James Hall Pitman. New Haven: Yale UP, 1921.

Overbury, Sir Thomas, et al. *The Overburian Characters.* Ed. W. J. Paylor. Oxford: Basil Blackwell, 1936.

Ovid. *Ovid's Elegies.* Trans. Christopher Marlowe. In Stephen Orgel, ed., *Christopher Marlowe: The Complete Poems and Translations.* New York: Penguin, 1979.

————. *Heroides and Amores*. Trans. Grant Showerman. Cambridge, U.S.: Harvard UP, 1977.

Oviedo, Gonzalo Fernandez de. *Natural History of the West Indies*. Trans. Sterling Stoudemire. Chapel Hill: U of North Carolina P, 1959.

Paré, Ambroise. *On Monsters and Marvels*. Trans. Janis Palliser. Chicago: U of Chicago P, 1982.

Plato. *Lysis. Symposium. Gorgias*. Trans. W. R. M. Lamb. Cambridge, U.S.: Harvard UP, 1925, rpt. 1996.

————. *The Republic*. Trans. H. D. P. Lee. Harmondsworth: Penguin, 1955.

Pliny the Elder. *Natural History*. Trans. H. Rackham. 10 vols. London: William Heinemann, 1938–1963.

Plutarch. *Plutarch's Moralia*. Trans. Harold Cherniss and William C. Helmbold. Cambridge, U.S.: Harvard UP, 1957. 15 vols.

Purchas, Samuel. *Hakluytus Posthumus or Purchas His Pilgrimes*. New York: AMS, 1965. 18 vols.

Sales, Saint Francis de. *Introduction to the Devout Life*. Trans. Michael Day. London: Burns and Oates, 1956.

Sanderson, Sir William. *A Compleat History of the Lives and Reigns of Mary Queen of Scotland, and of Her Son and Successor James*. London, 1656.

Shakespeare, William. *The Riverside Shakespeare*. Ed. G. Blakemore Evans et al. Boston: Houghton Mifflin, 1997.

Skelton, John. *The Poetical Works of John Skelton*. Ed. Alexander Dyce. 1843; rpt. New York: AMS, 1965.

Statutes at Large from the First Year of King Edward the Fourth To the End of the Reign of Queen Elizabeth. London: King's Printer, 1786–1866. 67 vols.

Stow, John. *The Annales of England*. London, 1592.

————. *The Survey of London*. London, 1633.

Stubbes, Philip. *The Anatomie of Abuses*. London, 1583.

Swinburne, Henry. *A Brief Treatise of Testaments and Wills*. London, 1637.

Tatham, John. *Fancies Theater*. London, 1640.

Taylor, John. *Works of John Taylor the Water Poet*. New York: Burt Franklin, 1876, rpt. 1967.

Tobin, J. J. M. *Shakespeare's Favorite Novel: A Study of "The Golden Asse" as Prime Source*. Lanham: UP of America, 1984.

Tyndale, William. *Obedie[n]ce of a Christen Man*. [Antwerp], 1528.

Vespucci, Amerigo. *The Four Voyages of Amerigo Vespucci*. In Martin Waldseemuller, *Cosmographiae Introductio*. Trans. Joseph Fischer and Franz von Wieser. Ann Arbor: University Microfilms, 1966.

Wager, Lewis. *Mary Magdalene*. In Paul Whitfield White, *Reformation Biblical Drama in England*. New York: Garland, 1992. 1–66.

Weever, John. *Epigrammes*. Ed. R. B. McKerrow. London: Sidgwick and Jackson, 1911.

Weldon, Sir Anthony. *The Court and Character of King James*. London, 1651.

Wilson, Arthur. *The History of Great Britain*. London, 1653.

Wilson, George. *The Commendation of Cockes, and Cock-fighting*. London, 1607.

"Women Are Not Human": An Anonymous Treatise and Responses. Trans. Theresa M. Kenney. New York: Herder and Herder, 1998.

POST-1700

Adams, Carol J. *Neither Man Nor Beast: Feminism and the Defense of Animals*. New York: Continuum, 1994.

Adams, Carol J., and Josephine Donovan, eds. *Animals and Women: Feminist Theoretical Explorations*. Durham: Duke UP, 1995.

Agnew, Jean-Christophe. *Worlds Apart: The Market and the Theater in Anglo-American Thought, 1550–1750*. Cambridge, U.K.: Cambridge UP, 1986.

Ariès, Philippe. *Centuries of Childhood: A Social History of Family Life*. Trans. Robert Baldick. New York: Vintage Books, 1962.

Auster, Paul. *Timbuktu*. New York: Henry Holt and Company, 1999.

Bach, Rebecca Ann. "Bearbaiting, Dominion, and Colonialism." In Joyce Green MacDonald, ed., *Race, Ethnicity, and Power in the Renaissance*. Madison, NJ: Fairleigh Dickinson UP, 1997. 19–34.

Barber, C. L. *Shakespeare's Festive Comedy: A Study of Dramatic Form and Its Relation to Social Custom*. Princeton: Princeton UP, 1959.

Barish, Jonas. *Ben Jonson and the Language of Prose Comedy*. Cambridge, U.S.: Harvard UP, 1960.

Barton, Ann. *Ben Jonson, Dramatist*. Cambridge, U.K.: Cambridge UP, 1986.

Bate, Jonathan. "Poetry and Biodiversity." In Richard Kerridge and Neil Sammels, eds., *Writing the Environment: Ecocriticism and Literature*. London: Zed, 1998. 53–70.

Beadle, Richard. "Crab's Pedigree." In Michael Cordner, Peter Holland, and John Kerrigan, eds., *English Comedy*. Cambridge, U.K.: Cambridge UP, 1994. 12–35.

Bedini, Silvio. *The Pope's Elephant*. Nashville: J. S. Sanders and Company, 1998.

Belsey, Catherine. *The Subject of Tragedy: Identity and Difference in Renaissance Drama*. London: Methuen, 1985.

———. "Disrupting Sexual Difference: Meaning and Gender in the Comedies." In John Drakakis, ed., *Alternative Shakespeares*. New York: Methuen, 1985. 166–190.

Bentley, Gerald Eades. *The Jacobean and Caroline Stage: Dramatic Companies and Players*. Oxford: Clarendon P, 1941). 7 vols.

Benveniste, Emile. *Problems in General Linguistics*. Trans. Mary Elizabeth Meek. Coral Gables: U of Miami P, 1971.

Bingham, Caroline. "Seventeenth-Century Attitudes Toward Deviant Sex." *Journal of Interdisciplinary Study* 1 (1970–1971): 435–451.

Bloch, Iwan. *A History of English Sexual Morals*. London: Francis Alder, 1936.

Bloom, Harold. *Shakespeare: The Invention of the Human*. New York: Riverhead Books, 1998.

Boehrer, Bruce. "Behn's 'Disappointment' and Nashe's 'Choise of Valentines': Pornographic Poetry and the Influence of Anxiety." *Essays in Literature* 16.2 (Fall, 1989): 172–187.

———. "*Othello*'s Monsters: Kenneth Burke, Deleuze and Guattari, and the Impulse to Narrative in Shakespeare." *Journal x* 3.1 (Spring, 1999): 119–138.

———. "Shylock and the Rise of the Household Pet: Thinking Social Exclusion in *The Merchant of Venice*." *Shakespeare Quarterly* 50.2 (Summer, 1999): 152–170.

———. "The Case of Will Kemp's Shoes: *Every Man Out of His Humour* and the 'Bibliographic Ego.'" *Ben Jonson Journal* 7 (2000): 271–295.

———. "Milton and the Reasoning of Animals: Variations on a Theme by Plutarch." *Milton Studies* 39 (2000): 50–73.

Bogue, Ronald. *Deleuze and Guattari*. New York: Routledge, 1989.

Bourdieu, Pierre. *Outline of a Theory of Practice*. Trans. Richard Nice. Cambridge, U.K.: Cambridge UP, 1977.

Bradbrook, M. C. "Courtier and Courtesy: Castiglione, Lyly, and Shakespeare's *Two Gentlemen of Verona*." In J. R. Mulryne and Margaret Shewring, eds., *Theatre of the English and Italian Renaissance*. New York: Saint Martin's, 1991. 161–178.

Bray, Alan. *Homosexuality in Renaissance England*. London: Gay Men's Press, 1982.

Breitenberg, Mark. *Anxious Masculinity in Early Modern England*. Cambridge, U.K.: Cambridge UP, 1996.

Brooks, Harold. "Two Clowns in a Comedy (to say nothing of the Dog): Speed, Launce (and Crab) in 'The Two Gentlemen of Verona,'" *Essays and Studies 1963* (1963): 91–100.

———, ed. *A Midsummer Night's Dream*. By William Shakespeare. New York: Methuen, 1979.

Brown, Christopher. *Scenes of Everyday Life: Dutch Genre Painting of the Seventeenth Century*. London: Faber and Faber, 1984.

Bruster, Douglas. *Drama and the Market in the Age of Shakespeare*. Cambridge, U.K.: Cambridge UP, 1992.

Burg, B. R. "Ho Hum, Another Work of the Devil: Buggery and Sodomy in Early Stuart England." *Journal of Homosexuality* 6 (1980–1981): 69–78.

Burke, Kenneth. *A Rhetoric of Motives*. Berkeley: U of California P, 1950; rpt. 1969.

Canning, Peter M. "Fluidentity." *SubStance* 13.3–4 (1984): 35–45.

Chambers, E. K. *The Elizabethan Stage*. Oxford: Clarendon P, 1923. 4 vols.

Clark, Anne. *Beasts and Bawdy*. London: J. M. Dent, 1975.

Clarke, Paul A. B., and Andrew Linzey, eds. *Political Theory and Animal Rights*. London: Pluto, 1990.

Cobbett, William. *English State Trials 1163–1858.* London: 1809–1828. 34 vols.

Colette. *Ripening Seed [Le ble en herbe].* Harmondsworth: Penguin, 1993.

Colin, Susi. "Woodcutters and Cannibals: Brazilian Indians as Seen on Early Maps." In Hans Wolff, ed., *America: Early Maps of the New World.* Munich: Prestel, 1992. 175–181.

Conrad, Joseph. *Nostromo.* Ed. F. R. Leavis. New York: New American Library, 1963.

Coren, Stanley. *The Intelligence of Dogs: A Guide to the Thoughts, Emotions, and Inner Lives of Our Canine Companions.* New York: Bantam, 1995.

Coupe, Laurence. *The Green Studies Reader: From Romanticism to Ecocriticism.* London: Routledge, 2000.

Danby, John. *Shakespeare's Doctrine of Nature: A Study of "King Lear."* London: Faber and Faber, 1949.

Defoe, Daniel. *Robinson Crusoe.* Ed. Harvey Swados. New York: Penguin, 1961.

Dekkers, Midas. *Dearest Pet: On Bestiality.* Trans. Paul Vincent. London: Verso, 1994.

Deleuze, Gilles, and Félix Guattari. *A Thousand Plateaus: Capitalism and Schizophrenia.* Trans. Brian Massumi. Minneapolis: U of Minnesota P, 1987.

Dent, Alan. *World of Shakespeare: Animals and Monsters.* Reading: Osprey, 1972.

Des Maizeaux, Pierre. *Dictionnaire historique et critique par Mr. Pierre Bayle, . . . révue, corrigée, et augmentée . . . par Mr. Des Maizeaux.* Amsterdam, 1730. 4 vols. in 3.

Dolan, Frances. *Whores of Babylon: Catholicism, Gender, and Seventeenth-Century Print Culture.* Ithaca: Cornell UP, 1999.

Dollimore, Jonathan. *Radical Tragedy: Religion, Ideology and Power in the Drama of Shakespeare and His Contemporaries.* Chicago: U of Chicago P, 1984.

———. "The Cultural Politics of Perversion: Augustine, Shakespeare, Freud, Foucault." *Textual Practice* 4 (1990): 179–196.

———. *Sexual Dissidence: Augustine to Wilde, Freud to Foucault.* Oxford: Clarendon P, 1991.

Douglas, Mary. *Purity and Danger: An Analysis of the Concepts of Pollution and Taboo.* New York: Frederick A. Praeger, 1966.

Dubrow, Heather. *Echoes of Desire: English Petrarchism and Its Counterdiscourses.* Ithaca: Cornell UP, 1995.

Eagleton, Terry. *William Shakespeare.* Oxford: Basil Blackwell, 1986.

Elias, Norbert. *The History of Manners.* Trans. Edmund Jephcott. New York: Pantheon Books, 1978.

Emmison, F. G. *Elizabethan Life: Morals and the Church Courts.* Chelmsford: Essex County Council, 1973.

Engels, Friedrich. *The Origin of Family, Private Property, and the State.* In Robert C. Tucker, ed., *The Marx-Engels Reader.* New York: Norton, 1978.

Erickson, Carrolly. *The First Elizabeth*. New York: Summit Books, 1983.

Evans, E. P. *The Criminal Prosecution and Capital Punishment of Animals: The Lost History of Europe's Animal Trials.* 1906; rpt. London: Faber and Faber, 1987.

Fineman, Joel. "Fratricide and Cuckoldry: Shakespeare's Doubles." In Murray Schwartz and Coppelia Kahn, eds., *Representing Shakespeare: New Psychoanalytic Essays.* Baltimore: Johns Hopkins UP, 1980. 70–109.

Fish, Stanley. *John Skelton's Poetry.* New Haven: Yale UP, 1965.

Flandrin, Jean-Louis. "Distinction Through Taste." In Roger Chartier, ed., *A History of Private Life.* Trans. Arthur Goldhammer. Cambridge, U.S.: The Belknap Press of Harvard UP, 1989. 3 vols. 3:264–307.

Fleischer, Manfred P. "'Are Women Human?'—The Debate of 1595 Between Valens Acidalius and Simon Gediccus." *Sixteenth Century Journal* 12.2 (Summer, 1981): 107–120.

Forshaw, Joseph. *Parrots of the World.* Melbourne: Lansdowne, 1973.

Foucault, Michel. *The History of Sexuality—Volume I: An Introduction.* Trans. Robert Hurley. New York: Vintage Books, 1980.

Frantz, David O. *Festum Voluptatis: A Study of Renaissance Erotica.* Columbus: Ohio State UP, 1989.

Fryer, Peter. *Staying Power: The History of Black People in Britain.* London: Pluto, 1984.

Fuchs, Barbara. "Conquering Islands: Contextualizing *The Tempest*." *Shakespeare Quarterly* 48.1 (Spring, 1997): 45–62.

Fudge, Erica. *Perceiving Animals: Humans and Beasts in Early Modern English Culture.* New York: St. Martin's, 2000.

Fudge, Erica, Ruth Gilbert, and Susan Wiseman, eds. *At the Borders of the Human: Beasts, Bodies, and Natural Philosophy in the Early Modern Period.* New York: St. Martin's, 1999.

Fumerton, Patricia. *Cultural Aesthetics: Renaissance Literature and the Practice of Social Ornament.* Chicago: U of Chicago P, 1991.

Garber, Marjorie. *Dream in Shakespeare: From Metaphor to Metamorphosis.* New Haven: Yale UP, 1974.

———. *Dog Love.* New York: Simon and Schuster, 1996.

———. "Shakespeare's Dogs." In Jonathan Bate, Jill L. Levenson, and Dieter Mehl, eds., *Shakespeare and the Twentieth Century: The Selected Proceedings of the International Shakespeare Association World Congress, Los Angeles, 1996.* Newark: U of Delaware P, 1998. 291–305.

George, Wilma. *Animals and Maps.* Berkeley: U of California P, 1969.

Girard, René. *Violence and the Sacred.* Trans. Patrick Gregory. Baltimore: Johns Hopkins UP, 1977.

Glidden, David. "Parrots, Pyrrhonists, and Native Speakers." In Stephen Everson, ed., *Language.* Cambridge, U.K.: Cambridge UP, 1994. 129–148.

Glotfelty, Cheryll, and Harold Fromm, eds. *The Ecocriticism Reader.* Athens: U of Georgia P, 1996.

Goldberg, Jonathan. *Voice Terminal Echo: Postmodernism and English Renaissance Texts.* New York: Methuen, 1986.

Gould, Stephen Jay. *The Mismeasure of Man.* New York: W. W. Norton and Co., rev. 1991.

Greenblatt, Stephen. *Renaissance Self-Fashioning: More to Shakespeare.* Chicago: U of Chicago P, 1980.

———. *Shakespearean Negotiations: The Circulation of Social Energy in Renaissance England.* Berkeley: U of California P, 1988.

———. *Marvelous Possessions: The Wonder of the New World.* Oxford: Clarendon P, 1991.

Greenlee, William Brooks, ed. and trans. *The Voyage of Pedro Alvares Cabral to Brazil and India.* London: The Hukluyt Society, 1938.

Hall, Kim. *Things of Darkness: Economies of Race and Gender in Early Modern England.* Ithaca: Cornell UP, 1995.

Hanke, Lewis. "Pope Paul III and the American Indians." *Harvard Theological Review* 30 (1937): 65–102.

Hawkes, Terence. *Shakespeare's Talking Animals: Language and Drama in Society.* London: Edward Arnold, 1973.

———. *That Shakespeherian Rag: Essays on a Critical Process.* London: Methuen, 1986.

Head, Dominic. "The (Im)Possibility of Ecocriticism." In Richard Kerridge and Neil Sammells, eds., *Writing the Environment: Ecocriticism and Literature.* London: Zed, 1998. 27–39.

Hendricks, Margo. "'Obscured by Dreams': Race, Empire, and Shakespeare's *A Midsummer Night's Dream.*" *Shakespeare Quarterly* 47.1 (Spring, 1996): 37–60.

Hieatt, Constance. "Stooping at a Simile: Some Literary Uses of Falconry." *Papers on Language and Literature* 19 (1983): 339–360.

Hodgen, Margaret. *Early Anthropology in the Sixteenth and Seventeenth Centuries.* Philadelphia: U of Pennsylvania P, 1964.

Holland, Norman. "Hermia's Dream." In Murray Schwartz and Coppelia Kahn, eds., *Representing Shakespeare: New Psychoanalytic Essays.* Baltimore: Johns Hopkins UP, 1980. 1–20.

Huggan, Graham. "A Tale of Two Parrots: Walcott, Rhys, and the Uses of Colonial Mimicry." *Contemporary Literature* 35.4 (Winter, 1994): 643–660.

Jamieson, Philip. "Animal Liability in Early Law." *The Cambrian Law Review* 19 (1988): 45–68.

Jardine, Lisa. *Worldly Goods: A New History of the Renaissance.* New York: W. W. Norton, 1996.

Jordan, Winthrop. *The White Man's Burden: Historical Origins of Racism in the United States.* New York: Oxford UP, 1974.

Kahn, Coppélia. *Man's Estate: Masculine Identity in Shakespeare.* Berkeley: U of California P, 1981.

Kenney, Theresa, ed. and trans. *"Women Are Not Human": An Anonymous Treatise and Responses*. New York: Herder and Herder, 1998.

Kermode, Frank, ed. *The Tempest*. London: Methuen, 1954.

Kerridge, Richard, and Neil Sammells. *Writing the Environment: Ecocriticism and Literature*. London: Zed Books, 1998.

Kete, Kathleen. *The Beast in the Boudoir: Petkeeping in Nineteenth-Century Paris*. Berkeley: U of California P, 1994.

Kiefer, Frederick. "Love Letters in *The Two Gentlemen of Verona*." *Shakespeare Studies* 16 (1983): 65–85.

Kinney, Arthur. *John Skelton: Priest as Poet*. Chapel Hill: U of North Carolina P, 1987.

Kolodny, Annette. *The Lay of the Land: Metaphor as Experience and History in American Life and Letters*. Chapel Hill: U of North Carolina P, 1975.

Kott, Jan. *Shakespeare Our Contemporary*. Trans. Boleslaw Taborski. New York: Doubleday and Doubleday, 1964.

———. *The Bottom Translation*. Trans. Daniela Miedzyrzecka and Lillian Vallee. Evanston: Northwestern UP, 1987.

Lacan, Jacques. *Feminine Sexuality*. Ed. Juliet Mitchell and Jacqueline Rose. New York: W. W. Norton, 1982.

Laqueur, Thomas. *Making Sex: Body and Gender from the Greeks to Freud*. Cambridge, U.S.: Harvard UP, 1990.

Lecercle, Ann. "Epics and Ethics in *1 Henry IV*." In Jean-Marie Maguin and Michele Willems, eds., *French Essays on Shakespeare and His Contemporaries: "What Would France with Us?."* Newark: U of Delaware P, 1995. 175–188.

Le Comte, Edward. *The Notorious Lady Essex*. New York: Dial, 1969.

Lee, Sir Sidney. "Bearbaiting, Bullbaiting, and Cockfighting." In C. T. Onions, ed., *Shakespeare's England: An Account of the Life and Manners of His Age*. Oxford: Clarendon P, 1916. 2 vols. 2:428–436.

Leech, Clifford, ed. *The Two Gentlemen of Verona*. London: Methuen, 1969, rpt. 1997.

Leehrsen, Charles. "My Child or Your Child?" *Newsweek* 112.19 (November 7, 1988): 103.

Leggatt, Alexander. *Ben Jonson: His Vision and His Art*. London: Methuen, 1981.

Lehms, Georg Christian. *Teutschlands Galante Poetinnen*. Frankfurt, 1714–1715. 2 vols. in 1.

Leinwand, Theodore. "Negotiation and New Historicism." *PMLA* 105.3 (May, 1990): 476–490.

Lewis, C. S. *The Allegory of Love: A Study in Medieval Tradition*. Oxford: Clarendon P, 1936.

Love, Glen A. "Revaluing Nature: Toward an Ecological Criticism." In Cheryll Glotfelty and Harold Fromm, eds., *The Ecocriticism Reader*. Athens: U of Georgia P, 1996. 225–240.

Lupton, Julia Reinhard. "Creature Caliban." *Shakespeare Quarterly* 51.1 (Spring, 2000): 1–28.

Mack, Phyllis. *Visionary Women: Ecstatic Prophecy in Seventeenth-Century England.* Berkeley: U of California P, 1992.

Mann, Jill. "Beast Epic and Fable." In F. A. C. Mantello and A. G. Rigg, eds., *Medieval Latin: An Introduction and Bibliographic Guide.* Washington: Catholic U of America P, 1996. 556–561.

Martin, Gregory. *The Flemish School circa 1600–circa 1900.* London: The National Gallery, 1970.

Masson, Jeffrey Moussaieff, and Susan McCarthy. *When Elephants Weep: The Emotional Lives of Animals.* New York: Delacorte, 1995.

Masten, Jeffrey. *Textual Intercourse: Collaboration, Authorship, and Sexualities in Renaissance Drama.* Cambridge, U.K.: Cambridge UP, 1997.

Maus, Katharine. "Horns of Dilemma: Jealousy, Gender, and Spectatorship in English Renaissance Drama." *ELH* 54.3 (Fall, 1987). 561–583.

McIntosh, Gregory C. *The Piri Reis Map of 1513.* Athens: U of Georgia P, 2000.

Metzger, Mary Janell. "'Now, By My Hood, a Gentle and No Jew': Jessica, *The Merchant of Venice,* and the Discourse of Early Modern English Identity." *PMLA* 113.1 (January, 1998): 52–63.

Millar, Oliver. *Van Dyck in England.* London: The National Portrait Gallery, 1982.

Milton, Giles. *Nathaniel's Nutmeg.* New York: Farrar, Straus and Giroux, 1999.

Montrose, Louis Adrian. "*A Midsummer Night's Dream* and the Shaping Fantasies of Elizabethan Culture: Gender, Power, Form." In Margaret Ferguson, Maureen Quilligan, and Nancy Vickers, eds., *Rewriting the Renaissance: The Discourses of Sexual Difference in Early Modern Europe.* Chicago: U of Chicago P, 1986. 65–88.

Murphy, Patrick. *Literature, Nature, and Other: Ecofeminist Critiques.* Albany: State U of New York P, 1995.

Neill, Michael. "'Mulattoes,' 'Blacks,' and 'Indian Moors': *Othello* and Early Modern Constructions of Human Difference." *Shakespeare Quarterly* 49.4 (Winter, 1998): 361–374.

Nichols, John. *The Progresses and Public Processions of Queen Elizabeth.* London, 1788. 2 vols.

———. *The Progresses, Processions, and Magnificent Festivities of King James the First.* London, 1828. 4 vols.

Olson, Paul. "*A Midsummer Night's Dream* and the Meaning of Court Marriage." *ELH* 24 (1957): 95–119.

Orgel, Stephen. *The Illusion of Power: Political Theater in the Renaissance.* Berkeley: U of California P, 1975.

———. "Nobody's Perfect: Or Why Did the English Stage Take Boys for Women?" *South Atlantic Quarterly* 88 (1989): 4–16.

———. *Impersonations: The Performance of Gender in Shakespeare's England.* Cambridge, U.K.: Cambridge UP, 1996.

Ortner, Sherry. "Is Female to Male as Nature Is to Culture?" In Michelle Zimbalist Rosaldo and Louise Lamphere, eds., *Woman, Culture, and Society.* Stanford: Stanford UP, 1974. 65–87.

Orwell, George. *Burmese Days.* Ed. Richard Rees. New York: New American Library, 1963.

Parker, Patricia. *Literary Fat Ladies: Rhetoric, Gender, Property.* New York: Methuen, 1987.

Paster, Gail. *The Body Embarrassed: Drama and the Disciplines of Shame in Early Modern England.* Ithaca: Cornell UP, 1993.

Patterson, Annabel. "Bottom's Up: Festive Theory in *A Midsummer Night's Dream.*" *Renaissance Papers* (1988): 25–40.

———. *Shakespeare and the Popular Voice.* Oxford: Basil Blackwell, 1989.

———. *Fables of Power: Aesopian Writing and Political History.* Durham: Duke UP, 1991.

Pepperberg, Irene. "The African Grey Parrot: How Cognitive Processing Might Affect Allospecific Vocal Learning." In Russell Balda, Irene Pepperberg, and Alan Kamil, eds., *Animal Cognition in Nature: The Convergence of Psychology and Biology in Laboratory and Field.* San Diego: Academic P, 1998. 381–410.

———. *The Alex Studies: Cognitive and Communicative Abilities of Grey Parrots.* Cambridge, U.S.: Harvard UP, 1999.

Phipson, Emma. *The Animal-Lore of Shakespeare's Time.* London: Kegan Paul, Trench, and Co., 1883.

Pollet, Maurice. *John Skelton: Poet of Tudor England.* Trans. John Warrington. London: J. M. Dent and Sons, 1971.

Pope, Alexander. *"The Rape of the Lock" and Other Poems.* Ed. Geoffrey Tillotson. London: Routledge, 1993.

Ranald, Margaret Loftus. "The Manning of the Haggard; or The Taming of the Shrew." *Essays in Literature* 1 (1974): 149–165.

Riggs, David. *Ben Jonson: A Life.* Cambridge, U.S.: Harvard UP, 1989.

Ritvo, Harriet. *The Animal Estate: The English and Other Creatures in the Victorian Age.* Cambridge, U.S.: Harvard UP, 1987.

Roberts, Jeanne Addison. *The Shakespearean Wild: Geography, Genus, and Gender.* Lincoln: U of Nebraska P, 1991.

Salisbury, Joyce E. *The Beast Within: Animals in the Middle Ages.* New York: Routledge, 1994.

Schama, Simon. *The Embarrassment of Riches: An Interpretation of Dutch Culture in the Golden Age.* Berkeley: U of California P, 1988.

Sharpe, J. A. *Defamation and Sexual Slander in Early Modern England: The Church Courts at York.* York: Borthwick Papers 58, 1980.

Shattuck, Charles. *Shakespeare on the American Stage: From Booth to Sothern to Marlowe.* Washington, DC: Folger Books, 1987. 3 vols.

Shell, Marc. "The Family Pet." *Representations* 15 (Summer, 1986): 121–153.

———. *The End of Kinship: "Measure For Measure," Incest, and the Ideal of Universal Siblinghood.* Stanford: Stanford UP, 1988.

Silverstein, Helena. *Unleashing Rights: Law, Meaning, and the Animal Rights Movement*. Ann Arbor: U of Michigan P, 1996.

Singer, Peter. *Animal Liberation: A New Ethics for Our Treatment of Animals*. New York: Avon Books, 1975.

Singer, Peter, ed. *In Defense of Animals*. Oxford: Basil Blackwell, 1985.

Slights, Camille Wells. "*The Two Gentlemen of Verona* and the Courtesy Book Tradition." *Shakespeare Studies* 16 (1983): 13–31.

Smith, Bruce. *Homosexual Desire in Shakespeare's England: A Cultural Poetics*. Chicago: U of Chicago P, 1991.

Smith, S. C. Kaines. *The Dutch School of Painting*. London: The Medici Society, 1929.

Snow, Vernon F. *Essex the Rebel: The Life of Robert Devereux, the Third Earl of Essex*. Lincoln: U of Nebraska P, 1970.

Snyder, Susan. "Mamillius and Gender Polarization in *The Winter's Tale*." *Shakespeare Quarterly* 50.1 (Spring, 1999): 1–8.

Somerset, Anne. *Unnatural Murder: Poison at the Court of James I*. London: Weidenfeld and Nicolson, 1997.

Spencer, Theodore. *Shakespeare and the Nature of Man*. New York: Macmillan, 1942.

Spurgeon, Caroline. *Shakespeare's Imagery and What It Tells Us*. Cambridge, U.K.: Cambridge UP, 1952.

Stallybrass, Peter, and Allon White. *The Politics and Poetics of Transgression*. Ithaca: Cornell UP, 1986.

Stern, Jane and Michael. "Parrots." *The New Yorker* 66 (July 30, 1990): 55–73.

Stewart, Alan. "Humanity at a Price: Erasmus, Bude, and the Poverty of Philology." In Erica Fudge, Ruth Gilbert, and Susan Wiseman, eds., *At the Borders of the Human: Beasts, Bodies, and Natural Philosophy in the Early Modern Period*. New York: St. Martin's, 1999. 9–25.

Stone, Lawrence. *The Family, Sex and Marriage in England 1500–1800*. New York: Harper and Row, 1977.

Summers, Joseph R. *Dreams of Love and Power: On Shakespeare's Plays*. Oxford: Clarendon P, 1984.

Tennenhouse, Leonard. *Power on Display: The Politics of Shakespeare's Genres*. London: Methuen, 1986.

Thomas, Elizabeth Marshall. *The Hidden Life of Dogs*. Boston: Houghton Mifflin, 1993.

Thomas, Keith. *Man and the Natural World: Changing Attitudes in England 1500–1800*. London: Allen Lane, 1983.

Thurston, Herbert. "Has a Council Denied that Women Have Souls?" *The Month* 559 (January, 1911): 1–11.

Tiffany, Grace. *Erotic Beasts and Social Monsters: Shakespeare, Jonson, and Comic Androgyny*. Newark: U of Delaware P, 1995.

Tobin, J. J. M. *Shakespeare's Favorite Novel: A Study of "The Golden Asse" as Prime Source*. Lanham: UP of America, 1984.

Turner, James Grantham. *One Flesh: Paradisal Marriage and Sexual Relations in the Age of Milton*. Oxford: Clarendon P, 1987.

Weimann, Robert. *Shakespeare and the Popular Tradition in the Theater: Studies in the Social Dimension of Dramatic Form and Function*. Ed. Robert Schwartz. Baltimore: Johns Hopkins UP, 1978.

Welsby, Paul. *George Abbott, the Unwanted Archbishop*. London: SPCK, 1962.

Wendorf, Richard. *The Elements of Life: Biography and Portrait-Painting in Stuart and Georgian England*. Oxford: Clarendon P, 1990.

Wheelock, Arthur J., Jr. *Dutch Paintings of the Seventeenth Century*. Washington: National Gallery of Art, 1995.

Whigham, Frank. *Ambition and Privilege: The Social Tropes of Elizabethan Courtesy Theory*. Berkeley: U of California P, 1984.

White, Lynn, Jr. "The Historical Roots of Our Ecologic Crisis." In Cheryll Glotfelty and Harold Fromm, eds. *The Ecocriticism Reader*. Athens: U of Georgia P, 1996. 3–14.

Willems, Michèle. "'Women and Horses and Power and War': Worship of Mars from *1 Henry IV* to *Coriolanus*." In Jean-Marie Maguin and Michèle Willems, eds., *French Essays on Shakespeare and His Contemporaries: "What Would France with Us?."* Newark: U of Delaware P, 1995. 189–202.

Williams, David. *Deformed Discourse: The Function of the Monster in Mediaeval Thought and Literature*. Montreal: McGill-Queen's University Press, 1996.

Wiseman, Susan. "Monstrous Perfectibility: Ape-Human Transformations in Hobbes, Bulwer, Tyson." In Erica Fudge, Ruth Gilbert, and Susan Wiseman, eds., *At the Borders of the Human: Beasts, Bodies, and Natural Philosophy in the Early Modern Period*. New York: St. Martin's, 1999. 215–238.

Wyrick, Deborah. "The Ass Motif in *The Comedy of Errors* and *A Midsummer Night's Dream*." *Shakespeare Quarterly* 33.4 (1982): 432–448.

Yoder, Audrey. *Animal Analogy in Shakespeare's Character Portrayal*. 1947; rpt. New York: AMS, 1975.

INDEX